The Evolution of the Prehistoric State

The Evolution
of the
Prehistoric State

JONATHAN HAAS

New York Columbia University Press *1982*

As a dissertation, this book was awarded the Bancroft Dissertation Award
by a committe of the faculty of the Graduate School of Arts and Sciences
of Columbia University.

Chapter 4 appeared in somewhat different form in
*The Transition to Statehood in the
New World*, Grant Jones and Robert
Kautz, eds. (New York: Cambridge University Press, 1981).
Reprinted by permission.

Library of Congress Cataloging in Publication Data
Haas, Jonathan, 1949–
The evolution of the prehistoric state.

Based on the author's thesis—Columbia University.
Bibliography: p.
Includes index.
1. Government, Primitive.   2. State, The
3. Olmecs—Politics and government.   4. Indians of South America—Peru—Politics
and government.
5. Indians of Mexico—Politics and government.
I. Title.
GN492.6.H2   301'.74   82-1229
ISBN 0-231-05338-X   AACR2

Columbia University Press
New York *and* Guildford, Surrey

*Clothbound editions of Columbia University Press books are
Smyth-sewn and printed on permanent and durable acid-free paper*

*To my parents
for providing their love
and the warmth of El Rito*

Contents

Acknowledgments

This book began with a fairly simple graduate paper on the Olmec. I modestly wanted to solve the problem of Olmec origins, but ultimately wound up writing about the "Evolution of the Olmec State." That paper grew into a larger one on power and stratification, which in turn grew into a dissertation. The latter finally evolved into the present manuscript. In the course of this evolution, many people have contributed support, encouragement, advice, and motivation.

My first thanks go to the entire Anthropology Department of Columbia University for providing an exciting environment in which to do graduate work. While the storm clouds got a bit nasty at times, they were always fun to watch. The lightning that accompanied them also enlivened as well as shocked. I could not have asked to be in a better place at a better time.

Each of the members of my committee has my gratitude for helping get my dissertation through, as well as for providing specific assistance. I have a debt to Morton Fried I cannot hope to repay. He has given stimulation, wisdom, and patience in unlimited quantities, along with a sense of direction I hope to always retain. Richard Keatinge also provided a constant source of advice and guidance, though he might not always have been aware of it. His ideas have been an ever-present backboard against which I could bounce off my own. I think my awareness of the nature, limitations, and possibilities of the archaeological record has benefited enormously from his input. Myron Cohen brought to my attention the cross-cultural depth of the conflict/integration debate by steering me to the literature on the Confucianists and Legalists. He also helped me clarify my definition of the state. Michael Coe provided me with abundant information about San Lorenzo before it was published, and broadened considerably my knowledge of the Olmec. Andrew Nathan helped me to look at the state from the point of view of a political scientist, and to emerge from some of the confines of an archaeological perspective.

Much of my thinking about power and the state stems from early interaction with Shirley Gorenstein. Chapter 7 in particular represents much of what I got out of our discussions, though I must, of course, accept any blame for its peculiar formulation and inherent problems. My colleague Neil Goldberg provided immeasurable help in grinding out parts of this work. Several years of verbal sparring kept lots of people awake, but many good ideas came out in the process. Although Bill Ehrlich suffers from that rare malady of sinological linguistics, his grasp of the archaeology of politics has led me to see things in new and exciting ways. He also commented on several of the present chapters, and helped me try and glean data from a number of Chinese sources. Other people who read various chapters as I tried to work them out include Jack Bernhardt, Ashraf Ghani, Nguyen Quan, Paul Steinfeld, Harry Silver, John Chance, and Pamela Cressey. Their ideas and criticisms helped me over a number of hurdles and are greatly appreciated. My students at the University of Denver have also had to suffer through interminable lectures on state evolution, and their grasp of critical problems has forced me to rethink a number of issues. Finally, though we have never met, I wish to thank Elman Service. He has read and criticized drafts of the manuscript and provided many useful observations. We still do not agree on several major points, but without the foundation he laid, I would have had precious little to start with.

The Evolution of the Prehistoric State

Introduction

One of the favorite pastimes of social scientists over the course of the past century has been to theorize about the evolution of the world's great "civilizations." These grand and glorious ancient societies have held a certain fascination for both professionals and the public at large. People want to know how these societies came into being, and what kinds of factors led to their efflorescence and rise to greatness. Explanations of how and why the civilizations rose to prominence in the murky past have run a full gamut from alien intervention and divine creation to more sophisticated theories involving economic, environmental, and demographic variables. In more recent years, the latter kinds of explanations have originated most frequently in the anthropological community, and have tended to focus not so much on the ambiguous concept of "civilization" as a whole, but on a central concomitant of civilization, the "state." The increased sophistication of anthropological endeavors has certainly contributed more to the understanding of state origins than have the numerous romantic and bizarre attempts at explanation; however, harmony and cohesion do not prevail in the anthropological study of early states.

Scholars have difficulty agreeing on exactly what it is they are studying, and differing definitions of the "state" abound in the literature. Conflicting theories are offered to explain state evolution, and to defend them scholars make conflicting interpretations of the same data. Cultural anthropologists generate macro-theories of state evolution without sensitivity to the nature of the archaeological record of early states. Obversely, archaeologists develop micro-theories to account for state development in particular areas, without concern for cross-cultural applicability. Furthermore, the actual data base that can be appealed to in studying the origin and development of the state is woefully incomplete. There have been few research projects aimed at systematically collecting data directly relevant to questions of state evolution, and the data not so collected often offer little in the way of useful information.

In bringing up problems such as these, no condemnation is implied of either the research or the researchers in the field of state studies. Rather, I wish to emphasize that the field is undergoing growing pains as it begins to come to grips with complex issues. At the same time, the anthropological investigation into the evolution of the state has the vigor of youth and a tremendous potential to progress rapidly in the near future. It is by no means my intention in this book to solve the problems of the evolution of the state and pick up the flag of progress. I do see a need, however, to reexamine the study of state evolution within anthropology, and to bring together the theoretical and empirical research of political anthropologists and archaeologists into a more agreeable whole. I would like to critically evaluate competing higher and lower level theories of state evolution, and take an initial step toward synthesizing anthropological and archaeological work on the emergence of the world's first state societies. Building on this existing base, I would also like to offer a new framework centered on the concept of "power," which can help to explain developmental processes in newly emergent states.

With these ends in mind, the first problem that needs to be confronted concerns the concept of the "state" itself. The myriad definitions presented in the literature tend to be either idiosyncratic or tied to a particular theoretical perspective. On a general level, the individual definitions fall into three basically different conceptions.

First, "state" is seen as representing the discrete complex of social institutions that operate together to govern a particular, highly evolved society. Under this conceptualization, *the* state operates as a concrete entity within the social whole. Lenin, for example, argues that "the state is an organ of class *domination*, an organ of *oppression* of one class by another" (1932:29, emphasis in original; see also Fried 1967; White 1959).

The second notion of "state" sees it as referring to a particular *kind* of society characterized by specific attributes. In an evolutionary sense, this conception uses "state" as a label to classify societies that have reached a particular level of cultural development. It is thus analogous to the "tribal" or "ranked" stages of evolution (Steward 1955; Service 1971a; Fried 1967).

Finally, "state" is used in a way that is somewhat complementary to the second usage. Specifically, it is used to simply identify individual bounded societies that are characterized by a "state" level of organization. In this sense, a "state" is analogous to a "tribe" or a "chiefdom." For example, one might refer to the Aztec *state* or the Zulu *state*, just as one might refer to the Zuni *tribe* or the Kwakuitl *chiefdom*. In contrast to the idea of the state being a part of a society, the third conception sees the state as the entire society.

These three notions of "state" do refer to different things, and lack of awareness of the distinctions between them has introduced a degree of confusion in the literature. What is one person's "state" is another person's "government" and vice versa. I tend to lean toward the second conceptualization in that I see the state as a type of society, with the member units of this type sharing certain broad characteristics. Specifically, I will define the state initially in the most general terms as a society in which there is a centralized and specialized institution of government. This definition does not contradict any of the three notions of "state," but it removes some of the confusion between them. I should also point out that this is not offered as a *final* definition in any sense. It is offered as a tentative *working* definition, serving primarily to delimit the field of interest and to provide a nonpartisan base for comparing various general and specific theories of state evolution.

In emphasizing the institution of government, I deliberately exclude certain variables—particularly economic stratification and the centralized application of coercive sanctions (force)—that are widely held as definitive of the state (see, for example, Service 1975:10; Fried 1967:186; Krader 1968:25; Johnson 1973:4; Flannery 1972:400; cf. Wright 1977a:383). However, I believe that the a priori inclusion of these variables in the definition automatically biases any attempt to evaluate competing theories of state evolution. As I perceive them the crucial differences between theories are related to questions of how formalized institutions of government first developed and what role such institutions played in the organization of society. This is not to say that a more concrete and precise definition of the state is not possible, but I would rather defer making a more detailed definition until after competing theories have been compared and examined in light of available empirical data.

It should also be pointed out that with the above working definition, I see the state as representing a distinct "advanced" stage in the political

evolution of society. While there is an aging debate over whether or
not all societies are in some sense "states," the issue appears to be
more semantic than substantive (see Cohen 1978:2; Fried 1967:228; cf.
Lowie 1927). Generally, there is agreement in anthropology today that
the state is not a cultural universal, nor is it to be found in all stages
of cultural development. Where exactly the state level lies on an evolutionary scale is open to question at this point, but is clearly lies
toward the upper end of a developmental sequence.

While there is little current debate over the universality of the state,
there is less agreement over whether certain attributes, which some
consider to be unique to states, are to be found in prestate societies
as well. For example, some scholars, such as Bohannon (1968, 1977),
Pospisil (1971, 1972) and Hoebel (1954), consider "laws" to be univer-
sals; while others, such as Diamond (1974) and Fried (1967), see true
"laws" as occurring only in states. Similarly, some scholars believe that
territorial organization is to be found in prestate societies while others
maintain that such organization is, again, unique to states. These
questions are not totally semantic (cf. Koch 1977:302), and they do
have a bearing on the general process of state evolution. However, I
believe they represent subsidiary issues in the broader debate over how
and why the state first evolved. We do not need to prove or disprove
the uniqueness of laws and territorial organization to grasp the basic
form and nature of emergent state societies. Since my primary focus
here is only on the broader debate, these two subsidiary questions will
not be answered here. This is perhaps a convenient avoidance, but
I think that overall, far too much attention has been paid particularly
to the question of territoriality at the expense of more important central
issues.

To further delimit the field of interest, I will not be looking at all
state societies, but only at the first states that emerged in a very few
crucibles of advanced political development. These early states might
be considered "pristine" (Fried 1960), but only in the most general
sense that they evolved without major economic, military, or technological influence from more highly developed external states. This
usage abuses to some degree Fried's original definition of the term
"pristine," but it still serves to distinguish those societies whose evolution can be attributed primarily to indigenous factors, from those
whose evolution resulted from direct exogenous influences. While it
might be theoretically preferable to look at only truly pristine states

(being those societies that first broke through to statehood before any of their neighbors followed suit), there would be no workable data base to appeal to. As yet, we have uncovered no state-level societies in the archaeological past or ethnographic present that can be conclusively shown to have developed without being in contact with societies at a similar evolutionary stage. As will be discussed below (chapter 5), one of the effects of state emergence in a particular area is the stimulation of state development in surrounding areas. (Price 1977:210 discusses this general phenomenon in the context of a "cluster-interaction" model.) Thus, if doctrinaire restrictions are placed on the notion of pristine, we would be left with no more than four or five societies whose "pristineness" would have evaporated in less than a generation.

By allowing some latitude in the concept "pristine," it still provides a useful tool for studying state evolution. It allows us to focus on those elements and institutions that are basic to newly emergent states rather than impositions or imitations of more highly developed external state societies. In terms of the present analysis it is important to determine whether such phenomena as economic stratification or systematic application of coercive sanctions develop initially in conjunction with the earliest states or represent secondary developments arising much later in the evolutionary process. On a more pragmatic level, concentrating only on the earliest states makes it possible to exclude from consideration a tremendous range of "secondary" states that have evolved under highly individualized historic circumstances. While the evolution of such states undoubtedly involves certain nomothetic processes, the influence of more advanced external states introduces causative variables that are not going to be found in more pristine processes of state evolution (Price 1978:161). Secondary and pristine processes may be similar in their end result (though this is also open to question), but they require substantially different explanatory models. The various theories of secondary versus pristine state development, expectably are also quite different, and it would be of questionable value to try and compact both into the present analysis (see Price 1978; Claessen and Skalnik 1978; Salzman 1978; Sanders 1974; Renfrew 1972; Webb 1965, 1968; Lewis 1978). My main concern here is with how the first states came about of their own accord and what they looked like after the initial stages of emergence.

This focus on the earliest states carries with it certain baggage in terms of the kinds of data that can be appealed to in testing and evaluating various theories that have been offered to explain state evolution. The few known cases of pristine states all evolved prior to the advent of a sophisticated system of writing; consquently, the only record of these states is their material record—the material remains of past human behavior and environment. This fact places rather severe limitations on the kinds of data that are available for use in analyzing the evolution and organization of these societies. We can make no direct observations of people's behavior; we cannot talk to them or ask them insightful questions; we cannot listen in on their conversations. Our informants are all dead, and we can only pick up what they left behind and observe when and where they left it. Unless we are going to throw up our hands in disgust and abandon any hope of empirical analysis (which, admittedly, some people are willing to do), we are going to have to approach the early states through the methodology of archaeology.

Often viewed as the younger sibling of cultural anthropology, archaeology has been struggling of late to find its proper niche in the social sciences. With dusty stones, bones, and other assorted artifacts as their primary empirical meat, archaeologists are faced with the problem of deciding how their time and energy can best be expended to further the understanding of patterns of human behavior. Coming to grips with this problem has generated a wide range of debate in the field. Should archaeology be descriptive or explanatory, inductive or deductive, nomothetic or particularistic, idealistic or materialistic? These individual debates will not be addressed at length here, though it is necessary to make my own biases clear. The approach followed below falls generally into the research strategy of cultural materialism outlined by Marvin Harris (1979). As such, it is explanatory and nomothetic. The ultimate goal is to seek cross-cultural and cross-chronological explanations of patterns of human behavior by appealing to technological, economic, environmental, and demographic variables. While controversy rages over the universal applicability of Harris' materialist strategy in archaeology (e.g., Conrad 1981; Isbell 1981; Paulsen 1981). I have found it to be a useful framework for understanding certain broad patterns found in the evolution of early states. It is thus used only as a tool, not a miracle panacea.

Another reason for using the materialist strategy is that it lends itself particularly well to archaeological analyses of prehistoric societies. In looking for explanation primarily in the material foundations of culture, Harris' materialism appeals to those variables that can be most readily extracted directly from the archaeological record. Things such as technology, subsistence, past environments, and certain aspects of demography will frequently have overt manifestations in the archaeological record of past societies. Tools, field systems, subsistence remains, biological and geological markers of past climates, skeletal remains, and settlement patterns, for example, are commonly excavated and/or recorded by archaeologists. However, because archaeology can most easily retrieve information on the material foundations of past societies, does not mean that less-material structural and superstructural aspects of culture can be conveniently ignored.

This brings up another major hurdle that must be faced in any archaeological analysis of past sociopolitical institutions such as states. Namely, to what extent can nonmaterial phenomena, specifically, social and political organization and ideology, be indirectly inferred from the archaeological record? Perhaps the most radical answer to this question comes from Lewis Binford:

> The position being taken here is that different kinds of phenomena are never remote; they are either accessible or they are not. "Nonmaterial" aspects of culture are accessible in direct measure with the testability of propositions being advanced about them. Propositions concerning any realm of culture—technology, social organization, psychology, philosophy, etc.—for which arguments of relevance and empirically testable hypotheses can be offered are as sound as the history of hypothesis confirmation. The practical limitations on our knowledge of the past are not inherent in the nature of the archaeological record; the limitations lie in our methodological naivete, in our lack of development of principles determining the relevance of archaeological remains to propositions regarding processes and events of the past. (1972:95–96)

What Binford essentially argues is that it cannot be assumed from the start that *any* aspect of past societies is gone forever, and that the only way to make viable inferences about such societies is through a process of deductive reasoning and hypothesis testing.

In this and earlier writings, Binford presented a challenge and stimulated archaeologists to go out and begin exploring the potentials and limitations of their discipline. The process of exploration is still going on, but the results of fifteen years of work have tended to point out some patterns of what archaeologists can and cannot expect to get out of the archaeological record. Generally, the farther up they move on the "layer cake of culture," from base to structure to superstructure, the less successful archaeologists have been in making inferences about the nature of prehistoric societies. Increasingly sophisticated reconstruction and analyses of past subsistence systems, demographic patterns and warfare patterns, for example, have been blossoming in the literature in recent years (e.g., Euler and Gumerman 1978; Sanders et al. 1979; Johnson 1973; Flannery 1976; Buikstra 1976).

Studies of past ideologies, in contrast, are still in a stage of relative infancy in that they lack a clearcut methodology and have a tendency to arrive at conclusions from an intuitive rather than scientific route. This is not to say that such attempts have been wholly unsuccessful, nor that success is unattainable. However, the results to date have been somewhat less than totally convincing. In between the ample achievements at inferring the material base of prehistoric cultures and the scarcity of such achievements with regard to inferring ideological superstructure, attempts to reconstruct the middle ground—social and political organization—have met with variable success. While a number of such attempts dealing with prehistoric states will be discussed at greater length in subsequent chapters, examples of some of the work done on prestate societies helps to illustrate the kinds of problems and possibilities inherent in the archaeological reconstruction of prehistoric social and political organization.

Some of the first efforts to delve into the structural component of past cultures, largely inspired by Binford, were aimed at reconstructing kinship systems and post-marital residence rules—two of anthropology's pet subjects. Implicitly, these early works were supposed to show that archaeologists could indeed work with the same subject matter as cultural anthropolgists (Longacre 1970; Hill 1970; Deetz 1965). However, these initial efforts have been strongly criticized for being overly ambitious and anthropologically naive (Allen and Richardson 1971; see also Longacre 1973:333 for a reconsideration of his earlier analysis). They essentially pushed the archaeological data too far, and made unwarranted assumptions about the relationships between material remains, behavior, and patterns of social organization and ideology. Subsequent to these initial forays, a number of less ambitious and more rigorously formulated attempts to elucidate patterns of social and political organization have produced more successful results.

Perhaps the best of the work done by archaeologists along these lines has been carried out by David Thomas and his associates in the Great Basin (Thomas 1972, 1973, 1974; Williams et al. 1973). Briefly, they have tried to determine, archaeologically, whether aboriginal groups in western North America were characterized by a "family band" type of organization, as argued by Julian Steward (1938, 1955; cf. Service 1971a; Sahlins 1968; Fried 1967). As a starting point for their analysis, they deduced from Steward's ethnohistoric model of the Shoshoni family band certain patterns of behavior that should be found in a society characterized by this type of organization. These patterns were then operationalized in terms of their expectable manifestations in artifact types, distribution of artifacts, and the size and distribution of settlements. With this operational model of the Shoshoni family band, they went out into the field to test the model in the archaeological record. Without going into specific details, their field research appears to show fairly conclusively that the Shoshoni pattern of organization was not a recent development in the Great Basin, but in fact prevailed for several thousand years prior to the arrival of the Europeans, thus providing empirical confirmation for Steward's argument.

While Thomas looked at a relatively simple form of prehistoric sociopolitical organization, other archaeologists have taken on more complex forms. For example, data are beginning to be collected which have a direct bearing on whether the *tribe* is a truly aboriginal form of social organization, as argued by most cultural anthropologists (see Service 1971a, 1971b; Sahlins 1968), or a secondary construct resulting from contact between simpler societies and advancing states, as argued by Fried (1975). Specifically, in the southwestern and northeastern United States, work has uncovered groups of prehistoric villages that appear to be bounded together into discrete multicomponent systems (Dean et al. 1978; Tuck 1971). Warfare appears to have been the binding agent that brought and held the villages together in both cases. These bounded, multicomponent units thus have the primary earmarks of a tribal form of organization, and they appear several hundred years prior to the intrusion of European states into either area.

At the same time, however, there is also evidence from the southwest demonstrating that bounded tribes may be a relatively isolated phenomenon in horticultural societies, found only under conditions of intensified warfare. In particular, at a number of sites located in transition zones between major culture areas (i.e., between the Hohokam,

Mogollon, and Anasazi), archaeologists have found an intermingling of culture traits. In other words, house types, ceramics, and lithics of two different culture groups are found together contemporaneously on the same site. One interpretation that has been made of this pattern is that intermarriage, rather than conflict, took place when people of the different culture groups came together (Haas 1980). This interpretation would tend to support Fried's notion that unranked horticulturalists tend to be organized in relatively loose, unbounded social networks. Again, as with Thomas' analysis of the family band, archaeologists working with tribes have complemented and supplemented the work of cultural anthropologists on patterns of social and political organization (see also Braun and Plog 1980 and Voss 1980 for additional archaeological analyses of tribal forms of organization).

Moving beyond tribes, a number of other scholars have looked at material manifestations of organization in chiefdoms or ranked societies. Differences in mortuary offerings and the distribution of sumptuary goods, in particular, have been analyzed to make inferences about the nature and degree of social and political ranking in such societies (Levy 1979; Hatch 1976; Rothschild 1975; Peebles 1974; Tainter 1973, 1975; Brown 1971; Saxe 1970). Peebles and Kus (1977) and Earle (1977) have also used subsistence and settlement patterns to look at the nature of political and economic relationships between communities within chiefdoms. The results of their work have brought directly into question the time-honored notion that centralized collection and redistribution of diverse resources play a key role in both the emergence and organization of chiefdom societies (cf. Service 1971a; Fried 1967). Basically, they have found that rather than redistributing resources between environmentally different ecozones, the primary role of the chief is to process information and manage interaction between communities.

Another somewhat more comprehensive attempt at reconstructing prehistoric chiefdom organization has been made by Colin Renfrew for societies in the Wessex area of south Britain and in the Aegean (1972, 1973a). Much of his work in these areas has been outstanding and has taken archaeology into new frontiers, however, his analyses also suffer from a number of critical problems, and a more detailed review here helps to illustrate several of the major pitfalls archaeologists may run into. As in Thomas' use of Steward's family band model, Renfrew relies on the anthropological models of Service (1962) and

Sahlins (1968) to provide him with a list of the features frequently found in chiefdom societies. While such a list, in and of itself, is an acceptable starting point in investigating prehistoric social and political organization, Renfrew makes a number of logical and methodological errors in using this list to interpret his archaeological data.

1. In establishing twenty features that supposedly characterize a chiefdom level of cultural evolution, Renfrew fails to distinguish those features which may be definitive of a chiefdom from those which may be found in simpler or more complex evolutionary levels. Such features as "greater productivity" and "frequent ceremonies and rituals serving wide social purposes," which may be found at any evolutionary stage, are placed on the same level as "ranking" and "no true government to back up decisions by legalized force," which taken together will distinguish a chiefdom from other types of societies (Renfrew 1973a:543; cf. Service 1971a, 1975; Fried 1967). Consequently, in looking at the archaeological data base he concludes that the prehistoric societies were at a chiefdom level even though they lack critical features separating them from bands, tribes, or states. In the Wessex case, for example, he concludes the society was probably a chiefdom on the basis of what he sees as evidence for about fourteen of the twenty features. At the same time, he states "wc have almost no direct evidence among the artifacts found for personal ranking" (1972:556), and he never addresses the question of whether there was an absence of "true government to back up decisions by legalized force" (1972:554–57). Thus, aside from his intuitive assurances there is no objective basis for accepting his conclusions.

2. He fails to rigorously define the various features of the chiefdom and operationalize them such that they can be recognized in the archaeological record. He simply looks at the archaeological record to see what general evidence might be found for each of them. For example, communally constructed monumental architecture (1973a:554) and large-scale storage facilities (1972:390) are alternately interpreted as constituting evidence of the redistributive economy of a chiefdom. In the first case, he does not clarify why communal architecture is an indication of redistribution, and in the second, he does not suggest a distinction between a voluntary system of redistribution and an enforced system of taxation (see Earle 1977). The abundance of administrative seals and other recording devices in association with the extensive storage facilities in the Aegean case would, in fact, appear to

indicate a formalized taxation system rather than a simple redistributive economy (1972:386–90). Basically, Renfrew interprets his data in a way that supports his conclusions but that does not allow for deductive confirmation or refutation. The result is little more than a "Just So" story.

3. The final general problem with Renfrew's analysis is one often encountered in attempts by archaeologists to utilize various anthropological models of social and political evolution, such as those offered by Steward, Service, Sahlins, Fried, and others. In making up and using his list of chiefdom features, Renfrew falls into the trap of accepting specific anthropological models as fact. He fails to recognize that these models represent theoretical arguments that have not been definitively "proven" in any sense in the ethnographic record, let alone in the archaeological record. Thus, he considers such things as redistribution, monumental architecture, a specialized priesthood, and other divisions of labor to be characteristics of chiefdoms, solely on the basis of assertions by two anthropologists, Service (1962) and Sahlins (1968) (Renfrew 1972:363–65; 1973a:542–43). Yet as noted above, other archaeologists have thrown into doubt the central role of a redistributive economy in chiefdoms, and additional serious questions can be raised about the presence of truly monumental construction or major specialization in any prestate society (see Fried 1967:115; also chapters 6 to 9 below).

This third problem entangling Renfrew's analysis brings up a point that needs to be discussed further; namely, how can the theories and models of cultural anthropologists be most profitably utilized by archaeologists in the investigation of cultural evolution? In all of the examples given above of archaeologists working with prehistoric social and political organization, the work of cultural anthropologists has played a key role, either as a guide to research or as an idea to be challenged. Such use of anthropological constructs in either role has certain dangers as well as advantages. Neither should be underestimated. The dangers lie in both *overreliance* on the anthropological models and in *overreacting* to them. These two possibilities present a Scylla and Charybdis for the archaeologist. The research of Thomas, Tuck, Peebles and Kus, Earle, and other archaeologists clearly illustrates that anthropological models based primarily on ethnography cannot be accepted at face value, as they are by Renfrew and many other archaeologists. They need to be rigorously operationalized and tested in the material record of past societies. They cannot be used, nor were they ever intended to be used, blindly as an independent magical means of interpreting that material record. If archaeologists do nothing more than parrot the theories of cultural anthropologists, then the discipline will inevitably be relegated to a rather obscure existence in the basement of the social sciences.

Equally dangerous, however, is the apparently primal need of some archaeologists to be totally independent of the work done by cultural anthropologists. At a recent convention of archaeologists, one of the grand statesmen of the discipline proclaimed that it was high time archaeologists went beyond Fried and Service and got on with new and better things. Amidst the loud applause for this proclamation, there was an undercurrent of cynical whispers to the effect that such an idea was hardly new, and that Fried's and Service's evolutionary models has been passé for years! This may well be true, but the critical issue is whether these models and others offered by cultural anthropologists are to be simply thrown out so we can start with a "fresh" slate, or if we are to use them as a start and progress beyond them in a constructive way. Recent literature would seem to indicate there is a movement toward abandonment and a search for wholly new alternatives.

Yoffee (1979), for example, argues that the entire evolutionist model of Fried, Service, and others "is at best nonuniversalistic and at worst theoretically sterile" (1979:24). In its place, he offers what he calls a "growth model." His criticisms of "evolutionism" are based on two things: first, he claims that a supposed analogy between social and biological evolution is "inappropriate, since sociocultural change is not discrete and limited to jumps in homeostatic adaptations depending on responses to external conditions" (1979:25); and second, evolutionary models have not been adequately operationalized in the field and have not productively focused archaeological research.

The first criticism might be a valid indictment of evolutionism except that it has the distinct ring of a straw-man type of argument. While some anthropologists do make a direct analogy between social and biological evolution, most would argue for a much looser analogy to the effect that cultures adapt to their total social and natural environment (internal and external) in a process similar to that of biological adaptation (see, for example, Service 1971a:6; cf. Peters 1980). The stages offered in various evolutionary models are not analogous to biological speciation or differentiation, but rather reflect similar kinds of adaptive processes that occur cross-culturally in response to similar kinds of circumstances. These stages may also represent "homeostatic adaptations" (although not always, as in the case of Fried's "stratified" stage—1967:225), but only in the sense that certain basic organizational changes allow diverse cultures considerable flexibility in adjusting to a wide variety of environmental conditions. No one argues that once a "tribal" or "chiefdom" stage has been reached a society settles in for a period of equilibrium with no change or further adaptation. Anyone coming to such a conclusion seems to me to have misread the evolutionist literature.

Yoffee's second criticism is not really a charge against the evolutionists, so much as it is a charge against the archaeologists who have tried to use the evolutionary models. As I pointed out above, there has been abuse of the models, and research has been misdirected, but this can hardly be taken as a flaw in the models. Yoffee's criticisms are not invalid, and he presents some real problems with current evolutionary theory. But his decision to abandon evolutionism and strike out on a new path comes too close to throwing out the baby with the bath water. We need to attack current models in the field, keeping some parts, revising others, and throwing out still others as research provides us with increasingly greater understanding of the processes of cultural evolution.

The primary advantage to using anthropological models, particularly in the field of cultural evolution, is that they provide a foundation upon which to build and focus archaeological research. Morton Fried and Elman Service, specifically, as well as others such as Marshall Sahlins, Richard N. Adams, Ronald Cohen, Robert Carneiro, and Marvin Harris, have established a theoretical framework that has excellent potential for exploitation and utilization by archaeologists. Furthermore, the work of these individuals is built on earlier foundations laid by Leslie White, Julian Steward, and Walter Goldschmidt, who in turn looked to the work of Karl Marx, Lewis Henry Morgan, Edward Tylor, Herbert Spencer, etc. I am not trying to say that the word of modern cultural anthropologists should be accepted because they are coming from a long tradition with eminent forefathers. I wish simply to point out that cultural anthropologists have done a great deal of work in the field of cultural evolution, and archaeologists do not have to start out from scratch. The discipline with only material remains to work with also has the ability to look at processes that take hundreds or thousands of years to complete and to examine the full range of extinct culture types that have inhabited the world at one time or another. These are abilities that cultural anthropology forsakes in exchange for its living informants. The two siblings complement each other and can share theory and data to their mutual benefit without endangering either's independence.

To return to the evolution of the state, what follows is a mix of both cultural anthropology and archaeology. I will be focusing first on two current anthropological schools of thought regarding the evolution of the state: a "conflict" school and an "integration" school. The philosophical foundations and historical development of each school will be discussed to provide a background and general perspective on the debate being waged within anthropology. The most recent and comprehensive presentations of the two positions will be outlined and critically evaluated in terms of their internal cogency. Their central differences will be abstracted, operationalized, and subjected to an empirical test in the archaeological records of areas where the world's first states are believed to have arisen—specifically, Mesopotamia, China, Mesoamerica, and Peru.

To expand the theoretical picture beyond the conflict/integration debate, more specific theories of state formation will also be examined. The latter theories have most often been proffered to explain the rise of the state in one particular area, but they can be shown to have cross-cultural applicability as well. Furthermore, while these theories appeal to different primary causal variables—trade, warfare, or irrigation—they all have one feature in common: a ruling body controlling production or procurement of basic resources and exercising economic power over its population.

The ubiquity of this economic power base in all the theories provides a starting point for constructing a broad framework for looking at the evolution of states in terms of power. Beginning with the economic power base, certain predictions can be made about the development of subsequent power bases, and the interaction of these bases in the process of governing a population. Once formulated, the framework will be applied to the emergence and development of state societies in the New World. Thus, in the first part of the book I will be looking at the theoretical arguments that have been offered to explain the origins of the state, and where possible examine these arguments in the light of relevant data. In the second part I will offer a "power framework" which takes off from previous work and attempts to deal with those developmental processes that can be expected to occur after the state has come into existence.

Before turning to the philosophical background of the conflict/integration debate, I should issue one caveat. The present work is not only about the evolution of political organization, it is in a very real sense political itself, as are virtually all scientific enterprises. In addressing advocacy in the social sciences, Wallerstein by happenstance selected archaeology as an example, and I think he has struck a nerve not often felt in the discipline.

> When I say the "present reality" of phenomena, I do not mean that in order to strengthen the political claims of a government, an archaeologist for example should assert that the artifacts he uncovers belong to one group when he in fact believes them to belong to another. I mean that the whole archaeological enterprise from its inception—the social investment in this branch of scientific activity, the research orientation, the conceptual tools, the modes of resuming and communicating the results—are functions of the social present. To think otherwise is self-deceptive at best. Objectivity is honesty within this framework. (Wallerstein 1976:9)

[Part I]

ANTHROPOLOGISTS AND ARCHAEOLOGISTS IN PURSUIT OF STATE ORIGINS

[Chapter 1]

The Philosophical Background

Throughout the modern social sciences there are broad problem areas which are found to co-occur in virtually all of the major disciplines. One of these common problem areas, shared by sociology, economics, political science, history, and anthropology concerns the role of government in the organization of complex societies. While the separate disciplines may approach government from different perspectives, there are certain basic similarities which can be found to cut across discipline lines. In particular, there are two outstanding schools of thought regarding the role of government. The political scientist David Apter has succinctly described the two schools in terms of opposing models of society:

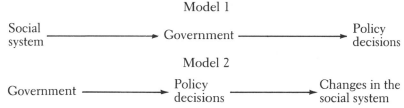

In the first model government is the dependent variable and social system or community is the independent variable. Power is seen to inhere in the public, which creates the inputs of stimuli to which government must cater (Easton 1957, 1965). In the second model government is the independent variable and social system the dependent one. Such systems tend to elevate the goals of the government into norms and make them sacred and ethical precepts, through which legitimacy is defined. Governments resembling the first model tend to be competitive, pluralistic, and democratic; those resembling the second tend to be monopolistic, monistic, and totalitarian. . . . As opposing paradigms, these two generalized types, in their various concrete formulations, are perpetually vulnerable to each other. Indeed, one can see over time that they form a permanent dialogue of conflict. They represent two fundamentally different approaches to government. (Apter 1968:217–18)

Within anthropology, these two "fundamentally different approaches to government" have recently been manifested in a debate over the origins of the state. Along the lines of Apter's first model, Elman Service (1975, 1978) argues that the governing institutions of the state first developed as integrative mechanisms to coordinate and regulate the different parts of complex societies. This argument may be called the "integration" theory (also "contract," "benefit," "consensus," or "conservative" theory—Service 1978; Lenski 1966; Yoffee 1979; Claessen and Skalnik 1978a). Following Apter's second model, Morton Fried (1967, 1978) argues that the governing institutions of the state initially developed as coercive mechanisms to resolve intra-societal conflict arising out of economic stratification. This argument may be called the "conflict" theory (also "coercive," "class," or "radical" theory—Service 1978; Lenski 1966; Carneiro 1979; Claessen and Skalnik 1978a).

These two opposing theories have generated a great deal of discussion in anthropology and archaeology, but they are often considered to be just two more theories among many offered in the last fifteen years to explain the origins of the state (e.g., Wright 1977b; Johnson 1973; Yoffee 1979). However, it is important to realize that contained within Service's and Fried's specific arguments are the most recent and clearest anthropological statements of major opposing philosophical/theoretical positions on the origins and primary role of government. Furthermore, the arguments they present, while modernized and clarified, are in no sense "new," but rather have deep historical roots in philosophy and the social sciences in general.

To provide a background to the current debate between Fried and Service, I will briefly outline below the philosophical and historical underpinnings of the conflict and integration positions. This outline will also provide some insight into the broader ramifications of archaeological research on the origins of the state. With a few notable exceptions (e.g., Childe 1936, 1942), archaeologists have tended to ignore any possible relationships between their research and the work of political philosophers and other social scientists. However, the questions of why states first arose and what role government may have played in those first states do have relevance outside the boundaries of the discipline of archaeology.

From Ancient Greece to China

Going back more than two millennia, the political and anthropological debates of the twentieth century are clearly manifested in the earliest philosophical writings. In these early works the state was not analyzed as a type of political organization distinct from other types, nor were its origin and developmental process discussed. Rather, the focus was either on what constitutes an ideal state, or on what kinds of contemporary states existed at that time. When the earliest states were described, however briefly, they were contrasted to extant states, which were considered to be corruptions or deviations from earlier, near-ideal forms.

Historically, most recurrent themes in Western political philosophy are first exhibited in the work of the early Greek philosophers. Writing on the Peloponnesian War in the fifth century B.C., Thucydides approaches the study of government and the state from a descriptive rather than strictly philosophical standpoint. From the specific societies he witnesses, Thucydides abstracts certain ideal forms of government. The two basic kinds of state constitutions he arrives at are the democratic and the oligarchic. While never directly comparing their salient points in his historical study, he treats these two forms as polar opposites.

Democracy, represented by the government of Athens according to Thucydides, and best exemplified by the rule of Pericles, is characterized by government through cooperation. All the citizens of the Athenian state, both those with property and those without, participate in the process of governmental decision making. Concurrently, all people mutually benefit from the positive services provided by a just and responsive ruler. Thus, Athens, at least as interpreted by Thucydides, can be seen as a model of the *integrative* type of state. Conversely, the oligarchy of Sparta implicitly represents a *conflict* model of the state, since Thucydides characterizes it as government by the few over the many. Only the propertied class in Sparta control the process of governmental decision making, and it uses that control to maintain its property rights.

Going beyond the basic descriptive analysis of Thucydides, Plato, in *The Republic*, presents a model for the development of an ideal state. He argues that men of different skills and professions must unite in a community to enjoy the mutual benefits inherent in specialization and the division of labor. Yet, once united, men must submit to the rule of a central governing authority to provide order in the complex and heterogeneous community, and to insure just and equal treatment of all segments of society. In this hypothetical model, Plato takes basically an *integrative* position.

However, it is of interest to note that at a later point he also presages the basis of the *conflict* argument. He argues that the ideal state with its beneficient government must at some time decay into a plutocratic form of government. The first step in this decay is the accumulation of private property and wealth by some members of the ruling class (in Plato's ideal state all property is communally owned, and other forms of wealth are strictly controlled.) This accumulation leads to marked economic inequality and ultimately to conflict between the rich and poor. While he does not proceed to analyze the role of government in this conflict situation, it can be seen that the basic premises of the conflict position are visible in Plato's exposition.

In contrast to Plato, Aristotle does not philosophize about the "ideal" form of state, and he does not question the basic structure of known governments at that time. He accepts ownership and unequal distribution of private property, and he supports the basic institution of slavery. However, in what is one of the first attempts at comparative political science, Aristotle compares and contrasts the governmental forms of different contemporary communities (see Weissleder 1978:187). On the basis of this comparative analysis, he finds that there are two basic kinds of governmental institutions: the democratic, in which the rulers are drawn from the entirety of the citizenry, regardless of property status; and the oligarchic, in which the rulers are drawn only from the propertied class. However, despite their differences, both types of governments are based on the resolution of *conflict* between economic classes:

> But the same people cannot be rich and poor, and that is why the prime division of classes in a state is into the well-to-do and the property-less. Further, owing to the fact that the one class is for the most part numerically small, the other large, these two appear as antagonistic classes. So constitutions reflect the predominance of one or other of these and two types of constitution emerge—democracy and oligarchy. (*The Politics*, book V, ch. 4).

Accompanying this emphasis on class antagonism in both types of governments, Aristotle uses the supremacy of enforceable laws as another critical element in his analysis. The function of these laws is to protect the basic rights, including property rights, of all citizens. Laws operate to keep the rich from abusing the rights of the poor, and the poor from abusing the property rights of the rich (as in his "monarchical demos" or what might be called today the "dictatorship of the proletariat") (Book IV, ch. 4–6). In addition to recognizing the conflict in state society, Aristotle does acknowledge the potential integrative benefits of a centralized government (Weissleder 1978). However, in accepting the inevitability of economic inequalities, slavery, and strife between classes, as well as in advocating the rule of law, Aristotle's overall position is clearly an early presentation of a conflict model of the state (see Lenski 1966:5–7; cf. Cohen 1978:13–14).

While the classical Greeks provide the foundations of most modern Western political philosophy, early recorded philosophers in other parts of the world are addressing similar subjects and engage in parallel political debates. Perhaps the most well-documented analyses of the nature and role of government and the state in the nonwestern world come from early China. (There are, however, relevant materials from the Middle East as in the Old Testament, and from India as in *The Laws of Manu*.) In the wealth of material from China, opposing positions analogous to those of Plato and Aristotle are manifested in the Confucianist and Legalist schools of thought.

Confucius and his followers in the fifth and sixth centuries B.C. maintain that the ideal form of government is dependent upon voluntary adherence by all members and segments of society to certain rules of propriety of *li*. In the Confucian model of government, laws backed by sanctions are not applied to enforce the rules of propriety; rather, the application of sanctions would itself be an impropriety. In place of government by laws, the process of governing is a moral one and obedience to the government is a voluntary action. These principles can be seen in the following statements attributed to Confucius in the *Analects*:

> If a ruler himself is upright, all will go well without orders. But if he himself is not upright, even though he gives orders they will not be obeyed.

> Lead the people by laws and regulate them by penalties, and the people will try to keep out of jail, but will have no sense of shame. Lead the people by virtue and restrain them by the rules of decorum, and the people will have a sense of shame, and moreover will become good. (DeBary et al. 1960:32)

There is no sense of an ideal social, economic, or political equality in the Confucian model of government. The *li* or appropriate behavior is different for different groups or classes of individuals, as are the concomitant privileges and hardships enjoyed or endured by each (Ch'u 1961:228–29). The inequities of life are not to be questioned or rectified in any way, but they are to be recognized as necessary for the beneficial operation of a harmonious system of government. For Confucius there is no sense of conflict between the parts of a heterogeneous society. Clearly an integrative model of government, the Confucian position contains remarkable similarities to certain twentieth-century anthropological schools of thought.

The early Legalists in Chinese philosophical thought contrasted sharply with the Confucianists. Shang Yang, a prime minister in the Ch'in dynasty in the fourth century B.C., and Han Fei in the third century B.C., are the first recorded proponents of the Legalist political philosophy (DeBary et al. 1960:122). The basic tenet of this early Chinese Legalism is the need for laws, backed by positive and negative sanction, to maintain social order. Accordingly, the role of government is in enforcing laws to insure the continuous orderly operation of society. To paraphrase Han Fei, the state government must inflict some small pain on the people to ensure them the greater benefits of social order (DeBary et al. 1960:129).

The possibility that the enforcement of laws might operate to the greater benefit of some than of others is not an active topic of consideration in the early Legalist thought. The Legalists also do not address the question of how economic and political inequalities may have come about in society, nor what specific role the laws and the government may have had in maintaining the system of inequality. However, there is some acknowledgment that the social, economic, and political inequalities in society create a situation of potential conflict between segments of society. The reason for this conflict, and the need for laws to resolve it, lie in the natural tendency of people to strive to improve their own position and that of their relatives in relation to the accumulation of wealth and power (Ch'u 1961:243–47; DeBary et al. 1960:124–36). Given this situation, the laws would operate ideally to keep the rich and powerful from totally exploiting the poor and weak, and at the same time they would effectively serve to prevent the latter from seizing the wealth and power of the former. Thus, the basic elements of a conflict-based state are present in the Legalist school of thought.

It is significant to note that private property, which plays a primary role in Aristotle's conflict position in the West, is of relatively minor importance in the Legalist position in China. This decreased role of private property is not unexpected in the light of Wittfogel's argument (1957:228–29, 291–94) that private property was "weak" (a minimum of freedom to dispose of property) in the hydraulic society of China and relatively "strong" (a maximum of freedom to dispose of property) in the nonhydraulic societies of the West. It is important to keep this point in mind when considering the prominent role of private property in later Western philosophies.

In comparing the philosophies of early China with those of ancient Greece, the Confucianist school is directly analogous to the philosophy of Plato, and the Legalist school is consonant with the basic philosophy of Aristotle. Plato and the Confucianists on the integration side hold that in the ideal government the recognized benefits of an orderly society, regardless of inherent inequalities, are sufficient incentive to insure the obedience of the populace to a just and moral governing body. Aristotle and the Legalists on the conflict side counter that because of the realities of economic and political inequality in the complex society, social order and the obedience of the people can only be successfully achieved through enforceable laws which govern behavior. While there are many differences between the philosophies of early China and Greece, the fundamental similarities between them indicate how the conflict/integration debate in political philosophy cross-cuts both time and culture.

The Beginning of Modern Theories

Beyond the elementary statements of the conflict and integration positions by the early Greek philosophers, the direct antecedents of modern Western theories of the state are to be found in the work of Enlightenment philosophers of the seventeenth and eighteenth centuries. During this period, a major focus of attention is on the origin of government. Scholars attempt to gain insight into the primary function of government by looking at how and why people first submitted to the rule of a central governing authority. Within this discussion on governmental origins there are clear manifestations of the conflict and integration positions, although there is considerable diversity on both sides of the debate. On the integration side, most theories present one of several alternative theories of the "social contract."

Integration

The basic premise of the social contract theorists in the seventeenth and eighteenth centuries is that men join together under a mutually agreed upon "contract" in order to enjoy the benefits of an organized society. As Barker (1947:xii–xiii) points out, the primary interest of these theorists is on the contract of society, rather than on the contract of government. In other words, they are interested in why men first come together to form social units, not necessarily why they come together under a governing agency. However, inherent in each of the respective theories of societal contract is the basis of a theory of governmental contract in which a form of contract is entered into by a ruler and a body of subjects. In both the societal and governmental contracts, the contract is entered into by mutual consent. One of the earliest comprehensive theories of social contract is presented by Thomas Hobbes.

As a social and political philosopher, Hobbes has a certain renown for his conception of basic human nature. He presents a logical statement on the quality of life prior to the development of the civil state, and gives reasons why the civil state developed out of the preceding "state of nature." For Hobbes, the basic elements of human nature are that people naturally compete for dominance over one another, while they simultaneously seek to avoid death (Hobbes 1651a; Macpherson 1968:39). From these basic human qualities, Hobbes deduces a vision of life prior to the civilizing effects of a state government and its accompanying body of laws. This vision has come to be a cliché of the bad life: such life in a state of nature was "solitary, poore, nasty, brutish, and short" (Hobbes 1651b:186). To escape such a life and to control the competitive chaos of human nature, people need government, and any form of government is better than none. Consequently, according to Hobbes, in exchange for the benefits of being governed, people must give up their natural right to pursue well-being at the expense of others. In giving up this right, they subsume their individual wills to a collective will, which is transferred to a sovereign ruler (Hobbes 1651b:227). In doing so, the people must agree to accept the rules of behavior, the laws, dictated by this sovereign (Hobbes

1651b:chs 14, 16, and 26; Macpherson 1968:39–45). Thus, to gain the benefits of an orderly society, the people fully abdicate governing authority to the ruling body of the state.

Other social contract theorists following Hobbes do not maintain such a polar position on the omnipotent role of government. John Locke, for example, holds that when men entered into the contract of society they entrusted authority to the government; but they did not contract with that government, so the authority to govern could be withdrawn should the government act contrary to the majority will of the population (Locke 1690:455–66; Laslett 1960:121–22; Barker 1947: xiii). Locke also differs from Hobbes in the reasons why men originally enter into the social contract and thereby submit to a central government. According to Locke, the primary reason for the contract was for the protection of rights to private property: "The great and *chief end* therefore, of Mens uniting into Commonweaths, and putting themselves under Government, *is the Preservation of their Property*" (Locke 1690:395, emphasis in the original). To fulfill its function of protecting property rights, the government provided adjudicatory services for resolving disputes over property between society members. This was achieved through a system of laws which emanated from a legislative body, but which ultimately represented the will of the majority (pp. 319–23).

Another version of the integration position, that offered by David Hume, is not tied to the notion of the social contract. Hume, to some extent, follows Locke in asserting that the right of property is at the base of all governments, but he eschews the idea that men initiated the institution of government by entering into a form of contract or formal agreement. He does argue that men cannot live outside society, and that in all societies there is an informal agreement or "convention" between men to allow everyone the secure enjoyment of those goods which one may attain either by "fortune or industry" (Hume, p. 32). However, this informal agreement does not give rise to government.

Government, according to Hume, originated under conditions of extended warfare in "savage" society (pp. 41, 49). The efficiency gained by unification in times of war induced people to consent voluntarily to the governing authority of a ruler. Eventually, the people recognized the benefits of a ruler who could serve as an arbiter of differences and prevent disorder, and the submission extended to him in time of war was gradually extended to him in times of peace as well. But stable government cannot be based solely on the voluntary consent of the people, so the ruler is obliged to exact revenues to support his governing bureaucracy and to punish "the refractory and disobedient" (p. 41). Hume, not unlike Hobbes and Locke, holds that at least the origin of government lay in a form of consensual agreement between the rulers and the ruled. However, Hume feels that beyond those first governments which arose out of consent in prehistoric times (Hume was the first philosopher to recognize that the first government "Preceded the use of writing and all the other civilized arts of life," p. 44), all subsequent governments were based on conquest or usurpation "without any pretense of a fair consent or voluntary subjection of the people" (p. 42). Nevertheless, regardless of whether it is based on consent, conquest, or usurpation, Hume maintains that all government has "no other object or purpose but the distribution of justice" (p. 39). This justice is achieved through a system of laws, backed by force, which serve to secure the constant possession of property.

In addition to Hume, Hobbes, and Locke, there are a number of other political philosophers in the seventeenth and eighteenth centuries who stress the integrative role of government in complex state societies. However, most of these scholars, such as James Harrington, Francis Hutchinson, and Adam Smith, are concerned primarily with modern politics and economics. Furthermore, they do not hold qualitatively differing positions from those outlined above concerning the origin and basic function of government. Of all the different theories of the time, Hume's outline of political evolution comes closest to the later integration theories in the nineteenth and twentieth centuries. In particular, his argument for the role of warfare in the origin of government is essentially the same in almost all aspects as the more recent arguments offered by such integration theorists as Herbert Spencer and Elman Service (see chapter 3).

Conflict

In contrast to the relative abundance of integration theorists, there are few conflict theorists in the Enlightenment period. By far the most comprehensive conflict theory of the origin of government is offered by Jean-Jacques Rousseau in *Discourse on the Origin of Inequality*. Rousseau, however, is also known for his advocacy of the "social contract," and it is useful to clarify his basic position. In *The Social Contract*, a philosophical statement about the ideal form of government, Rousseau expresses many ideas similar to those of Hobbes and Locke concerning the desirability of a social contract. While believing that basic human nature is good and that the prestate form of society was idyllic, Rousseau nevertheless agrees with Hobbes that there must be some form of sovereign governmental power with supreme authority (Winch 1972:223). He feels that some form of sovereign government is necessary to protect the freedom of all individuals in the face of potential inequities inherent in complex societies (Rousseau 1762:20–23, 215–28). Rousseau's ideal form of protective government involves a social contract similar to that of Locke. The people submit their individual wills to a common will, and they exchange their natural liberty for a civil liberty. Rousseau's ideal ruler, upon assuming power, is still dependent upon the common will of the people. The rules of behavior are expressions of that common will, they are not laws enforced solely at the command of the ruler. The process of governing, therefore, consists of interpreting and carrying out the common will.

In this conception of the ideal government, Rousseau does not differ widely from the integrationist position of other contract theorists of the time. However, in his ideas about the actual historical development of formal government, Rousseau stands in polar opposition to the integrationist position. He hypothesizes that as intensive agriculture and metallurgy developed at some time in the past, the avenue to economic and political inequality was opened. In time, both population size and inequality increased until a point was reached where all material wealth was privately owned; therefore, a gain in one person's wealth meant a loss in another's. Since some people were totally dispossessed of land and material wealth, they were forced to either beg or steal their subsistence from the wealthy. As more people fell into the latter condition, there was increasing social disorder. The circumstances resembled a "state of war," and no person could feel assured of the possession of his property. Within this context of disorder, Rousseau asserts it was the rich who realized the need for a formal means of social control:

> The rich in particular must have soon perceived how much they suffered by a perpetual war, of which they alone supported all the expense, and in which, though all risked life, they alone risked any property. (1755:226)

To resolve this problem and retain his wealth,

> the rich man, thus pressed by necessity, at last conceived the deepest
> project that ever entered the human mind: this was to employ in his favor
> the very forces that attacked him, to make allies of his enemies, to inspire
> them with other maxims, and make them adopt other institutions as
> favorable to his pretensions, as the law of nature was unfavorable to them.
> (p. 227)

This "project" was the establishment of a formal system of government with a strict body of laws. This new political institution did
provide the advantages of social control to all, and abolished the "state
of war" which endangered the lives of all; but the primary advantages
were gained only by the rich and powerful. The new system

> gave new fetters to the weak and new power to the rich; irretrievably
> destroyed natural liberty, fixed forever the laws of property and inequality;
> changed an artful usurpation into an irrevocable right; and for the benefit
> of a few ambitious individuals subjected the rest of mankind to perpetual
> labor, servitude, and misery. (p. 228)

In this hypothetical reconstruction of the origins of formal government, Rousseau thus establishes himself as one of the first political
philosophers to present a comprehensive conflict theory of the origin
of the state. Also, just as Hume's analysis contains the basic outline
of modern integrationist theory, Rousseau's analysis represents a ru-
dimentary facsimile of the major conflict theories of Marx and Engels
and their twentieth-century successors.

A Blend of Theories

In addition to the general integration and conflict theories, a number
of Enlightenment philosophers offer theories of the state that combine
both integration and conflict elements. One of those to offer such an
eclectic theory is Giambattista Vico. Vico analyzes the origins of formal government in the specific historical context of Rome. In his
pseudo-historical reconstruction of events, he asserts the presence of
men of naturally different temperaments in the world: there are impious and weak men, who prior to the state were living in a Hobbesian
state of nature; and there are "pious, chaste, strong, and even pow-

erful" men who originally lived in a state of the family (Vico 1744:12). To escape the anarchy of the state of nature, the impious fled to the cities, wherein the pious and strong were ensconced. Once in the cities, they were taken in by individual families and provided with protection and the means of subsistence. In return, these weak individuals assumed a position of submission to the family father, and were obliged to support their protectors by cultivating their fields (pp. 12–14, 79–82).

Up to this point in Vico's reconstruction, he presents an organismic model of society based on a natural division of labor, and places stress on integrative benefits and consensual agreements. However, in the successive stage of political development, he makes a shift over to a conflict model. After a "long period" of passively submitting to the rule of the fathers, Vico states that the subordinate individuals began to "chafe" at their servile state, and rose up in rebellion against the ruling fathers (p. 210). In response to the unrest and rebellion of their subjects, the fathers then united under a single governing authority, the king. It was the function of the king to administer laws which protected the property rights of the fathers, and to conduct war in the protection of the state. Thus in Vico's scheme, the origin of a dominance-submission political relationship is based on a consensual agreement with mutual benefits for all parties. But the maintenance of that relationship is based on the physical suppression of the subordinate members of the society.

The Scots philosopher Adam Ferguson offers another theory of governmental origins combining both integration and conflict elements that is somewhat more viable than the postulated reconstruction of Vico. Ferguson briefly outlines a model of political evolution that proceeds from savagery to barbarism to civilization. In the earlier stages of development he argues that there was an absence of private property (aside from immediate personal belongings), no true subordination in political relationships and no form of recognizable government. He also holds that the transition from savage society to barbarous society was marked by the initiation of private property, leading to economic inequalities. This in turn led to the subordination of some individuals under others, based on the distribution of property (Ferguson 1819:179–81). The transition from barbarism to civil society and the establishment of true government was accomplished in the face of continued warfare, when people submit to a sovereign authority to gain the military advantages of unification and internal social order. Ferguson thus follows Hume in claiming that the integrative benefits in time of war are a primary impetus in the formation of government (pp. 38–43). At the same time, Ferguson also recognizes that "the sword which was whetted against foreign enemies may be pointed at the bosom of fellow subjects," and because of abuses of power by a sovereign, "every interval of peace from abroad, [may] be filled with domestic war" (p. 228). It is apparent that Ferguson rides the fence, seeing both conflict and benefit in the initial development of government, and giving priority to neither side.

Taken as a whole, the work of the political philosphers in the seventeenth and eighteenth centuries provides a wide and diverse base upon which virtually all modern theories of the origin of the state have been founded. With very few exceptions, even the most creative of new ideas or hypotheses about how and why the state first developed can be found to have direct intellectual antecedents in the Enlightenment period. This is not to say, of course, that no progress has been made in the study of state origins. But the main themes have been expressed early, and subsequent efforts in the nineteenth and twentieth centuries have provided elaboration, clarification, and sophistication to the nascent theses of Rousseau, Hume, Ferguson, and the others.

In the course of the last two centuries there has been a constant growth in studies of the development of the state and related political and economic institutions. The predominantly theoretical analysis of political philosophers has given way to more empirically based studies of anthropologists and other social scientists. There has also been increasing recognition that formal government first developed prehistorically, and this recognition has been accompanied by the greater incorporation of archaeological data into the study of state origins. The opposing conflict and integration schools of thought have been presented in increasingly greater detail by a large number of scholars. Following the initial framework of Rousseau, major contributions to the conflict school have been made by Morgan, Marx, Engels, Childe, White, and Fried. Fried has presented the most comprehensive conflict theory specifically dealing with the origin of the state. With a philosphical foundation in the theories of social contract and government by consent, the integration school has matured with the major works of Spencer, Sumner, Durkheim, Moret, and Davy, and most recently Service. The latter's work is a direct counterpoint to that of Fried, and represents the most extensive treatment of the integration theory of the origin of the state.

Since each of these schools has its own intellectual development in the nineteenth and twentieth centuries (though with some interrelationships), they will be examined individually below. To assess the usefulness of the two schools in explaining the origin of the state in prehistory, the most comprehensive presentations of each will also be subjected to a more intensive critical analysis.

Chapter 2

The Conflict Position

During the nineteenth century the notion that the state evolved in response to conflict between unequal social classes was championed most forcefully by Karl Marx and Friedrich Engels. With a primary focus on the structure of nineteenth-century capitalism, the basic position of Marx and Engels is that the state is physically repressive governing institution, which serves a basic function of protecting the privileged position of a propertied ruling class. Although they are chiefly interested in the factors underlying contemporary class stratification and repressive government, they turned to the origins of the state to obtain a historical perspective on modern government. For their analysis of the original development of government and the state, Marx and Engels depend on the evolutionary model of the American anthropologist, Lewis Henry Morgan.

Lewis Henry Morgan and Henry Maine

In *Ancient Society* (1877) Morgan traces the development of culture through several succeeding developmental stages. Using the same nomenclature as Ferguson and Montesquieu (Harris 1968:29), Morgan divides the evolution of human society into the stages of savagery, barbarism, and civilization. In what is the first extensive use of ethnographic as well as historic data, he systematically documents the evolution of complex cultural forms out of simpler antecedent forms. He outlines the evolution of kinship systems, subsistence systems, and organizational systems (the manner in which people are organized to maintain order). In regard to the latter, the single qualitative evolutionary step in Morgan's model comes in the transformation from "social" to "political" organization (Leacock 1963: II:xi–xx). This transformation was marked by a move from organization "founded upon persons, and upon relations purely personal" (1877:6) to organization "founded upon territory, and upon property" (1877:6). In this evolutionary shift from a kin-based "social" organization to a territory-based "political" organization, Morgan borrows heavily from the writings of the legal historian Henry Maine.

In his attempt to trace back the origins of law in ancient society, Maine argues that in all ancient societies the basis of political relationships was kinship, whether real or fictive (Maine 1861). Specifically, kinship was the means by which smaller social groups originally joined together to form larger political units. Families joined to form houses, houses joined to form tribes, and tribes joined to form commonwealths or states (1861:124–27). Within each of these larger units political relations were based on real or imagined kin ties. The point when political relations come to be based on something other than kinship represents an organizational revolution in Maine's analysis:

> At some point of time—probably as soon as they felt themselves strong enough to resist extrinsic pressure—all these states [or commonwealths] ceased to recruit themselves by fictitious extensions of consanguinity. They necessarily, therefore, became Aristocracies, in all cases where a fresh population from any cause collected around them which could put in no claim to community or origin. Their sternness in maintaining the central principle of a system under which political rights were attainable on no terms whatever except connection in blood, real or artificial, taught their inferiors another principle, which proved to be endowed with a far higher measure of vitality. This was the principle of *local contiguity*, not recognized everywhere as the condition of community in political functions. (1861:128)

Thus, Maine argues that under conditions of population growth through immigration, the resident population, organized along kin lines, would assume a position of political superiority over incoming persons who could not establish a link to the kin network.

Morgan retains Maine's emphasis on the importance of the shift from kin-based to territory-based organization, but he offers a somewhat different and more extended explanation of why the shift took place. Morgan's explanation is tied to the development of private property. He argues that increasingly efficient argiculture and the domestication of animals provided the necessary conditions for the growth of private property. With this growth of property, and the movement of people into urban areas, the means of maintaining social control within a system of "social" organization, were insufficient to cope with the increased complexity of society:

> It is evident that the failure of gentile [kin-based] institutions to meet the now complicated wants of society originated the movement to withdraw all civil powers from the gentes, phratries and tribes, and reinvest them in new constituencies. (1877:263)

These "new constituencies" were the separate and permanent political institutions of a formal government.

In general Morgan's analysis of the transformation to a territorially based "political" organization represents only a rough sketch of evolutionary development. He does not specifically take up the nature of the relationship between the rise of private property and the state. In *The Origins of the Family, Private Property, and the State*, Engels, drawing heavily on the notes of Marx, builds on parts of a foundation laid by Morgan, and details the nature of that relationship in more explicit detail (Leacock 1972:11–12).

Friedrich Engels and Karl Marx

According to Engels, the sequence leading to the formation of the state starts with increasingly efficient means of agricultural production. In circumstances of increased agricultural efficiency, a substantial economic surplus was possible, because people were able to produce more than their immediate subsistence and reproductive needs required. Over time, Engels argues, the economic surplus, coupled with continuing advances in subsistence technology, resulted in a multiple division of labor, increasingly centralized control over the means of production, and the concentration of economic wealth in the hands of a few. This division of labor and unequal distribution of wealth, in turn, resulted in "the cleavage of society into classes" (Engels 1891:228). Furthermore, this new class society was fraught with internal conflict:

> Here was a society which by all its economic conditions of life had been forced to split itself into freemen and slaves, into the exploiting rich and the exploited poor; a society which not only could never again reconcile

these contradictions, but was compelled always to intensify them. Such a society could only exist either in the continuous open fight of these classes against one another or else under the rule of a third power, which, apparently standing above the warring classes, suppressed their open conflict and allowed the class struggle to be fought out at most in the economic field, in so-called legal form (p. 228).

The third power which emerged to suppress the open conflict between classes was the state (here used in the sense of a separate institution of government). However, the state did not serve to resolve this conflict in an impartial, bipartisan fashion; rather, it served the needs of the rich at the expense of the poor:

As the state arose from the need to keep class antagonisms in check, but also arose in the thick of the fight between the classes, it is normally the state of the most powerful, economically dominant, class, which by its means becomes also the politically dominant class and so acquires new means of holding down and exploiting the oppressed class. The ancient state was, above all, the state of the slave owners for holding down the slaves. (p. 31)

As a new means of organizing society, the state differed qualitatively in a number of ways from the preceding form of kin-based or "gentile" organization, according to Engels. The new qualities possessed by the state in his model include: the territorial base emphasized by Maine and Morgan, the levying of taxes, state debt, and a new means of enforcing social control—force (pp. 229–30). Engels argues that with the development of the state, a public armed power arises to physically control the behavior of the members of the society: "This public force exists in every state; it consists not merely of armed men but also of material appendages, prisons and coercive institutions of all kinds, of which gentile society knew nothing" (p. 230). The presence and role of force will assume increased significance in later analyses of the origin and development of the state.

In the combined work of Marx, Engels, and Morgan, there is the first concerted attempt to analyze and empirically document the historical development of formal governmental institutions. They look at the mechanisms of social control found in simpler societies without formal governments, and compare these mechanisms with the formal political institutions found in what they perceive to be the earliest examples of societies organized under true governments. They conclude that government first developed to resolve economically based class conflict. The resolution provided by the institution of government involved the application of force to check the ambitions of the nonpropertied majority and secure the wealth of the propertied minority.

John Austin

The general conflict theory offered by Morgan and Engels is complemented in the nineteenth century by John Austin's analysis of law. In *Lectures on Jurisprudence* (1873) Austin discusses the relationship between positive laws and the state, and distinguishes between the customary law of prestate societies and the positive law of state societies. In Austin's analysis a state society is an independent political community in which the majority of the population habitually obeys a sovereign authority (1873:225–27, 249). Within such state societies, positive laws are the body of rules of behavior established by the sovereign authority. These positive laws take the form of commands which express the desire of the sovereign authority, and are enforced by the application or threat of application of negative sanctions (pp. 89–98). In contrast, the customary laws of prestate societies were rules of behavior set by an indeterminate body of persons and enforced by "mere opinion" (p. 89). Thus, in Austin's analysis there is not only a positive one-to-one correlation between true laws and the state form of political organization, but also a qualitative difference between the positive laws of the state and the customs of the prestate.

In addition to making these two points on the relationship between law and the state, Austin also provides insight into why the people in state societies habitually obey the commands or laws of the sovereign. His basic argument is that all governments are dependent upon the voluntary obedience of the people. If the majority of a population refuses to obey the laws, no government could continue to exist, regardless of the force it could bring to bear on that population (p. 302). However, because of population consents to obey a government does not mean that there is a population approval or appreciation of the government:

> But a special approbation of the government to which they freely submit,
> or a preference of that government to every other government, may not
> be their motive to submission. Although they submit to it freely, the
> government perhaps is forced upon them: that is to say, they could not
> withhold their submission from that particular government, unless they
> struggled through evils which they are loath to endure, or unless they
> resisted to the death. Determined by a fear of the evils which would follow
> a refusal to sumbit, they freely submit to a government from which they
> are specially averse (pp. 306–7).

In making this argument, Austin points out that a population giving
open obedience to a government may do so out of a fear of negative
sanctions, as opposed to their perception of the positive benefits of
government (cf. Service 1975:291–99; see also chapter 3 below).

V. Gordon Childe and Leslie White

The first half of the twentieth century witnessed the first concerted
efforts by conflict theorists to address questions of the origins and
initial development of the state using archaeological data. The British
archaeologist V. Gordon Childe uses prehistoric and protohistoric
materials from Mesopotamia, Egypt, and India in an attempt to confirm an evolutionary sequence similar to that of Morgan. Childe's
concern is not with the state specifically, but rather with the sequence
of events accompanying the emergence and efflorescence of ancient
civilization in the Old World. In his analysis, the origin of the state
is but one of these events. Since social phenomena such as the state
cannot be directly observed in the archaeological record, Childe makes
note of certain recurring patterns in the material remains of ancient
societies, and then infers the social processes that probably produced
those patterns. He also utilizes early written materials from the societies in question, and relies on ethnographic and historic analogy to
support his inferences about the nature of prehistoric social organization. In regard to the initial development of the state, Childe's interpretation contains elements of both integration and conflict.

Childe observes that the development of agriculture laid the foundation for a major revolution in politics and economics. One of the concomitants of agriculture was the means of producing a food surplus. Such a surplus could be used not only to tide a community over in bad years, but also to support non-food-producing individuals in the community. Recognizing that the ability to produce a surplus does not necessarily result in the production of a surplus, Childe argues that a surplus beyond immediate community needs (as a protective "cushion") was first produced in order to obtain certain essential resources by trade (1936:115). Since the broad river valleys of Mesopotamia, Egypt, and India were lacking in basic resources, such as timber, ores, building stones, and flint, the inhabitants of these areas had to import them from other regions. This importation was accomplished by exchanging surplus foodstuffs for the required resources. Accompanying the development of an extensive trade network, the first major division of labor also arose. On the one hand there were the primary food producers, and on the other there was a complex of administrators, soldiers, merchants, and craftsmen who procured, processed, and distributed the imported resources.

Childe also argues that in order to produce sufficient surplus for exportation and for the support of this non-food-producing trade complex, the farmers of the river valleys had to engage in large-scale irrigation agriculture (1942:98–99). Irrigation, in turn, resulted in a major revolution in the system of social control in these primitive societies:

> Conditions of life in a river valley or other oasis place in the hands of society an exceptional power for coercing its members; the community can refuse a recalcitrant access to water and can close the channels that irrigate his fields. Rain falleth upon the just and unjust alike, but irrigating waters reach the fields by channels that the community has constructed. And what society has provided, society can also withdraw from the unjust and confine to the just alone. The social solidarity needed by irrigators can thus be imposed owing to the very circumstances that demand it. And young men cannot escape the restraint of their elders by founding fresh villages when all beyond the oasis is waterless desert. So when the social will comes to be expressed through a chief or a king, he is invested not merely with moral authority, but with coercive force too; he can apply sanctions against the disobedient. (1936:90)

In addition to this change in the means of maintaining social control, the combination of trade and irrigation also required that the local population submit to a much more restrictive political organization than had existed before. The consolidation of smaller communities into larger political bodies was necessary to provide the requisite manpower for major canal construction and maintenance. Centralization under a ruling body was also necessary to effectively coordinate the systems of trade and irrigation. The centralized governing authority which emerged in response to these organizational demands of trade and irrigation was the theocratic state (1936:115–25; 1942:107–10). Childe does not define exactly what he means by "state," but he appears to use it synonymously with the small body of ruling elite who were in control of the systems of production, trade, warfare, and ideology.

Up to this point in his analysis, Childe assigns priority to integrative and economic benefits as causal variables in the emergence of the state. However, he proceeds to argue that the state also arose to resolve intrasocietal conflict resulting from the division of labor and the concentration of the economic surplus in the hands of a theocratic ruling class. In this regard, Childe observes that the surplus expropriated from the peasantry was not used exclusively for the economic benefit of the entire community. The ruling class, clothed in the ideology of a state religion, used a sizable portion of the surplus entrusted to them to build their personal wealth in foodstuffs and trade goods. Luxury goods imported from foreign areas or manufactured by local craft specialists were enjoyed by only the minority upper stratum of the society. Childe points out that this pattern is manifested archaeologically by the highly restricted distribution of luxury goods in temples, palaces, royal tombs, and the craft workshops where they were produced (1936:115–16, 130–31; 1942:106–7, 124–25). He also argues that the unequal distribution of goods resulted in conflict between the ruling class and the working class peasantry:

> However necessary the concentration of the surplus really was with the existing forces of production, there seemed a glaring conflict of economic interests between the tiny ruling class, who annexed the bulk of the social surplus, and the vast majority who were left with bare subsistence and effectively excluded from the spiritual benefits of civilization. (1972:50)

In support of this argument, he offers limited documentation drawn from early historical records of social conflict between the ruling elite and the laboring poor (1942:107–8). Without empirical documentation, however, he continues to argue that this conflict was resolved in favor of the wealthy by the state. Using ideological mechanisms, the state attempted to legitimize the system of inequality, and backed these attempts by the application of forceful economic and physical sanctions (1936:90, 124–25; 1942:108–9; 1972:50). The only support he offers for this argument is the theoretical analysis of Engels, in which the latter concludes that it is a primary function of the state to maintain economic stratification and resolve class conflict by the active repression of the working classes (Engels 1972:229–31). Childe appears to believe that archaeology cannot contribute supporting evidence for his argument, nor does he hold much hope for historical documentation, as he asserts that "the records are silent" on this point (1936:125).

There is no question that Childe's analysis of the origin and development of the state sets a precedent in his use of the archaeological record. He recognizes that the initial development of the state was a prehistoric not a historic phenomenon, and he attempts to integrate a large body of existing archaeological data into a cohesive theory of cultural evolution. However, there are a number of problems with his analysis that limit its utility in the general study of the origin of the state. While nominally working in an evolutionary framework, Childe emphasizes the description of particular sequences of historical events, rather than the elucidation of general evolutionary processes. Within this descriptive analysis, the origin of the state was but one of the events, along with others, such as urbanization, writing, and monumental architecture, which accompanied a new economy based on a surplus of foodstuffs. While he discusses such things as warfare, class conflict, religion, and economic administration, Childe fails to provide a coherent explanation of how and why the institution of the state developed similarly in different areas.

He also does not take up the question of when the state first arose in any of the world areas he analyzes. His only observation is that by the time of the first historical records, the state was already in existence (1942:108). In thus neglecting to place the emergence of the state within the evolutionary sequence of events, Childe provides no basis for distinguishing between those events which produced the state, and those which resulted from its development. Cause and effect are inseparable in his analysis.

Another problem with Childe's analysis is a symptom of the state of archaeology as a science at that time. Although he makes greater use of archaeological data than any of his contemporaries, Childe still makes only passive use of the archaeological record. If it speaks to him, he listens, but he does not ask it any questions. In other words, Childe makes no attempt to actively test any of his theoretical propositions in the archaeological record. His reconstruction of past events and his interpretations of archaeological data are largely informal and intuitive, with little effort made to provide logical confirmation. Consequently, though Childe's attempt to draw conclusions about the nature of prehistoric political organization is highly innovative and advanced for the time, much of his analysis never proceeds beyond the level of sophisticated guesswork.

In an analysis similar in many respects to that of Childe, Leslie White attempts to modernize and elaborate the evolutionary schemes of Morgan and Engels. The causal model outlined by White (1949:379–82; 1959:293–302) to explain the development of the state, like Childe's, begins with a marked increase in agricultural efficiency.

According to White, this increased efficiency led to population growth and the development of occupational specialization. As specialization continued, greater numbers of people were removed from subsistence production, and society moved from an economy based on kinship relations to an economy based on access to property. The shift to a property-based economy in turn led to a concentration of wealth in the hands of a minority, and an economic division of society into the rich and the poor. Increased warfare, arising out of competition for accumulated wealth and limited natural resources, also contributed to the class structure, by dividing the society into military leaders and their subordinate followers. Extensive irrigation systems, an important factor in the initial increase in agricultural efficiency, further solidified the partitioning of society by giving rise to administrative and laboring classes. Basically, White holds that the intensification of agriculture produced a system of dominant and subordinate classes based on a combination of economic, military, and administrative variables.

Once society was divided into these classes, White argues that there was a need for a new organizational means to "maintain and perpetuate" the system (1959:300). This process of maintenance and perpetuation involved three things:

> (1) co-ordinating, correlating, and integrating the various parts and functions of which the new sociocultural system was composed, namely, the various public works and community enterprises . . . ; co-ordinating and integrating the various social structures that comprise the system as a whole, namely, the occupational groups. . . . (2) It would have to reconcile the two basic classes of society, the dominant, ruling class and the subordinate class, whose interests were not only different but opposite and conflicting at many points, and prevent the subordinate class from disrupting society and reducing it to anarchy and chaos through insurrection and civil war . . . ; (3) it must maintain its autonomy and independence by successful military operations of offense and defense with reference to its neighbors. To accomplish all this, the new society would have to have a special mechanism, a special political device, for coordination, integration, regulation, and control. Such a special mechanism was developed. We shall call it the *state-church* (1959:301).

White treats the "state-church" governing mechanism in terms of the functions served by each of its aspects. The state aspect, operating through the secular governmental machinery or bureaucracy, served to integrate, regulate, and control the secular realm of public activities, e.g., legal activities, warfare, subsistence management, etc. (1959:314–23). The church aspect, operating through a sacred bureaucracy (which may or may not correspond to the secular bureaucracy), paralleled and supplemented the function of the state. The church served to legitimize the actions of the state, and to support those actions with supernatural sanctions (1959:323–27). As a whole, the causal model outlined by White stresses the resolution of class conflict as the critical variable in the origin of the state; however, the model also recognizes the important function of the state in providing integrative benefits to the population at large. As was the case with Childe, the role of integration is not automatically excluded from the conflict-based theory of White.

Viewed critically, White's theoretical model of state development contains basic problems similar to those found in Childe's analysis. On an empirical level, White provides only a minimum of evidence to support and illustrate his model; furthermore, the evidence he does use is not directly germane to his argument. Although the recognizes that the initial autochthonous development of the state took place only in prehistoric societies (1949:372), he does not turn to the archaeological record to sustain his argument of initial state development. Instead, he looks only to the historical record drawn from those world areas where states are believed to have first arisen. In doing so, he is restricted to using data from highly developed states that have undergone extensive internal evolution.

White's failure to utilize evidence from the earlier stages of state development results in his inability to establish potential causal priorities among related variables associated with the evolution of the state. The significance of this inability is most evident in regard to the initial generation of class stratification. By viewing states solely in advanced stages of development, White can see only that warfare, labor management, and private property all serve as bases for the division of society into classes. Like Childe, he fails to address the relative importance of each of these as potentially independent causal agents in the origin of the state. This question, raised early by political philosophers, assumes a critical position in later anthropological debates about the initial development of the state (see, for example, Adams 1966; Wittfogel 1957; Fried 1961; Carneiro 1970; Webb 1975; Service 1975; Harris 1977; also chapter 6 below).

Related to White's failure to utilize the relevant archaeological data base is a more serious problem with his overall theoretical analysis. White's causal model of the evolution of the state is essentially a historical reconstruction of state development, with causality inferred between the variables. White starts with ethnographically known prestate polities and with historically known, highly developed states. Noting the organizational differences between these disparate types of political systems, he constructs a logically valid evolutionary sequence of causality, which explains how the simpler form evolved into the more complex. The problem is that the sequence he outlines is based more on intuition than on an analysis of the process of political evolution. He does not engage the questions of how and why particular phenomena actually developed; instead, he observes that they did develop, and then argues, without evidence, that they must have done so in a particular way.

The weaknesses resulting from White's intuitive analysis are most readily apparent in his discussion of state forms of economic systems. Based on logical argumentation alone, he asserts that "the division of society into occupational groups required a profound transformation of economic system" (1959:294). Then, using an inductive line of reasoning, he concludes that the resultant new economic system could have been one of two types: a system of state-controlled production and distribution; or a commercial system of free markets and mediums of exchange (1959:294–95). Using examples from Mexico and Peru at the time of contact, White argues that these two fundamentally different systems of economic organization evolved out of similar economic antecedents. However, when an explanation is sought for how this could have happened, White is at a loss: "Why the Agricultural Revolution produced a state-controlled system in one culture, or country, and a commercial system in another is a question for which we have no adequate answer" (1959:296). The reason he has no answer is that he treats the evolution of the state as a series of events and not as a series of processes. He is able to show that particular phenomena did develop in the course of political evolution, and by applying one line of logic he can indicate why he thinks they developed; but by focusing on events rather than processes, he cannot explicate how they developed (see Steward 1955:16–18).

The problems with White's analysis do not in any way invalidate his model, but they do weaken its applicability as an explanatory or even heuristic device. They also illustrate the status of anthropological studies of the evolution of the state at the middle of the twentieth century. The emphasis is on reconstruction and description rather than on explanation of how and why the state first developed. There is also little attempt to distinguish state institutions as a pivotal variable in the development of complex societies. It is treated as but one of a number of social and political variables associated with the evolution of "civilizations." To achieve a greater understanding of the primary role of state institutions in the evolution and organization of society, the general models of White and Childe would have to be reformulated with a new focus on *process*, in order to explain how, why, and when the different steps transpired in the emergence and subsequent development of state level societies. Furthermore, any model of state formation should be constructed in such a way that it can be illustrated and confirmed using archaeological evidence from the first states to have evolved prehistorically. The work of Morton H. Fried represents a reformulation of the basic conflict model presented by Morgan and updated by White and Childe, and it resolves some of the problems inherent in the latter analyses.

Morton H. Fried

In his introduction to *The Evolution of Political Society*, Fried states that his goal is to outline a "unified theory of the *emergence* of ranking, social stratification, and the state" (1967:xi, emphasis added). Thus, his emphasis is on the process of political evolution, not on the reconstruction of historical events in an evolutionary sequence. Fried's evolutionary model is also presented in a deductive logical form, so the different elements can serve as hypotheses through which the model can be tested and confirmed or disconfirmed. In relation to White and Childe, Fried provides a fuller and more useful analysis of how and why the state develops out of simpler evolutionary antecedents. He also combines the unilinear evolution of White with the multilinear evolution of Steward (1955), to provide alternative routes by which different societies may arrive at politically analogous evolutionary stages. To some extent, then, he addresses the question of why there may be different bases of class stratification in different societies.

In Fried's model, the first step in the eventual development of formal institutionalized government was the emergence of "ranked" society out of "egalitarian" society (1967:109–84). A ranked society is one in which there are "fewer positions of valued status than individuals capable of handling them" (1967:109–10; see also 1960). According to Fried, ranking developed in different societies primarily in response to ongoing changes in the material conditions of life. These changes, related chiefly to population growth and agricultural efficiency, created pressures on the respective social systems to develop more efficient means of production and distribution of resources. Fried sees this increased efficiency as being achieved through the concentration of responsibility and authority in particular individuals. In turn, these latter individuals then assumed positions of superior status and rank in their respective societies. Fried outlines alternate processual paths which different societies may traverse in going from the egalitarian to the more hierarchical ranked stage of political organization (1967:183–84).

In succeeding political evolution, ranking serves as an organizational base for the development of "stratification" (1967:154). The stratified political level proposed by Fried is characteristic of societies in which "members of the same sex and equivalent age status do not have equal access to the basic resources that sustain life" (1967:186). In other words, in stratified society, some members have unrestricted access to all the resources necessary for subsistence and reproduction, while other members have various impediments barring direct access to such resources. The processual shift from ranking to stratification involves the conversion of basic resources from communal property, accessible to all, to some form of private property, openly accessible to only a portion of the population. How and why this conversion takes place differs in individual circumstances, as illustrated in Fried's analysis.

He proposes two general ways in which access to basic resources may be restricted in the development of stratification: 1) restricted access may result when some portion of the population less than the whole monopolizes control over certain limited resources, such as land, water, or technological raw materials, through organizational, geographical, or physical means; 2) restricted access may also come about in a complex society when some portion of the population specializes in an occupation other than subsistence production and, therefore, must depend on others to provide necessary subsistence resources (1967:188–90). The variables that produce these bases of stratification are materialistic and found primarily in the environment, demography, and economic structure of the society. Specific material circumstances that Fried outlines as conducive to the conversion to private property and, concomitantly, stratification include: population pressures (both from endogenous growth and from exogenous influx); contraction of the resource base; organizational systems (particularly irrigation) requiring centralized managerial control and responsibility (1967:191–213). Fried specifically rejects war as an avenue for the emergence of stratification on the logical and ethnological grounds that systematic warfare for expansion and conquest is a result of stratification and restricted access to basic resources, rather than their cause (1961; 1967:213–16).

Once stratification has occurred in a particular society, Fried argues that there is inherent instability in the nascent stratified hierarchy:

> The stratified society is torn between two possibilities: It builds within itself great pressures for its own dissolution and for a return to a simpler kind or organization, . . . lacking differential access to basic resources. . . . On the other side, the stratified community, to maintain itself, must evolve more powerful institutions of political control than ever were called upon to maintain a system of differential ranking. (1967:225–26)

The "more powerful institutions" which evolve to maintain the stratified system are the formal governmental institutions of the "state" (1967:227–40; see also 1968).

Following the basic tenets of conflict theory, Fried maintains that the initial impetus in the emergence of the state is a need to maintain social order in the face of built-in conflict in a system of differential access to basic resources (1967:230). In meeting this need and resolving the conflict, the state is characterized by institutionalized physical and ideological control mechanisms. Of primacy in the state are institutions of coercive control (army, police, militia, etc.) which can apply physical force in the defense of the stratified system and the sanctity of private property (1967:230–31); see also 1978). Through institutional control over information and systems of communication, the state also attempts to achieve ideological legitimization of the system of stratification (1967:238, 1968). In addition to the internal maintenance of stratification, the state also serves secondary functions in providing general social order through a formal judicial system, and external defense through a military organization. The combination of state institutions with the preexisting system of stratification provides the rulers of the state with qualitatively greater power than the leaders in any prestate society. Likewise, stratification and the state represent an evolutionary development which is qualitatively distinct from all preceding political forms in Fried's model.

Taken as a whole, Fried's analysis of the development of the state level of political organization has both strong and weak points. One of the greatest strengths lies in the logical rigor and parsimonious nature of his argument. Based essentially on materialist principles of causality, Fried presents a general causal model which explains how changes in material variables will lead to specific patterns of political evolution. Within this model, the evolutionary stages represent theoretically distinct types of organization. Thus, the definitive characteristics of these stages are not inductively derived generalizations based on observed patterns in many cultures; rather, they are significantly different principles of political organization, corroborated by examples drawn from the ethnographic record. Each of these organizational stages is precipitated by specific patterns of material change. In turn, the definitive patterns of political organization result in additional organizational and ideological changes in other aspects of society. In outlining both the causal and resultant effects of the emergence of each evolutionary stage, Fried provides the "processual flesh" for the basic skeletal conflict model of White, Childe, Morgan, and Engels.

Another strength in Fried's analysis is that most aspects of the evolutionary model can be readily recognized in the empirical record. Furthermore, the numerous cause-and-effect relationships he hypothesizes are directly amenable to testing with empirical data from any number of societies. Fried thus provides a solid theoretical base for the orientation of research into the origins and nature of the state. Confirmation for the utility of his model in this regard is seen in its widespread practical application (e.g., Sanders and Price 1968; Price 1977; Rathje 1972; Grebinger 1973; Peebles and Kus 1977; and others). In fact, the elegance and credibility of Fried's logical analysis make his model so useful, that it is often accepted as a given, rather than as a comprehensive but tentative *theory* of political evolution. Researchers, particularly archaeologists, have simply assumed the validity of his model, and used it to typologically pigeon-hole societies. Its strength, however, is not as a given typological model, but as a potential explanatory model of political evolution.

While the misuse of Fried's model is not evidence of an internal problem, his analysis does contain certain weaknesses. These weaknesses lie at both the empirical and methodological levels. The main empirical problems stem from his failure to recognize the critical importance and utility of the archaeological record. Like White before him, Fried recognizes that the emergence of stratification and the state under "pristine" conditions probably has taken place only in prehistory, and can be illustrated only with events drawn from the prehistoric past (1967:185). Yet he does not turn to prehistory to illustrate and confirm his theories about the emergence and organizational nature of the stratified and state levels. At one point, Fried attributes the absence of such an appeal to gaps in the archaeological record (1967:198); however, there is a clear implication of other junctures that he considers the archaeological record as somehow inadequate for proper illustration and confirmation. For example, in discussing the impact of irrigation on the emergence of stratification, he states:

To discuss fully the identity of pristine states and to attempt to describe the precise nature of their emergence is not possible in these pages. It may be that the task is ultimately impossible in any context for the reasons alluded to earlier: Literacy appears only with the emergence of the earliest states, and recorded history is much younger. The kinds of evidence we have are essentially archaeological and inferential. Although the general patterns of emergence may be discerned, details are fragmentary at best (1967:232–33).

Examining this statement, it would seem that the impossibility of adequately describing the emergence of the pristine state lies in the inferential and fragmentary nature of the archaeological evidence. However, it can be easily argued that the ethnographic and ethnohistoric evidence Fried uses to illustrate the evolution of simpler political levels is equally inferential and fragmentary. To explain the emergence of ranking, and to a lesser extent, stratification, Fried appeals to material conditions and patterns of organization in extant or historically known societies. From these, he *infers* the processes which led to the emergence of each stage. For example, in discussing the process in which ranking develops, his conclusion that "one of the major developments is the emergence of a clearly distinguished descent principle requiring demonstration of relationship" (1967:116) is an inference based on observations of living or historically known societies. Fried's use of logical inference is a methodological necessity, dictated by the nature of the subject matter. Evolution is a process requiring time; in most cases, it requires a great deal of time. Practical opportunities to observe a society actually evolving from one political stage to another, either ethnographically or in the ethnohistoric record, are rare. Furthermore, even these rare opportunities have limited value, since in every case in which emergence of a new political level has been recorded in simple societies, the situation has been "contaminated" by the presence of outside complex societies. Consequently, any analysis of the emergence of the different levels of political organization under pristine conditions can *only* be inferential.

The charge that archaeology can provide only fragmentary details of state development is, of course, true. While all social science disciplines can provide only fragmentary details of any social process or event, it must be recognized that the archaeological fragment is qualitatively smaller. However, as pointed out in the Introduction, archaeologists, using material data alone, have made substantial contributions to the study of cultural evolution. In specific regard to the evolution of the state it is to be expected that changes involving the material foundations and broad patterns of sociopolitical organization of past societies will be open to archaeological investigation. In Fried's explanatory model of state development the primary causal variables are to be found in the environment, the economy, the technology, and the demographic composition of the evolving society. They are predominantly material variables, and as such should be manifested either directly or indirectly in the artifactual and ecological records of past societies. Likewise, there are certain patterns of behavior and etic organizational patterns, which Fried hypothesizes as being concomitant with the development of the state. These behavioral and organizational patterns should have a direct and recoverable impact on the nature and distribution of artifactual remains. In particular, such patterns as economic stratification, specialized institutions of coercion, increased internal conflict, and systematic exploitation and repression, should be detectable in some form in the archaeological record.

On the other hand, there are undoubtedly some patterns associated with state development (e.g., changes in kinship organization, emergence of laws and a legal system, and the internalization of governmental rules), which are much less likely to be manifested archaeologically. Generally, in spite of the fragmentary data base, it can be expected that archaeology can provide considerable insight into the material and behavioral aspects of state development; but it cannot be expected to provide equal insight into the changes in emic organizational principles and ideal patterns that may also be associated with state development. Exactly how much detail on the emergence of the state can be provided through archaeological analyses is a question which cannot be answered until numerous attempts are made. There would seem to be little reason, however, to accept Fried's dour predictions based on a priori assumptions about the limited nature of archaeological evidence.

The criticism, that Fried has not made sufficient or proper use of the archaeological record in his analysis of political evolution, may seem minor when related to the totality of his work. Nevertheless, it must be realized that questions of how and why stratification and the state first arose are *archaeological* questions. They can only be answered effectively through the use of archaeological materials, not through complex logical argumentation or through convoluted extrapolation from protoliterate historical documents or late secondary states. The point to be made here is not that Fried's model is in need of additional archaeological documentation. He makes no pretense that the model is in any way fully documented. Rather, the point is that Fried has demonstrated an ethnographic chauvinism in constructing his logical evolutionary model. As a result, the model is not only void of appropriate documentation for the stratified and state levels, but more importantly, primary emphasis is placed on ethnographic elements which would assume secondary importance in an archaeologically sensitive model.

There are two points at which Fried's analysis shows weakness when viewed from an archaeological perspective. The first concerns the significance of kinship in the emergence of stratification and the state; the second concerns the separation of stratification and the state into two distinct evolutionary levels. In regard to the former, Fried follows the precedent set early by John Locke, and later elaborated by Henry Maine, Paul Vinogradoff (1920:299), William Seagle (1946:43–57), and others, in arguing that the transition to stratified society and the state was associated with a transition from kin-based to non-kin-based systems of organization (Fried 1967:224–25). He in fact takes this argument and incorporates it into his basic definition of the state. According to Fried, the state developed to maintain a system of stratification, and is to be viewed as "the complex of institutions by means of which *the power of the society is organized on a basis superior to kinship*" (1967:229, emphasis added). Thus, in Fried's model, the demise of kinship as the prime organizing principle is seen as a critical variable in the emergence of the state. For the archaeologist, however, kinship is anathema.

Dealing solely with material evidence, archaeology is ill-equipped for an analysis of kinship, which is essentially nonmaterial in nature. Harris provides a materialist definition of kinship as follows: "The domain of ideas constituted by the beliefs and expectations that kin share with each other is called *kinship*. Kinship is the paramount ideology of domestic life" (1975:331). To the extent that kinship thus falls within the realm of ideology, it is expressed in the material record only indirectly, insofar as it is expressed in patterns of behavior. The few archaeological attempts to elucidate prehistoric kinship patterns have, by and large, been unsuccessful. Consequently, if an understanding of the development of the state requires an understanding of the shift from kinship to nonkinship principles of organization, then Fried is right: archaeology can provide only highly fragmentary details of the evolutionary process. However, when his model is examined for the rationale for the central position asserted for kinship, there appears to be still some hope for archaeology.

Fried's argument that the rise of the state must be accompanied by the fall of kinship as the principle of organization is an argument based more on guesswork than logic: "While a model of stratified nonstate society can be built within the confines of a congruent model of kin relations, the probability is slight that the kin model will in fact contain it" (1967:224). Also: "It is possible for such applications of power [physical power found in a state] to be made in the context of a preexisting set of kin relations, but it is not likely that this will long remain the case" (1967:226). Thus, the central place accorded kinship in Fried's analysis is based on an intuitive sense of likelihoods and probabilities. He does not present a cogent logical or empirical argument explaining why a society could not have all the economic and material characteristics of a state, and yet still be organized along kin lines.

His predecessors, such as Maine, Vinogradoff, and Seagle, make the distinction between kin and non-kin principles of organization primarily on the basis of comparison of primitive societies and advanced historically known states. Their conclusions are based primarily on inductively derived generalizations, and they do not preclude the possibility of a state organized in some way along kin lines. In fact, Maine concludes that the *first* states probably did have a kin-based organization, and the territorial base came shortly after initial state development:

> It may be affirmed then of early commonwealths that their citizens considered all the groups in which they claimed membership to be founded on common lineage. What was obviously true of the Family was believed to be true of the House, next of the Tribe, lastly of the State (Maine 1861:124–25).

It might be "improbable" or "unlikely" that a state organized along kin lines could exist on a permanent basis, but there are no a priori reasons why such a society *could not* exist. Furthermore, in an analysis of the process of political evolution, it would seem counterproductive to exclude by definition all kin-based societies from treatment as states.

In Fried's basic analysis, primary emphasis is given to the importance of economic factors. He argues that the state develops to maintain a system of economic stratification through the exercise of coercive control mechanisms. Changes in emic principles of organization, whether they be kinship or non-kinship principles, have no causal impact on the basic process of state development. Such changes are, at best, secondary in an explanation of how and why the state emerges. Thus, the relative inability of the archaeologist to recognize whether or not a society was kin-based, is not a major limitation on the utility of archaeological evidence.

The second area where an awareness of the nature of archaeological evidence calls into question a major element of Fried's model is in regard to his distinction between the stratified and the state levels of political organization. As briefly outlined by Fried, the stratified non-state society is highly unstable and empirically short-lived (1967:224–26). Since such societies would have developed under pristine conditions only in prehistory, their emergence can only be directly analyzed through archaeology. However, the inference that stratified nonstates were relatively short-lived sharply decreases the likelihood that they can be identified and adequately defined using only archaeological evidence. Thus Fried hypothesizes an evolutionary stage which cannot be tested, confirmed or described empirically. By asserting the necessity of such a stage preceding the emergence of the state, he places a virtually undemonstratable link in his causal chain, and accordingly weakens the totality of the model. Given the ephemeral nature of the stratified nonstate, and the difficulty of documenting such a stage, it is not unreasonable to question the necessity of inserting it in the sequence of political evolution.

The definitive characteristic of stratified society is that there is restricted access of some members of the society to basic resources. This basis of stratification does not have structural analogs in the economic organization of antecedent ranked level societies. The emergence of stratification is, therefore, a process of qualitative, and not quantitative, evolutionary change. When stratification is compared to the state, the process of state development does not represent a qualitative change. The underlying organizational base of both types of polities is essentially the same in Fried's model. They are both based on economic stratification with unequal access of members to basic resources. The primary distinction offered by Fried is that the stratified nonstate lacks the "specialized institutions" of social control that characterize the stratified state (1967:229–37). Although his discussion of the nature and function of these state institutions is very brief, it can be inferred from his analysis that the distinctive quality of these institutions is that they maintain the order of stratification through the application of instruments of coercion. However, consideration of two additional factors brings into question the distinctiveness of the specialized institutions of the state in Fried's model.

The first factor which must be considered is the fact that coercive control mechanisms are to be found in any stratified society, regardless of its level of development. In any situation in which some members of a society do not have unrestricted access to the basic resources necessary for subsistence and reproduction, there is an undeniable instrument of coercion present. This instrument is derived from the economic control some members of the society have over access to the basic resources. In exercising this control, these members can apply sanctions which are just as forceful as a policeman wielding a club (Haas 1977; see also chapter 3 below for an elaboration of this point). Fried's point is well taken that those who restrict access to basic resources must develop additional physical means of coercion to stabilize and maintain their control over the resources. However, it must be realized that any additional physical mechanisms of coercion are supplementary to the already existing mechanisms of economic coercion.

The second factor to be considered concerns the development of the specialized institutions of the state. According to Fried, these state institutions will have direct antecedents in stratified society. The internal pressures in stratified society lead to increased emphasis on existing nonkinship mechanisms of political and economic power. These mechanisms then "mature, coalesce, and form the state" (1967:225). In this sense, the transition from what Fried calls the stratified nonstate to the state is a process of quantitative growth and development. This then brings up the question of where to draw the line between the stratified nonstate and the stratified state. Fried provides no answer, and it would appear that the decision is ultimately an arbitrary one. If such is the case, what is the point of separating a stratification stage, characterized by a qualitatively distinct principle of organization, from the state, characterized by quantitative epiphenomenal precipitates of stratification?

Fried implicitly answers this question by using the stratified stage as a functional, heuristic device to make the transition from ranking to the state. By first establishing the priority of stratification, he can then make a logical argument for the development of the specialized institutions of the state. However, in separating stratification from the state, he obscures the fact that the definitive elements of the state must develop in concert with the emergence of economic stratification. In an emergent stratified society, those at the top of the socio-political hierarchy are going to make immediate use of any and all available kinship and nonkinship mechanisms of control to maintain their position and privileged access to resources. Since the emergence of stratification is not an instantaneous event, it is to be expected that increasing control over basic resources will be accompanied by the development of more stringent mechanisms of social control. The maintenance of an order of stratification embedded with conflict is not accomplished through the independent *development* of specialized institutions of control. Rather, it is accomplished through the ultimate *success* of specific types of control mechanisms. The growth and elaboration of the specialized institutions of the state is a reflection of the success of control mechanisms which are already operating at the inception of stratification. Fried maintains that "the state forms in embryo in stratified society" (1967:225). A more accurate analogy would be that the state is born with stratified society and grows as an integral part of the order of stratification.

In spite of the lack of appropriate documentation, and the methodological problems of formulation, Fried's analysis of political evolution represents the most viable and complete exposition of a conflict model of state development. The weaknesses in his formulation do not negatively affect any of the central premises of the conflict position (i.e., class stratification leading to class conflict, which is resolved through coercive repression). To improve on the conflict model presented by Fried would entail a reformulation with increased awareness of the archaeological nature of the relevant data, and documentation with material from prehistoric societies. Furthermore, before any conflict model of state development is to be accepted, it must be subjected to testing and verification in the archaeological record of early state societies. A logical model such as that presented by Fried must be considered as an hypothesis, and examined critically. It cannot be simply accepted as fact and used accordingly. There have been few attempts to actively test parts of Fried's model, and still fewer attempts in the field of anthropology to challenge the basic conclusion that the resolution of class conflict is central to the initial development of the state. However, in a recent work by Elman R. Service, not only is Fried's analysis taken to task, but the entirety of the conflict position is challenged. In opposition to Fried and the conflict position, Service offers an integration argument, which also has extensive intellectual antecedents dating back to the middle of the nineteenth century. The development of this integrative position culminating in Service's analysis can now be examined.

[Chapter 3]

The Integration Position

The integration position of the Enlightenment, manifested in the general idea of the "social contract," assumes a number of different forms in the late nineteenth and early twentieth centuries. Despite their differences, however, most of these forms have a common theoretical foundation in the comprehensive works of the English sociologist Herbert Spencer.

Herbert Spencer

Spencer outlines two different evolutionary lines along which formal government and associated political institutions originally developed. Both are brought about primarily through the agency of warfare. In the first line, warfare stimulates endogenous social development, whereas in the second it leads to development through the addition of external elements into the social system. While these two lines are closely interrelated in Spencer's analysis, they must be examined separately to understand the influence of his work on subsequent studies of the evolution of the state.

Spencer's endogenous line of evolution is based on his analogy between society and the biological organism. Society, like the biological organism, is a system of specialized and interrelated parts, all operating together for the survival of the whole. Spencer supports this analogy as follows:

> [Society] undergoes continuous growth. As it grows, its parts become unlike: it exhibits increase of structure. The unlike parts simultaneously assume activities of unlike kinds. These activities are not simply different, but their differences are so related as to make one another possible. The reciprocal aid thus given causes mutual dependence of the parts. And the mutually dependent parts, living by and for one another, form an aggre-

gate constituted on the same general principle as is an individual organism. (p. 8)

The internal evolution of society is also analogous to organic evolution in that it follows a process of natural selection or the "survival of the fittest" (p. 78). Within this organic analogy, Spencer views evolution as a progression involving the aggregation of relatively small and simple groups into larger, "compounded" groups; concomitantly, the internal complexity of society increases (pp. 14, 48–53). His different stages of development range from simple to trebly compound, and from headless societies to societies with stable headship. The "state" is not a specific stage in this sequence, but its development is subsumed in his general treatment of the evolution of political institutions.

Spencer argues that the initial emergence of endogenous government was an adaptive response to the pressures inherent in a condition of regularized warfare (pp. 32–38). By uniting forces under a centralized regulatory agency, separate social groups gained a joint advantage, and were thus more likely to emerge victorious from a military conflict. Initially, this agency was composed of those warriors who demonstrated the greatest military skill and leadership ability. Over time, however, this impromptu military leadership became a permanent body with hereditary positions. As a result, the formerly independent subunits became permanently subordinate to the military body. Furthermore, with permanency this body served as a natural focal point for the regulation of nonmilitary activities both in times of war and in times of peace (p. 35).

The military advantages gained through centralization were also paralleled by economic advantages, since a centralized coordinating agency made possible a specialized division of labor and the more efficient production of resources. The subordination and loss of independence of the individual subunits was thus compensated for by the increase in economic and military benefits. Cooperation and obedience of the subordinate population, military necessities in times of war, were also freely given in times of peace.

Spencer reasons that this occurred since the political decisions of the governing authority were tightly controlled by the combined will of the public and the force of custom established in the past:

When a political agency has been evolved, its power, largely dependent on present public opinion, is otherwise almost wholly dependent on past public opinion. The ruler, in part the organ of the wills of those around him, is in a still greater degree the organ of the wills of whose who have passed away, and his own will, much retrained by the first, is still more restrained by the last. (pp. 104–5)

Hence, the initial development of an internal regulatory agency in Spencer's model resembles in many ways the formation of the social contract proposed by Locke, Hobbes, and Hume.

Subsequent to the development of a ruling body, Spencer sees the process of endogenous evolution as involving differentiation and specialization of the social organism's different parts. With growth in the size and complexity of society, the ruling body itself underwent internal specialization, and separate regulatory groups emerged with responsibility for military activities, and production and distribution of resources (pp. 44–47). These specialized groups were relatively independent of each other, but they were all subject to the common rule of the central authority. Under this complex of regulatory agencies, specialized tradesmen and merchants emerged who were responsible for distributing resources throughout the social system. At the bottom of the internally developing hierarchy were free craftsmen, food producers, and laborers. All these separate parts of the social system functioned together, like parts of a living body, to insure the continuing and efficient operation of the whole (pp. 30–31, 46–47).

As briefly outlined, it can be seen that in the process of endogenous political evolution, warfare serves primarily as an integrative mechanism in Spencer's analysis. In the face of external conflict, social groups voluntarily came together and submitted to a governing authority in order to gain the military and economic benefits of centralization.

In the second line of evolutionary development, however, Spencer sees warfare serving primarily as an exploitative mechanism. He argues that the first stage in this line is characterized by the capture of members of an enemy society in the course of warfare (pp. 83–85). These captives were then taken home and put to personal use as private slaves. As this capture of slaves regularized in habitual war, there eventually developed a distinct slave class separate from and subservient to a superior ruling class.

Beyond this master and slave dichotomy, the next step in the evolutionary development of classes involved a major change in the nature of warfare. Starting as simple aggressive contact between societies, warfare later was characterized by predatory expansion, conquest, and annexation as the conflicting social units became increasingly complex. With this change in warfare, entire societies, conquered in battle, assumed positions of inferior classes. Unlike the original slaves, however, these new subject classes were allowed to stay on their land and had a social status somewhat above that of the slave class and below that of the free laborers.

Spencer also argues that the source of authority exercised over this conquered groups is based on physical strength, and therefore was markedly different from that exercised over the groups within the endogenous hierarchy:

> We must not expect to find in a rule coercively established by an invader the same traits as in a rule that has grown up from within. Societies formed by conquest may be, and frequently are, composed of two societies, which are in large measure, it not entirely, alien, and in them there cannot arise a political force from the aggregate will. Under such conditions the political head either derives his power exclusively from the feeling of the dominant class, or else, setting the diverse feelings originated in the upper and lower classes one against the other, is enabled so to make his individual will the chief factor. (p. 106)

However, the relationship between the victors and the vanquished was not simply a unidirectional exploitation of the weak by the strong, according to Spencer.

Clearly, a subjugated territory, useless without cultivators, was left in the hands of the original cultivators because nothing was to be gained by putting others in their places, even could an adequate number of others be had. Hence while it became the conqueror's interest to tie each original cultivator to the soil, it also became his interest to let him have such an amount of produce as to maintain him and enable him to rear offspring, and it further became his interest to protect him against injuries which would incapacitate him for work. (p. 87) Thus to some extent, he reasserts the organic analogy of a mutually beneficial interaction between disparate parts of a social system.

Overall in Spencer's analysis, recognition is given both to integration and conflict in the development of political institutions. But the conflict is externally derived, it does not develop endogenously. Class differences are present in the social system, arising out of the unequal distribution of wealth and power as well as out of conquest, but interclass relationships are symbiotic and not necessarily antagonistic. While he maintains that all classes compete to improve their position and physical well-being, Spencer also argues that the lower subject classes tend to be passive, and accept rule by the wealthy and more powerful (p. 100). The role of government in his analysis is not to resolve internal conflict and govern by force, but to regulate the different components of a complex, heterogeneous society.

The Conquest Theorists

Spencer's conquest line of evolutionary development is further elaborated by a number of advocates in the late nineteenth and early twentieth centuries. Actually, the theory is said to have been first presented in the fourteenth-century writings of Ibn Khaldun, and again in the sixteenth century by Jean Bodin (Service 1978:24). Spencer's analysis revitalizes the conquest theory and provides the immediate foundation for the analyses of Ludwig Gumplowicz, Franz Oppenheimer, Friedrich Ratzel, Gustav Ratzenhofer, Henry Graham Sumner, Lester Ward, Albion Small, and others (Hofstadter 1944; Krader 1968:44–45; Service 1978:23–24). While there are specific differences in the theories of each of these scholars, they all share the basic argument that class stratification and the state arose out of the conquest of one society by another. To illustrate the later outline of the conquest theory, the comprehensive arguments of Gumplowicz and Oppenheimer can be examined in greater detail. The works of these two men complement each other, since Gumplowicz approaches the state as a sociological abstraction, and Oppenheimer approaches it within the context of an historical reconstruction. Both begin from the same starting point:

> The State is a social phenomenon consisting of social elements behaving according to social laws. The first step is the subjection of one social group by another and the establishment of sovereignty; and the sovereign body is always the less numerous. But numerical inferiority is supplemented by mental superiority and greater military discipline. (Gumplowicz 1899:199)

> The State, completely in its genesis, essentially and almost completely during the first stages of its existence is a social institution, forced by a

victorious group of men on a defeated group, with the sole purpose of regulating the dominion of the victorious group over the vanquished, and securing itself against revolt from within and attacks from abroad. (Oppenheimer 1914:15)

Both then see the state as starting by the imposition of governmental rule on a conquered society by their conquerors. To the extent that there is forceful rule of one group by another, their conception of the origin of the state resembles the contemporary conflict position of Marx and Engels. However, the overall analyses of the state by Gumplowicz and Oppenheimer exhibit major and minor differences from the analysis of Marx and Engels.

Gumplowicz, for example, argues that the development of private property was a result and not a cause of state formation (1899:198; cf. Engels 1891:170). Furthermore, it was the possession of private property, not the coercive actions of a police force, which served as the primary means of maintaining social control in the state according to Gumplowicz (p. 196). In possessing valued property, particularly in land, the conquering ruling class gained the obedience of the subject population by selectively providing access to that property.

Oppenheimer's historical reconstruction of how the first states came about also differs from that of the conflict theorists. Briefly, he argues that prior to the state there were three types of social groups: huntsmen, herdsmen, and peasants or agriculturalists (pp. 27–52). It was in the interaction of the latter two that class stratification and the state were born. When the nomadic herdsmen, skilled in warfare, came into contact with the land-bound peasants, the former quickly learned to prey on the goods of the latter. Over time, the peasants learned that resistance was futile, and came to accept the domination of the herdsmen. In turn, the herdsmen learned that it was to their advantage to spare the lives of the peasants and to appropriate only their surplus. They also provided the peasants with military protection and shared with them the spoils gained from raids on other societies (pp. 64–69). These two groups then represented the first social classes, joined together in a symbiotic relationship of submission and exploitation. The state, in turn, emerged only to concretize this relationship.

One major similarity between the conquest theory of Gumplowicz and Oppenheimer and the conflict theory of Marx and Engels lies in their common assertion that class stratification, whether endogenously or exogenously derived, inevitably leads to a struggle for power within the state (Gumplowicz, pp. 222–28; Oppenheimer pp. 92–105; Engels p. 228). However, unlike Marx and Engels, the conquest theorists maintain that after the initial military imposition of government, there eventually emerged a substantial unification of heterogeneous classes, and the struggle between them only took place within the limits of this overriding unity. The basic argument is that through such agencies as religion, common residence, and language, the subject and ruling classes in the state united to their mutual benefit. Oppenheimer describes this process of unification as follows:

> Those originally not of the same blood, and often enough of different languages, will in the end be welded together into *one* people, with *one* speech, *one* custom, and *one* feeling of nationality. This unity grows by degrees from common suffering and need, common victory and defeat, common rejoicing and common sorrow. A new and vast domain is open when master and slave serve the same interests; then arises a stream of sympathy, a sense of common service. Both sides apprehend, and gradually recognize each other's common humanity. . . . Gradually they learn to understand one another, first through a common speech, and then through a common mental habit. (1914:70–71)

Gumplowicz also saw economically and politically unequal social classes as unavoidable covariables of social complexity, and the state as an organizational umbrella under which the social classes struggled for power and position (1899:199–203; Horowitz 1963:37).

As briefly outlined, the arguments of Gumplowicz and Oppenheimer are fairly representative of the different conquest theories presented in the late nineteenth and early twentieth centuries. However, as pointed out by Service (1975:270), the specific theory of states formed by pastoral nomads conquering agriculturalists has been largely abandoned by anthropology. While there is at least one possible state, the Ankole of east Africa (Oberg 1940; Thurnwald 1935) that may have formed in this way, it is highly secondary in nature and heavily influenced by external colonial states. In other areas where pastoral nomads are juxtaposed with settled agriculturalists, the hypothesized conquest and state formation are not in evidence (see, for example, Nadel 1940; Asad 1973). An updated version of the conquest theory has been offered recently by Carneiro (1970), who follows Spencer's second line of evolutionary development, but appeals to a set of causal variables quite different from those argued by Gumplowicz and others. Carneiro does not see conquest leading ultimately to integration, however, and his theory represents a specific variation of the general conflict model. As such, it will be discussed at greater length in chapter 5, along with other more specific theories of state formation.

William Graham Sumner and Albert Keller

While Spencer's second line of evolutionary development led to a combination conflict/integration model of state formation, his first line of development (based on endogenous evolution and an organic analogy) provided the basis for more strictly integrative models. One variation of his thesis was presented by William Graham Sumner and his protege, Albert Keller. Making extensive use of ethnographic and ethnohistoric materials, Sumner and Keller (1927) outline in encyclopedic detail the evolution of many social institutions from primitive origins into the Greek states and the Roman empire. Directly following Spencer's argument, they maintain that there are two parallel lines of social evolution—one proceeding through internal development and the other through conquest. Leaving aside their conquest argument, which is basically a restatement of Gumplowicz (Sumner and Keller 1927:581–85, 703–7), their specific discussions of the internal development of government, the division of labor in society, and class stratification represent a clear version of the integrative position in the early twentieth century.

Starting with the premise that all social evolution proceeds through natural selection, Sumner and Keller see the institution of government as a coordinating mechanism that bestows an adaptive advantage on the governing society:

> The basic function of government has been the securing of coordination; of peace and order within the range of its authority. It is readily enough seen that such coordination constitutes an advantage in the struggle for existence; the society possessing it is better adjusted to its life-conditions than the one that has it not. (p. 459)

Government started with the informal concentration of authority in a war leader, priest, or head of a kin group. Through a gradual evolutionary process government became increasingly formalized with permanent offices and greater authority over the population. The state, first found in the Roman empire, was the end product of this process, and represented "the concentration by civil organization of a great group over a great territory, so that the total power for work or war could be directed with prompt reaction to selected ends" (p. 696). Throughout its developmental sequence, Sumner and Keller see government as a regulative agency that provides society with the benefits of external protection, and internal peace and organization.

As with government, Sumner and Keller also see the division of labor in society as developing through a process of natural selection. Some members of a society became governors because of their natural leadership qualities, while others remained subjects (pp. 460, 473–88). Subsequent divisions of labor, made possible by the coordinating role of government, were also based on natural differences of ability and were beneficial to the society as a whole:

> Society pursued its own massive interests by letting the socially fit attain their reward. Careers have always been open to talent; enterprise exhibited in the food-quest or in war or in the acquisition of property has had its reward; eminence in magic and religion has been acquired by study and inventiveness. All this has come out in the case of the chief and will appear in that of the medicineman. (pp. 562–63)

This process of intrasocietal differentiation, based on variation in age, sex, personal qualities, and wealth, eventually was manifested in a stratified system of social classes. These social classes provided complementary benefits to one another, and they coexisted in relative harmony. Furthermore, the lower strata came to accept their subjected position as "necessary and right" (p. 582). Thus in Sumner and Keller's model of endogenous development, class conflict is not a critical issue, and the resolution of such conflict is not a primary role of government. The only conflict in their model arose out of conquest, as outlined by Gumplowitz. But Sumner and Keller argue that even this conflict resolved itself into nonhostile competition between classes. With government acting as a regulative arbiter, the classes which were better adapted to their environment assumed supremacy over those less well adapted in a continuing process of natural selection (pp. 581–87).

Emile Durkheim

A second version of the integrative position, differing in a number of ways from the arguments of Spencer and Sumner and Keller, was presented by Emile Durkheim at the end of the nineteenth century. Durkheim does not specifically address the origin of the state nor the evolution of political systems, but his analysis of the basic role of government and the division of labor is relevant to the present discussion. Like Spencer, Durkheim follows a biological analogy and asserts that the different parts of a society are organically interrelated. In direct opposition to the thesis of Spencer, however, he argues that increased efficiency is only a by-product, not a cause, of the division of labor in society:

> The division of labor appears to us otherwise than it does to economists. For them, it essentially consists in greater production. For us, this greater productivity is only a necessary consequence, a repercussion of the phenomenon. If we specialize, it is not to produce more, but it is to enable us to live in new conditions of existence that have been made for us. (1893:275)

The "new conditions," which were inducive to a division of labor were increased population size and density (pp. 262–75). With more people living closer together and pursuing the same ends, rivalry and disunity developed. The division of labor arose under these conditions to increase social solidarity, and had as its primary function "the integration of the social body to assure unity" (1933:62). Except under what Durkheim considers abnormal circumstances (e.g., conquest), labor was divided spontaneously and peacefully in a society. Those who were most apt for a particular kind of activity naturally came to specialize in it:

> The only cause determining the manner in which work is divided, then, is the diversity of capacities. In the nature of things, the apportioning is made through aptitudes, since there is no reason for doing otherwise. Thus, the harmony between the constitution of each individual and his condition is realized of itself. . . . Normally, man finds happiness in realizing his nature; his needs are in relation to his means. (p. 376)

The different parts of the social organism would not inherently conflict with one another, since people were in harmony with their conditions in a naturally divided society.

The role of government in Durkheim's model, then, is not to resolve conflict, but to serve as a directive force that represents the collective conscience or will of the people. He states:

> Whenever a directive power is established, its primary and principal function is to create respect for the beliefs, traditions and collective practices; that is, to defend the common conscience against all enemies within and without. It thus becomes its symbol, its living expression in the eyes of all. Thus, the life which is in the collective conscience is communicated to the directive organ as the affinities of ideas are communicated to the words which represent them, and that is how it assumes a character which puts it above all others. (p. 84)

While he recognizes that governmental power may come to be controlled by a privileged class of people, he nevertheless maintains that it is the collective sentiment that governs society, and the privileged class is simply the interpreter of that sentiment (1933:77). The only repressive role of government is in the interest of justice, when it punishes criminals for committing acts that are "universally disapproved of" by the members of a society (1933:73). Thus, Durkheim's concept of government and his analysis of the division of labor is based on the overriding importance of integration. Any conflict present in the system is considered to be an aberration and represents a malfunction of the social organism. Under normal conditions, the different parts of society coexist in mutual harmony.

While Durkheim appeals to ideological rather than economic variables to explain the division of labor in society, his integrative analysis of the role of government and the organic nature of society is essentially the same as that of Spencer and his descendants. Together, the two lines of argumentation provide a common basis for subsequent integrative theories of state formation in the twentieth century. The first specific integrative attempt to outline the origins of the state in prehistory is presented by the French archaeologists A. Moret and G. Davy.

A. Moret and G. Davy

Using both archaeological and historical data, Moret and Davy (1926—it is of interest to note that the English translator of the Moret and Davy work was V. Gordon Childe) describe the development of civilization and the state in Egypt. Using an innovative approach for this period, they attempt to integrate contemporary sociological theory with the empirical evidence from past societies. Their interpretations of the archaeological data are based upon Durkheim's model; consequently, the conclusions they draw are basically restatements of those drawn by Durkheim, and their analysis does not stand as an independent empirical confirmation of the integrative position. However, they do make observations on the prehistoric and historic Egyptian data that add empirical depth to Durkheim's integrative argument.

Moret and Davy describe a sequence of several thousand years prior to the first states in Egypt, during which there was a constant population growth and an increasing aggregation of people into villages. Accompanying these demographic changes was a gradual centralization of authority into the hands of a chief, who resided in a distinct village that was a focal point for economic and religious activities (1926:129–30). The first Egyptian states represented larger political aggregations of villages under a single ruler. This ruler, as seen pictographically, was a god-king, who guided and protected the people under him. Following Durkheim, Moret and Davy argue that the king, like the chief before him, derived his power to govern from the combined consent and will of the people:

> The origin of sovereignty is neither violence nor despotism. True sovereignty—that of the feudal chief and, more universalized, that of the king, of Pharoah, . . .—has deep roots. It is in the fullest sense a national sovereignty, which means that it is rooted in the very heart of a group. It is not to be found at the point of a sword nor at the bottom of a sack of ducats. It is enshrined in the social body itself; it is its emminent tradition, will and consciousness. (p. 110)

In fact, they maintain that the state itself was the end product of a long search by the Egyptians "for an effective social organization to ensure the security and regularity of social labour in the valley" (1926:128). Thus, the state is seen as the result of the people's conscious need for centralized organization and regulation.

In spite of their general adherence to Durkheim's ideological model, Moret and Davy do recognize material variables as being conducive to the initial formation of the state. They point out that in order to successfully exploit the resources of the Nile Valley, the land had to

be irrigated and the river had to be controlled in times of periodic
flood. Irrigating and controlling a river the magnitude of the Nile
required the coordinated labor of a large group of people spread over
a wide area and organized by a central governing agency. The state
government then is seen to provide essential economic services in
organizing the water control efforts of the population. In addition to
water control, Moret and Davy argue that the state also provided
necessary services in the areas of trade, military protection, and adjudication of internal disputes (1926:154, 225–26). In exchange for the
economic and social services thus provided, the people voluntarily
submitted to the rule of the pharoah as the head of the state.

Other than the work of Moret and Davy, most twentieth-century
advocates of the integration position have not been concerned directly
with the origin of the state. Rather, integrationists, such as Max Weber,
Talcott Parsons, and Kingsley Davis in sociology and Lucy Mair, Mark
Swartz, Ronald Cohen, and many others in anthropology, have stud-
ied the organization and operation of modern industrial states, "primitive" states, or relatively late preindustrial states. Specifically addressing the question of the origin of the state, there are two relatively
recent anthropological theories that have incorporated elements of
the integration position. In the first of these, a revision of Spencer's
first endogenous line of evolution, warfare is seen as leading to the
integration of society under a centralized government (Webb, 1973,
1975; Webster 1975; Harris 1977). In the second theory, Karl Wittfogel
argues that extensive irrigation systems require the cooperation of the
population and their integration under a governing authority (1957).
However, these two theories diverge significantly from the main line
of the integration argument in that government is seen to assume a
repressive role after its initial development. Both theories, and their
relation to the conflict/integration debate, will be considered at greater
length in chapter 5. Leaving these two specific theories aside for the
moment, the most recent and complete presentation of an integration
theory of state formation is found in a major work by Elman R. Service.

Elman R. Service

In *Origins of the State and Civilization*, Service arrives at a general
integrative model of state development by first examining and rejecting

the opposing conflict model as it has been presented in general form by Fried and in more specific forms by other anthropologists. His rejection of the general and specific conflict theories is not based on a superior theoretical argument, but rather on an assemblage of apparently refutatory empirical data. Looking at the cultural areas of the earliest prehistoric state developments, and at known examples of historic "primitive state" formation, Service finds that structural and behavioral features expected to be found in the conflict-based state are not readily manifested in the archaeological and ethnohistorical records.

To test the validity of the conflict model, Service abstracts the essential elements of the model, and attempts to determine the presence or absence of these basic elements in the material and historical records of the early states (1975:36–46, 266–89). His search for validating evidence of the conflict model is concentrated on three features expected for of the conflict-based state: 1) the presence of an early propertied class; 2) indications of early class conflict as manifested in social unrest or revolution; and 3) extended exercise of physical force and repression by the rulers in the early states. In Service's analysis, the presence or absence of evidence for these three elements would serve to confirm or negate the validity of the general conflict model.

In regard to the first element, he asserts that the absence of a propertied class in the earliest states would eliminate the basis of class conflict proposed in the conflict model. Furthermore, the lack of an early propertied class would negate the proposal that the state first developed to maintain a system of class stratification. Considering the second element, Service argues that evidence for or against social unrest or open rebellion by the peasants of the early states would indicate whether or not the peasantry represented a physically repressed and exploited lower class, as proposed by the conflict theorists. The third element, the exercise of harsh negative sanctions (primarily physical force) by the governing body in the first states, has critical importance in Service's evaluation of the conflict position. Since force is an essential element in the conflict theory of state development, Service argues that if the early state rulers did not rely on force as a primary governing mechanism, then the validity of the conflict position as a whole is brought into question.

After reviewing the available archaeological and ethnohistorical data base for evidence of the essential elements of the conflict model,

Service concludes that the model cannot be confirmed:

> In all of the archaic civilizations and historically known chiefdoms and primitive states, the creation and extension of the authority bureaucracy was also the creation of the ruling class, or aristocracy. The "stratification" was thus mainly of two classes, the governors and the governed—political strata, not strata of ownership groups. And no where in the cases discussed do we find the power of force used in the maintenance of the position of the governing strata over the ordinary masses. At least this is not recorded in the historical cases, nor is it visible in the archaeological record. In other words, there apparently was no class conflict resulting in forceful repression (1975:285).
>
> . . . the few cases of "civil war" were wars over succession to power of rival claimants among the aristocracy; "wars of princes," not of classes. (1975:286)

As stated, the above conclusions stand as a relatively powerful negation of the conflict model of state development. Service then reinforces this rejection by offering an alternative model which he maintains is more congruent with the data: "A still more potent rebuttal to the stratification/conflict theory exists, however. A counter-argument about the rise of classes, it has to do with the origin and evolution of bureaucracy" (1975:286).

Service's counter-argument is that strong central government evolved gradually as an adaptive response to a need for increased integrative mechanisms in larger and more complex cultural systems:

> The alternative thesis to be presented here locates the origins of government in the institutionalization of centralized leadership. That leadership, in developing its administrative functions for the maintenance of the society, grew into a hereditary aristocracy. The nascent bureaucracy's economic and religious functions developed as the extent of its services, its autonomy, and its size increased. Thus the earliest government worked to protect, not another class or stratum of the society, but itself. It legitimized itself in its role of maintaining the whole society.
>
> Political power organized the economy, not vice versa. The system was redistributive, allocative, not acquisitive. Personal wealth was not required to gain personal political power. And these first governments seem clearly to have reinforced their structure by doing their economic and religious jobs well—by providing benefits—rather than by using physical force. (1975:8)

In Service's presentation of the evolution of formal centralized government, the first organizational inequality came with the development of the chiefdom level of sociopolitical integration (1975:71ff.). According to Service, chiefdoms developed in societies with relatively large populations exploiting diverse microenvironments, or engaging in complex subsistence activities (e.g., irrigation). In such situations there was a societal need to coordinate the efforts of the people, and this need was efficiently met through the concentration of authority in the hands of a leader or "chief." This leader then served as a focal point in a system of society-wide redistribution and organized group activities.

In the initial development of the chiefdom-type societies, the person who assumed the position of leadership was the one most capable of fulfilling the functions of the chief. However, Service maintains that such an ad hoc leadership organization is inherently unstable. With an increase in the size and complexity of society, greater stability and stronger means of integration were needed. This stability and integrative strength were provided by the institutionalization of leadership in an hereditary authority hierarchy. At the head of this hereditary hierarchy, the chief gained a degree of independence in the process of political decision making. However, this person would still be dependent upon the will of the people to maintain his/her politically superior position. Thus a chief is a servant of the people and must provide definite, observable benefits to the people (1975:293–94).

Once the centralized chiefdom has developed, Service argues that the chief's position served as a logical focal point for other types of coordinating and organizing activities, which may not have been parts of its original jurisdiction. Thus, the bureaucratic network set up to facilitate redistribution is "preadapted" to take over the management of other types of activities that require a centralized bureaucracy. According to Service, the types of activities which benefit from a centralized chiefdom bureaucracy include warfare, long-distance trade, irrigation and other types of water control, and intrasocietal adjudication (1975:290–308). With continued growth in societal size and complexity, the office of the chief was elaborated and strengthened through the preemption of additional functions.

It is to be expected that as the chief assumed greater control over a wider range of activities, leadership became increasingly independent of the will of the people. While Service recognizes this increased independence, he maintains that the chief did not impose his own will on the people through coercion. Rather, it is more effective and efficient to "engineer the consent" of the people through religious or supernatural means (1975:294). Ideological manipulation is thus the primary mechanism used in gaining the obedience of the population in chiefdoms.

Beyond the chiefdom stage of sociocultural integration, Service presents two alternate succeeding stages: the "primitive state" and the "archaic civilization." The primitive state is a particular historic development which is not a critical element in Service's analysis of general cultural evolution. Such states are the product of contact between an advanced modern state and a society at the chiefdom level (1975:289, 302, 304; see also Service 1971a). The primitive state is thus a secondary historic development which Service uses for illustrative purposes rather than as a separate level of evolutionary development.

The "archaic civilization," on the other hand, is a primary development evolving out of the chiefdom stage, and it is uninfluenced by more highly developed external societies (pristine situations as defined here). In Service's model, the evolution of the archaic civilization from the chiefdom is a quantitative, rather than a qualitative, change process. While he does not provide explicit details of this process, he asserts that the causal impetus for the change is to be found primarily in material variables: "The 'road to civilization' was the developmental career of a few bureaucracies, which under rather unusual environmental conditions fulfilled themselves eventually in ruling what finally must have been hundreds of former petty chiefdoms" (1975:306). The specific conditions which Service cites as being conducive to the development of the archaic civilization are social and environmental circumscription (1975:223). Such conditions of circumscription gave an adaptive advantage to those social systems with an increasingly centralized administrative hierarchy and bureaucracy. The increasing centralization of the pattern found in the chiefdom eventually resulted in the archaic civilization.

Service never provides a clear definition of the archaic civilization stage; rather, he leaves it as an open stage which is somehow recognized intuitively in the archaeological and historical record:

The term I have used—"archaic civilizations"—suggests the qualities of the advanced stage of primitive development. There was a point at which some few of the relatively simple hierarchical-bureaucratic chiefdoms grew, under some unusual conditions, into much larger, more complex bureaucratic empires. There seems to be no practical difficulty in the archaeological discrimination of the original archaic civilizations from the previous developments. At least, there seems to be no fundamental disagreement among archaeologists and historians as to the identity of the full-fledged developments. (1975:305)

Service maintains there are no definitive attributes, such as internal violence or writing, which demarcate civilization from preceding stages. In fact, he states that the archaic civilization has no distinguishing characteristics which are qualitatively different from the preceding chiefdom stage (1975:305). Both stages have centralized, instituted bureaucracies, redistributive economies, hereditary aristocracies with a mandate to govern, and a "thoroughly theocratic nature" (1975:307). Archaic civilizations did tend to have refined art styles, monumental architecture, writing, calendrical systems, laws, organized warfare, long-distance trade networks, and craft specialization. However, none of these traits were unique to the archaic civilization stage, since they were all to be found, at least individually, in certain chiefdoms (1975:178:290–308). In the final analysis, the archaic civilization, as described by Service, appears to be a larger, more elaborate, more powerful, and more complex version of the chiefdom.

One specific characteristic that Service maintains is *not* definitive of archaic civilizations is the political institution of the "state." According to Service, the state is an instituted polity in which "the basis of political organization is repressive physical force" (1975:10). In other words, the state is a political institution which uses repressive forceful mechanisms to govern the population. Service maintains that the formal institutionalized governments of the first archaic civilizations were not states as defined above. Instead of governing by forceful repression, these first governments ruled by "right of authority" and through the application of sacred sanctions (1975:10, 296–97). In Service's analysis of sociopolitical evolution, state development coincides with the secularization of the government. While he does not directly address the process of state development, he asserts that the state came relatively late in the evolutionary sequence of the early civilizations. Furthermore, the state form of government developed not in response to internal class conflict, but as a result of military expansion and conquest of foreign peoples (1975:190–94, 223–24, 285–86).

Even those [archaic civilizations] with the best claims to repressive state-hood, like Teotihuacan, the Western Chou, and Tiahuanaco, were ac-tually would-be empires: That is, the violence and repression was military and directed at neighboring ruling class rivals, not at a class or segment of their own original population. (1975:286)

In presenting a general integration model in conjunction with a substantial body of empirical evidence, there are definite strengths in Service's analysis of the origins of formal government. He strikes a convincing argument that there are major integrative benefits to be found in a strong centralized government. Furthermore, these benefits provided the rulers of the first governments with a peaceful means of ensuring the compliance of the population. Service thoroughly documents this argument with direct evidence from historically recorded primitive states, and indirect evidence from the early prehistoric civilizations. In the latter case, he uses archaeological data not only to illustrate aspects of his theoretical model, but also to generate a more complete model of state development than can be constructed solely through reliance on ethnographic and ethnohistoric records. Service's presentation thus represents the first major attempt in either the conflict or integration position to fully incorporate archaeological evidence into a comprehensive theoretical analysis of the origins and development of formal government and the state.

In spite of the fact that Service provides an in-depth argument with an abundance of documentation, there are certain flaws in the argument which warrant against its uncritical acceptance. The flaws are related not only to his positive conclusions about the integrative origins of government, but also to his negative conclusions about the conflict theory of the state. Since these conclusions are interdependent in Service's analysis and confirmation of the former is dependent on refutation of the latter, a critique of his argument provides a basis for assessing the relative validity of both positions. With such an assessment in mind, there are two major points in Service's argument open to criticism: 1) certain of his central conclusions are based on no data and faulty logic rather than on sound documentation; 2) he fails to recognize that when a government provides necessary goods and services to a population it has a forceful means of coercing that population.

To illustrate the first point, three of his central positive conclusions will be examined here and shown to be logically and empirically unsupported. The three conclusions are: 1) peasants in archaic civilizations conformed to traditional normative rules rather than to imposed governmental edicts; 2) peasants in archaic civilizations would not have considered improving their conditions by revolting against their societal rulers; 3) early theocracies could govern with positive sanctions without having to rely on coercion.

In reference to whether individuals in archaic civilizations conformed because of direct governmental pressures, Service concludes:

> As we have noted time and again, the pressure on individuals to conform is a property of the local kin group—at least in any primitive or peasant society, including the primitive states and archaic civilizations. The considerable conformity is to the norms of the traditional folk society, and not necessarily something imposed by a despotic state. (1975:301)

However, contrary to his statement, Service does not "note" this pattern "time and again" in the record of primitive states and archaic civilizations. He does note it in prestate chiefdoms and simpler types of polities, and briefly in the case of the weak secondary state of Ankole (1975:120); but he does not note it in any of the other ethnographically known states, nor in any of the archaic civilizations. His assertion is based on the assumption that the first states and civilizations could not differ significantly from prestate societies.

Therefore, the conclusion does not derive from a logical argument or from a behavior pattern manifested in the material record of those first states and civilizations. Whether individuals conformed in response either to kin or to governmental pressures is a question that cannot be adequately addressed through the archaeological record. It may be observed archaeologically that individuals *did* conform, and it may be inferred that their conforming behavior benefited themselves, their kin group, or the government. But it cannot be logically inferred why they conformed. Service's assertion that prehistoric peasants conformed to traditional normative rules cannot be dismissed; but neither should it be dismissed that the observed normative behavior of the peasants represents only the enforced acceptance of imposed governmental edicts (recalling Austin's statement). The direct pressures that the first governments may have exerted to insure the conformity of their subject populations will be discussed later.

A second conclusion reached by Service without documentation deals with the reasons why peasants did not revolt:

> Similarly, the perception of benefits was not what prevented "revolts of the masses." The chiefdoms and archaic civilizations were *caste* societies in the fullest sense of the word. Peasants, artisans, and rulers were all in their hereditary occupations and statuses. It is inconceivable that any peasants would have considered bettering their lot by their own political actions, for this would have to be done for them by their own hereditary rulers. It seems much more realistic to think of the push and pull toward integration and disintegration of the hierarchical society as being confined to the bureaucracy itself, with the "people" passively doing as they were told. (1975:301)

He provides no explanation of why it is "inconceivable" that peasants would even consider actively improving their position, or why they would "passively" do whatever they are told to do.

In a survey of twentieth-century revolutions, Wolf (1969) observes that the poorest peasants, do, in fact, often passively accept their position, but their motivations are other than those Service cites. Such peasants are highly fragmented and disenfranchized from all centers of power (Wolf 1969:289–90). They are politically and economically *incapable* of waging a successful revolution. In the examples of successful rebellions analyzed by Wolf, the peasant revolutions are initiated by the union of disenchanted intellectuals and an economically secure, but nevertheless oppressed, middle range of the peasant population (1969:291–93; cf. Fanon 1966; Wallerstein 1979). Once initiated, the poorer peasants have a focal point for their dispersed energies, and actively enter into the revolution. The intent here is not to infer that prehistoric peasants are necessarily the same as twentieth-century peasants, but that there are empirically more viable interpretations than Service's to explain why early peasants may not have revolted. (Whether or not there actually were peasant revolutions in the first states and civilizations will be examined more thoroughly below.)

The third critical conclusion reached by Service without logical or empirical support is that early theocracies effectively governed through positive sanctions and religious conditioning, making secular force (and therefore the state) unnecessary. This final example of the intuitive nature of Service's line of argumentation brings into question the validity of one of the fundamental premises of the integrative position: government by consent as opposed to by force. In discussing the first forms of true government, Service states:

> The classical forms had one particularly salient characteristic that we should never underestimate, a thoroughly theocratic nature. Economic and political functions were all overlaid or subsumed by the priestly aspects of the organization. As Hocart so cogently pointed out, the building of an irrigation canal was not "utilitarian" and a temple "religious"; both were efficacious, practical and necessary, and both probably seen as equally significant ritually. *Obviously the perceived benefits and other forms of reinforcement of such a theocracy can enable it to govern large aggregations without regular recourse to violent coercion.* Therefore the state as a repressive institution based on secular force is not coterminous with civilization in the classic, primary developments. (1975:307, emphasis added)

In concluding that the state and civilization are not coterminous because the latter was originally theocratic, Service makes several assumptions that cannot be justified on the basis of his preceding analysis.

Neither Service nor Hocart (1936:217) presents a cogent argument which supports the assumption that temples are as "efficacious, practical, and necessary" as canals. In an objective analysis, an irrigation canal can be empirically demonstrated to increase agricultural production and/or enable agriculture in arid lands (e.g., Boserup 1965; Hunt and Hunt 1974; Woodbury 1961). It might also be demonstrated ethnographically that some form of religious architecture is efficacious, practical, and necessary for purposes of social cohesion and control in primitive societies. However, this does not warrant the assumption that these same social reasons were instrumental in inducing the expenditure of enormous quantities of labor in the construction of monumental religious architecture in archaic civilizations. Since labor-cheap religious architecture can logically fulfill the same types of beneficial social functions as labor-expensive architecture, there must have been additional reasons why the latter was consistently chosen over the former in the archaic civilizations (see chapter 7 below). In intuitively assuming that canals and temples were constructed for comparable reasons, Service fails to face the question of why so much extra energy went into the latter.

Another assumption inherent in Service's statement is that since canals and temples were constructed under the supervision of a theocratic hierarchy, both must have been constructed voluntarily, without the application of coercion. This assumption is stated more explicitly at an earlier point:

> It may be, as well, that secular construction like the building of irrigation canals, usually thought of as compelled by the coercive power of government, is apparently as willingly undertaken as the building of temples and pyramids, *since the same theocratic authority presides equally over both.* (1975:297, emphasis added)

However, since Service fails to provide actual examples of willingly constructed temples or pyramids in prehistoric or historic societies, there is no empirical reason to accept this assumption.

He also offers no compelling reasons why a theocracy would not apply physically coercive mechanisms available to it in attempting to ensure the compliance of the populace. In fact, in a recent article David Webster (1976) convincingly argues that the theocratic orientation of all the early prehistoric governments was a religious facade used by the ruling class to maintain their privileged access to resources and legitimize the application of coercive sanctions. Thus, it is far from "obvious," as Service contends, that a theocracy can govern a large population without recourse to violent coercion. It should also be pointed out that not only has he failed to establish that a theocracy *can* build canals and temples without coercion, but he has failed to demonstrate that the theocratic governments of the archaic civilizations *did* govern without recourse to violence.

These weaknesses in Service's argument do not necessarily invalidate his conclusion. However, no answer is given regarding the integral role of physical coercion, and concomitantly the state, in the archaic civilizations in his intuitive analysis. This question must be subjected to an empirical investigation and will be discussed at greater length in the following chapter.

A second critical problem with Service's analysis is that he fails to recognize that coercive force is invariably present when a strong central government provides essential goods and services to a dependent populace. As noted earlier, Service defines the state as an instituted polity in which "the basis of political organization is repressive physical force" (1975:10). He subsequently defines force as "the physical power to coerce" (1975:12). He concludes that the state was not a characteristic of the first archaic civilizations, since he had not observed successful government based primarily upon violence in primitive states and archaic civilizations (1975:285–86, 302–8). Service contends that the early governmental leaders gained the compliance of the population through positive, not violent, means. Such means include: "engineering the consent" of the governed by the adroit use of supernatural powers; maintaining social control through an adjudicative or legal system; providing the offensive and defensive advantages of a centralized military; and providing the economic benefits of a redistribution system and/or trade network (1975:291–96).

Yet, Service fails to see that coercive force is covariable with a strong centralized government supplying essential benefits to a dependent populace. While it cannot be denied that in governing a population, the early rulers could have applied tremendous positive sanctions in providing beneficial ideological, judicial, military, and economic goods and services, neither can it be denied that those rulers could also have applied equally tremendous negative sanctions by *withholding* the same goods and services. Furthermore, if these goods and services are essential (as argued by Service), then withholding them is a negative sanction equally as forceful as the brute strength of a police force or militia.

Service does recognize that societal leaders have the power to withhold as well as to provide. For example, he states that in early civilizations the religious rulers utilized their control over the supernatural to apply both positive and negative sanctions in "engineering the consent" of the governed (1975:294). Since negative supernatural sanctions have no direct physical impact, Service's claim that force was not used by early governmental rulers is unaffected. However, when control over economic or military resources is considered, Service fails to recognize the potential physical impact of using that control to apply negative sanctions.

In his discussion on the evolution of leadership, Service states that the redistributive leaders in simple "big-man systems" have the power to reward and punish by giving out or withholding the goods they control. (1975:293). At the same time, he asserts that the leadership position of the "big-man" is dependent on his successful and judicious management of the redistributive system. In this sense, a leader is "created by his followers, not by their fear of him but by their appreciation of his exemplary qualities" (1975:293–94). However, as Service points out, such a leadership system is inherently unstable due to its dependence upon the success of the leader.

When a society increased in size and social complexity, the necessary stability was provided by transforming the leadership system into a permanent, institutionalized government. Such a transformation would indeed provide stability to a developing hierarchy as Service contends. However, it concomitantly frees the leaders from their critical dependence on the successful and judicious management of resources for the maintenance of their position. Freed of the dependency imposed on their evolutionary antecedents, permanent governmental rulers have qualitatively greater power to govern by reward and punishment through providing and withholding the economic goods and services they control. Viewed from this perspective, it is apparent that in "engineering the consent" of the governed, the early governmental rulers could have applied materially forceful economic sanctions along with the materially forceless supernatural sanctions inferred by Service.

Service's failure to recognize that coercive force is an inevitable covariable of an essential benefit is exacerbated in his discussion of the effects of circumscription. He maintains that in all examples of early governmental development, the societies were circumscribed either geographically or socially by the presence of external enemies (1975:298, following Carneiro 1970). In cases of geographical circumscription, the governments provided integrative benefits in the form of efficient production and distribution of subsistence resources. In cases of social circumscription, the government provided the benefits of protection from the enemy.

By observing the ubiquity of circumscription, Service draws the conclusion that due to circumscription "the benefits of membership in the society must have been very obvious" (1975:299). He then maintains that these obvious benefits helped enable the governmental rulers to govern without applying force. What he does not point out in his conclusions is that under conditions of circumscription, there are no viable alternatives to belonging to the society. The only "choices" available to the members of such a society would have been death at the hands of an enemy, starvation in a sterile desert, or submission to the demands of the societal rulers. As stated eloquently by the philosopher David Hume:

> Can we seriously say that a poor peasant or artisan has a free choice to leave his country when he knows no foreign language or manners and lives from day to day by the small wages which he acquires? We may as well assert that a man, by remaining in a vessel, freely consents to the dominion of the master, though he was carried on board while asleep and must leap into the ocean and perish the moment he leaves her. (1953:51)

Certainly the benefits of membership in the society would have been obvious to the populace; equally obvious would have been the physically deleterious or lethal alternatives to membership. Thus, the lack of reasonable alternatives provided the rulers with an indirect, but nevertheless forceful means of ensuring the obedience of the population. These means may not have entailed physical violence, but I fail to see how their impact would have been any less physically coercive.

When the basic logic underlying Service's integrative argument is critically examined, it is found to be less than compelling. He bases conclusions on assumptions that prove to be either unwarranted or arbitrary, and he fails to provide appropriate documentation at important junctures. While many of his conclusions are plausible, they are untested, and possible alternative hypotheses are not considered. In addition, when dealing with the key concept of force, Service fails to consider additional conclusions that follow logically from his analysis, but that contradict his integrative position.

It must also be acknowledged, however, that not all of Service's conclusions are unsound or logically unjustified on the basis of his empirical analysis. In a strong and cogent argument, he clearly demonstrates that a powerful centralized government does provide definite economic, military, and adjudicative benefits to a large and heterogeneous society. Since this is one of the central elements in the integrative position, the position can be considered to be at least partially confirmed on the basis of his analysis. However, he does not demonstrate that formal government developed solely in response to a societal need for such benefits, or that such benefits provided the first rulers with sufficient positive incentives to govern without recourse to coercion.

To more fully document and confirm the integrative position as presented by Service, it is necessary to return to the archaeological and ethnohistorical record for an empirical test. Since his rejection of the conflict position is an integral part of this argument, a test of his outline will provide a framework for comparing and evaluating both the integrative and conflict positions.

[Chapter 4]

Conflict Versus Integration: An Empirical Test

Before entering into a test of Service's conclusions concerning the conflict or integrative origins of state societies, it must be recognized that major elements in his integration argument are not open to empirical verification or refutation. Specifically, to the extent that he draws conclusions about prehistoric norms, values, beliefs or mental templates, his argument cannot be readily tested archaeologically. Such ideational variables are manifested indirectly, if at all, in behavior that has an impact on the manufacture, use, and distribution of artifactual remains, and thus are poorly reflected in the archaeological record. Given the relative inability of archaeology to reveal these variables, it is impossible to evaluate Service's statements about the normative reasons why people acted the way they did in the first states. Among his positive conclusions not open to empirical critique are: individuals perceived the benefits of being protected by the government from nomadic raids (1975:299); people willingly built temples and pyramids (pp. 296–97); people responded most positively to religious conditioning (p. 297); people did not revolt because of traditional norms (p. 301); canals were considered ritually significant, while temples were considered necessary and practical (p. 307); negative supernatural sanctions caused just as much terror as physical violence (p. 307); people were comforted in being told their gods were the best and that their religious representatives were holy (p. 297).

The logical problems in the argumentation used by Service to reach many of these conclusions have already been considered in chapter 3. However, it is necessary to point out that in addition to problems of logical formulation, these conclusions cannot be tested empirically with regard to the first states. The kinds of ideological and psychological evidence needed to conduct such a test are not to be found in the material record of past societies. While some indirect evidence may be gained through comparative ethnography, such evidence is of highly limited value because of radical differences between the sociopolitical environment surrounding all modern ethnographically known societies and that surrounding the few prehistoric pristine states. Thus, major portions of Service's integrative argument have to stand without evaluation. If his argument as a whole is to be accepted, it must be on the basis of his intuitive positive conclusions or, more importantly, on a documentation of his negative conclusions about the opposing conflict argument. Since much of the strength of his integration model is based on his prior rejection of the conflict model, an empirical test of the major premises of the latter can serve as a means of testing both models.

The basis of Service's negative conclusions about the conflict model lies in his observation that class stratification, internal social conflict, and forceful state repression do not appear to be manifested in the archaeological record of the first archaic civilizations. To assess the validity of these conclusions, two steps are necessary: First, each of the conflict-related features must be operationalized such that they are recognizable in the archaeological record. Second, after establishing how each feature would be manifested archaeologically, the material record must be examined for appropriate positive or negative evidence of each.

Unfortunately, a perusal of the published data from the areas of the first archaic civilizations rapidly reveals that the basic elements of the conflict position cannot be fully tested in the archaeological record. However, the problem is not that the elements lack material manifestations; it is that the requisite kinds of evidence have not been systematically collected. Archaeologists, traditionally, have not asked questions related to the nature of prehistoric political organization and, as a result, have not gathered the data needed to answer such questions. Nevertheless, it is possible to abstract some relevant data from the corpus of material collected in specific areas, and this abstracted data can be used for a preliminary test of Service's negative conclusions.

To make this preliminary test the total data base to be examined here will have to be restricted both temporally and areally for both methodological and practical reasons. Material will be examined only from those areas of the world where there is greatest probability of pristine state development, since this is the immediate subject of concern. Of the six probable areas of such development, Mesoamerica, Andean South America, Mesopotamia, China, Egypt, and India, the present investigation will focus on only the first four. The latter two are excluded partially to reduce an already unwieldy data base.

Additionally, in the case of Egypt there is substantial evidence that the Egyptian state was a secondary rather than pristine development (Daniel 1968:82; Frankfort 1951:97–98; Price 1977). At the time of initial state development Egypt was in extended contact with the already developed states of Mesopotamia, and the nature and impact of this contact has not yet been clearly determined archaeologically. In the case of India, there is again the problem of extended contact with Mesopotamia (Fairservis 1975:222–29; Allchin and Allchin 1968:125–56; Lamberg-Karlovsky 1972). Also, the archaeological data on the early stages of state development in India are even more limited than the data from other areas. While there are some data on the highly complex Harappan civilization, the developmental sequence preceding this culture is largely unknown. Thus it is impossible to determine what stage of development the Harappan civilization represents.

None of the four areas to be included in the test of Service's conclusions is free of problems. The few excavations of sites from the beginning stages of civilization in Mesopotamia have been extremely limited in scope. They rarely go beyond the level of large-scale test pits or "soundings" (e.g., Woolley 1956). China, like Egypt and India, did not develop totally isolated from the outside states to the west. However, China's contact with the Near East appears to have been more limited and indirect (Chang 1977; Ho 1976). Less likely, though still possible, the development of the Mesoamerican state may have been influenced in turn by China (Meggers 1975). There may have also been early contact between Mesoamerica and Andean South America at the time of early state development, though if there was such contact, it appears to have been of extremely limited scope (Coe 1962a; Lanning 1963; Lathrap 1965). In spite of their respective problems, these four world areas at present offer best data bases for the investigation of the development of the pristine state.

The present study will also focus temporally only on the earliest stages of development in each of the four world areas, to make the data base under investigation more manageable. It also increases the probability that the patterns observed in the archaeological record will represent basic elements in the initial stages of the development of complex forms of political organization. For example, Service asserts that widespread application of coercive sanctions is a secondary phenomenon characteristic of only the later, "empire" stage of civilization development. While any chronological cut-off point is to some extent arbitrary, Service's analysis can be used as a basic guideline. Since he argues that coercive sanctions are not introduced until the development of empires formed by political expansion and military conquest (1975:286), only the data from pre-empire stages will be used to test his conclusions about the conflict position. The cultural and chronological periods to be included in each area are given in table 4.1.

In each of the four world areas I have made an effort to examine the available literature (in English, Spanish and, in some cases, Chinese) on the full-time range under consideration and from the entire area. However, I have been able to find only a small number of surveys and excavations in which relevant kinds of data have been collected; thus, the body of material that can be used to test the premises of the conflict model is correspondingly small. A brief rundown of each of the areas provides a perspective on the range of available relevant data.

In Mesopotamia, with few exceptions, surveys and excavations have been highly limited in scope and there is little usable data of any kind. What there is comes from the areas around the sites of Ur and Uruk (Warka) in southern Iraq during the Jemdet Nasr Period and slightly later, and from southwestern Iran during the Uruk Period (Redman 1978).

In North China there is data for most of the time period under consideration, but it comes predominantly from only three sites in the northern part of Honan Province—Hsiao t'un, Cheng-chou, and Erh-li-t'ou. There are apparently comparable contemporaneous developments to the north and south of these sites, but there is scant information available on these developments (Chang 1977:258).

In Mesoamerica there is relevant data from a wider range of sites and from most of the time period under consideration. Specifically, data can be drawn from Formative Period sites in the Gulf Lowlands of Mexico; from a range of sites in the Mayan Lowlands and Highlands of Guatemala and Mexico; from a range of sites in the Valley of Oaxaca; and from the site of Teotihuacán in the Valley of Mexico.

In South America relevant data come almost exclusively from Early Intermediate sites on the coast of Peru. Work on Early Horizon sites

TABLE 4.1
Areas and Chronologies of the Early Pristine States

Area	Cultural Periods	Time	Reference
Mesopotamia	Ubaid (4) Uruk Jemdet Nasr	4000 B.C.–3000B.C.	Adams and Nissen 1972: Frontispiece; Redman 1978
China	Shang Dynasty (Erh-li-t'ou, Erh-li-kang, and Yin phases)	1850 B.C.–1100 B.C.	Chang 1977: 270
Mesoamerica	Formative (Early Horizon) Early Classic (First Intermediate)	1000 B.C.–A.D. 300	Weaver 1972: 38-39, 118-19; Price 1976: 16-17
Andean South America	Early Horizon Early Intermediate	800 B.C.–A.D. 700	Lumbreras 1974: 57, 95 Rowe and Menzel 1967: Introduction

and in the Andean highlands has simply not produced the specific kinds of information needed to test the conflict model. As a caveat, it must be noted that most of the Peruvian data used below will be drawn from only a single site, Pampa Grande. The reasons for this selectivity are twofold: I worked at the site and have knowledge about it that is generally unavailable in published literature; there has been more intensive research at the site aimed at elucidating sociopolitical organization that at any other early Peruvian site of which I am aware.

In general, the earlier periods in each area tend to be underrepresented, and none of the areas provides an adequate data base to satisfactorily test the conflict model. Consequently, it is presently impossible to provide definitive empirical confirmation or refutation of the model. From the little data available from the different areas, however, some apparent patterns can be discerned, and it is possible to make at least a preliminary evaluation of Service's negative conclusions about the conflict model.

Stratification

The first element basic to the conflict position is economic stratification. In Fried's model, stratification exists when there is unequal access to basic resources. Concomitant with stratification is the division of society into disparate economic groups. Those persons with unrestricted or increased access to basic resources constitute one group, while those with restricted or lesser access to those same resources constitute another. (I hesitate to call these "classes" because the term has much wider ramifications in political science than are intended here.) In reality, there may be a range of persons with greater or lesser access to basic resources, but it is expected that there will be a qualitative distinction between those persons with the greatest access and those with the least. To establish the presence or absence of economic stratification in prehistoric societies, it is necessary to operationalize the concept so it can be recognized in the material record. There are two central issues which must be considered in operationalizing stratification: the first is to define and distinguish basic resources; and the second is to determine how to recognize archaeologically differential access to those resources.

Fried's treatment of basic resources is on a theoretical level, and does not include a substantive analysis. In regard to the nature of basic resources, he makes two major points. First, basic resources will be variable from one culture to another, depending on environmental, technological, and historical circumstances (1967:186). Second, basic resources are not necessarily the actual goods and products needed for subsistence and reproduction but, rather, the means of attaining or making those goods and products. As stated by Fried:

> It should be emphasized that our concept of basic resources refers to what might be considered capital rather than consumer goods. Central are the things to which access must exist in order for life to be maintained for the individual. Given those things, or, better, given unrestricted access to those things, anyone can manage his own support, particularly given a domestic division of labor. We are less interested in such actual consumables as food itself, or specific tools, than in the ultimate source of food and the raw materials from which tools are fashioned. (1967:187)

In making these two points, Fried rules out a uniform list of items which may be considered basic resources in all cultures. Nevertheless, it is possible to distinguish types of goods and products which are either absolutely necessary for, or significantly contribute to the probability of, successful subsistence and reproduction in all societies. These are "consumer" goods and products, and represent the result of exploitation and utilization of the "capital" basic resources referred to by Fried. Without attempting to specify particular items, there are certain general types of consumer goods and products which must be derived from basic capital resources cross-culturally. Among the types of basic consumer items would be food, tools for acquiring or producing food, tools for preparing food, protective devices for coping with the physical environment, protective devices for coping with an aggressive social environment.

This is not intended as an exhaustive list of all types of necessary or adaptively advantageous consumer items, but rather as a tentative list to be used in an initial test of the presence or absence of stratification. In identifying these types of items which must be derived from basic resources, it becomes possible to make logical conclusions about the nature of specific basic resources in a particular society. For example, if food can be obtained in one society only through the practice of irrigation agriculture, then land and irrigation water can be considered as basic resources in that society. Or, if obsidian is the only material from which cutting tools are made in a society, then the obsidian quarries can be considered basic resources.

The identification of the general types of basic consumer resources and specific types of basic capital resources also provides a methodological mechanism for approaching the second central issue in the operationalization of stratification—the archaeological recognition of differential access. Since there are direct material manifestations of both consumer and capital resources, the unequal access of groups in a stratified society should be reflected archaeologically in differential use, consumption and/or proximity to those resources. Comparatively, however, consumer resources offer a more effective mechanism than do capital resources for observing possible stratification in prehistoric societies. Access to capital resources can only be determined either indirectly through the distribution of the consumer goods derived from the capital goods, or directly in those cases when a group is clearly in a superior geographical position in relation to the capital resources. However, even when a group occupies such a strategic position, stratification cannot be inferred without additional confirmation based on the distribution of consumer resources. This confirmation would be necessary to demonstrate that the group was able to successfully exploit their advantaged position. Thus, analysis of consumer resources is a necessary element in the archaeological investigation of stratification.

Focusing on consumer resources, the unequal distribution of each of the types of resources may be manifested in a number of different ways archaeologically. Theoretically, stratification can be inferred if *any* of the necessary or adaptively advantageous goods or products are found to be distributed differentially in a society. However, it is probable that stratification based on unequal access to one type of resource will be accompanied by unequal access to other types as well. In other words, there should be a pattern of differential access, not just an isolated instance.

Each of the five types of consumer resources listed above will be treated separately, in order to specify how each can serve as a means of identifying a pattern of stratification in the archaeological record. In each case, specific logical hypotheses will be presented, which provide an initial means of assessing available archaeological materials for evidence of early prehistoric stratification. Within the limitations of published materials these hypotheses will also be tested, using appropriate archaeological data. In reviewing the available materials the kinds of information necessary to make the empirical tests, when present at all, are found to be highly fragmentary and often inconclusive. There is no single world area from which there is sufficient data to adequately test for stratification using all five types of basic consumer resources given above. However, in each of the four areas presently being considered, there is enough relevant data to provisionally confirm or disconfirm the presence of stratification based on the distribution of one or more of the five types. Neither the logical nor the empirical analyses offered here is intended to be comprehensive or definitive; rather, the intent is to illustrate the type of logical argumentation which must be used to develop empirical tests for stratification, and to see whether Service's conclusions are confirmed given the present state of knowledge of prehistoric complex societies.

Food

This type of basic consumer resource includes those comestibles which contribute to basic subsistence and nutritional balance. Unequal access to such comestibles could be exhibited directly either in trash deposits or in skeletal remains. The upper levels of a stratified hierarchy should have trash containing food remains which reflect a better overall diet than that of the lower levels. The upper stratum's diet should have a higher nutritional content (protein, vitamins, minerals, etc.), and include more types of foods and perhaps higher quality items and better cuts of meat. Thus, a stratified society based on unequal access to foodstuffs should have trash deposits with qualitatively different comestible assemblages. Skeletal remains should also reflect differential access to a better diet in terms of the general health of individuals from different levels of the stratified hierarchy. If some members of a society have greater access to foodstuffs, particularly higher quality and nutritious foodstuffs, then it can be expected that these individuals would be healthier than individuals without such access. Thus, the skeletal population from a stratified society should exhibit qualitative physical differences between groups of individuals with unequal access to food resources.

Material pertinent to the relative access to food resources in complex prehistoric societies has been recovered in both China and Mesoamerica. In both cases the evidence is derived from skeletal populations.

The nutritional analysis of trash deposits is still in a state of relative infancy in most areas.

In China, there have been a number of elaborate Shang tombs found, which have been inferred to be interments of royal Shang kings or leaders. In addition to the central figure, each of these tombs contains a large number of human sacrificial victims. While some of these sacrificial victims may have been simply prisoners of war, others were accompanied by materials that would indicate that they were servants or retainers of the central figure (Kuo 1951; Kao 1959; Cheng 1960:72–77; Chang 1976:51–56). In an analysis of the dentition of the persons buried in the tombs, it was found that those who were sacrificed also suffered from malnutrition when they were living (Chang 1976:55; Mao and Yen 1959). Whether these people were indentured servants or war captives treated as slaves, the inference that they served the central entombed figure and had a nutritionally inadequate diet is indicative of internal stratification. Unfortunately, the skeletal material has not been subjected to sufficient osteological analysis to determine whether the malnutrition was prolonged over a lifetime or was limited to the period immediately prior to death.

Additional evidence of economic stratification comes from smaller graves adjacent to the larger tombs. In excavations carried out in 1976, archaeologists uncovered 191 burials clustered into 22 separate groups. Among these burials there were differences in burial goods and, in specific regard to access to food, one of the groups, consisting of three graves, "yielded skeletons more robust and taller than all the others" (Chang 1980:124).

Unfortunately, no further information is given on the morphology of any of the individuals. As with the case of the malnourished individuals in the tombs, more extensive analyses of these and other burials would have to be conducted before a more conclusive statement could be made about intrapopulation nutritional variation in Shang China. However, limited as they are, these data do begin to indicate a pattern of differential access to foodstuffs in Shang China. (Another indication of this pattern may be found in oracle bone records, where there are extensive accounts of large numbers of animals being taken on royal hunting trips (Chang 1980:142–43, 214–15). Here again, though there is no information on the distribution of these animals.)

In Mesoamerica, there are two skeletal populations which have a bearing on food as a variable in systems of stratification. From the

Mayan lowland site of Tikal, there is an in-depth study of burial materials, indicative of differential access to food resources. Haviland (1967) found that in the first century B.C. the men inhumed in elaborate burial tombs were approximately 7 cm taller than the men not buried in tombs. Furthermore, the difference between the tomb occupants and non-occupants was a qualitative one. There was an actual gap between the shortest occupants and the tallest non-occupants. If it were simply the case that superior status was bestowed on tall individuals, it would be expected that there would be a quantitative height scale, with no qualitative gaps. While other explanations may account for this pattern, stratification based on unequal access to foodstuffs best survives the cut of Occam's Razor (Haviland 1967:321).

More direct evidence of differential nutrition and access to foodstuffs comes from the Formative site of Chalcatzingo. In a recent study, Schoeninger (1979a, 1979b) analyzed the chemical composition of bone minerals from skeletons uncovered at Chalcatzingo. She specifically examined the bone strontium levels, which in turn reflect the relative meat intake of individuals. The results were striking. Basically, she found that individuals in the highest status graves, accompanied by jade artifacts, had the lowest bone strontium levels and thus the highest meat intake. Middle status graves, with some grave goods but no jade, had significantly higher bone strontium levels and lower meat intake. Individuals in the lowest status graves with no grave goods had the highest bone strontium levels and lowest meat intake. Clearly there was differential access to basic food resources at Chalcatzingo.

It is fairly obvious that the limited cases from Mesoamerica and China do not definitively prove that stratification based on unequal access to food was a widespread element in the worldwide development of early states. The problem of proving such a pattern, however, cannot be attributed to an overwhelming amount of *adverse* evidence; rather, there is an abysmal *absence* of necessary evidence. At the same time, what Schoeninger's study so nicely shows is that when the difficult but critical kinds of analysis are conducted, concrete evidence of stratification based on access to food *can* be found. Until such analyses are carried out on other sites in early complex societies, we will have no way of knowing if some members of the early states were consistently eating better than others. As things stand at present, we have no solid basis for making positive or negative inferences concerning the ubiquity of stratification based on access to food resources.

Tools

. . . FOR ACQUIRING OR PRODUCING FOOD

Tools for acquiring or producing food include those items necessary for extracting food from the environment—predominantly agricultural implements. Differential access to such tools may be reflected in diverse types of distributional patterns, depending on a variety of circumstances. In some situations, certain types of tools may be technologically superior to other types of tools (for example, metal vs. stone plows), and bestow an advantage on their possessors in the production of food. In this case, finding the superior tools in association with only a portion of the population, and the inferior tools in association with the remainder, would constitute evidence of a form of stratification. In circumstances of large-scale labor specialization, only a portion of the population would be directly involved with the extractive process. Consequently, those persons not engaged in subsistence activities would lack direct access to the basic resources of subsistence.

In the archaeological record, such a pattern would be evidenced in the complete absence of agricultural implements from the artifactual assemblages associated with a portion of the population. It should also be recognized that this pattern can be indicative of different forms of stratification. One possibility is that the persons in possession of the agricultural implements have greater ability to extract basic subsistence resources, and constitute an advangaged upper class. Another possibility is that some persons without agricultural implements have some means of inducing those with the implements to supply the requisite subsistence resources. In this case, the persons without agricultural implements would be in a superior position in a stratified hierarchy. Consequently, while differential distribution of tools for the production of food is indicative of stratification, supplementary data, perhaps derived from food, housing, or luxury goods, must be used to determine the relative significance of that distribution.

As with food resources, the archaeological evidence pertaining to relative access to productive tools is not totally conclusive in any one world area. In Mesopotamia, one of the few references to the distribution of productive tools is from the relatively late Early Dynastic Period (immediately after the Jemdet Nasr Period) at the site of Ur

(Woolley 1934; Adams 1966). In a large cemetery discovered at Ur, a minority of graves contained metal axes and adzes as funerary offerings. The majority of the graves contained no productive tools of any kind. Furthermore, those graves with metal tools were found to contain greater quantities of sumptuary items (gold, silver, semiprecious stones, fancy ceramics, etc.), which would indicate that increased access to productive tools accompanied a superior position in a stratified heirarchy. While the distribution of productive tools in the Ur cemetery is indicative of unequal access to those tools, it is extremely weak evidence of the role of stratification in the development of Mesopotamian civilization. Since there were highly complex polities in the area prior to the Early Dynastic Period, the relevant data on productive tool distribution can only be obtained from earlier periods. None of the grave materials recovered to date from earlier sites contain tools of production, and distributional analyses of tools in houses, work areas, manufacturing areas, and trash deposits have not been carried out for any of the early periods of Mesopotamian civilization.

In China, the evidence of productive tool distribution is slightly better than in Mesopotamia. At the central site of Hsiao-t'un in the An-yang area a cache of over 3,500 stone sickles, all showing signs of use, was found in association with luxury items and in an area of temples and elaborate housing (Shih 1933:727, cited in Cheng 1960:197). This physical concentration of sickles in an area of generally high status is an indication of restricted accumulation of necessary tools of production, from which may be inferred differential access. Where the requisite data are available, it is also apparent that a minority of the burials recorded in the An-yang area are accompanied by agricultural implements (which may be due to the possibility that most agricultural implements were made of wood—Chang 1980:224), and an even smaller number have metal implements (Kao 1959; Cheng 1960:64–77). Again, however, there has not been an analysis of the nonburial contexts of productive tools, and unequivocal conclusions cannot be made about relative access to them.

At the site of Pampa Grande (A.D. c.600–700) on the North Coast Coast of Peru, there is some direct evidence of unequal distribution of productive tools. In the lower status residential architecture, the associated artifactual assemblages contain some agricultural implements (Shimada 1976; Day 1975), while in the high status residential area, there are no such implements (Haas 1975). From this distribution it can be inferred that the persons in the higher status residence did not produce their own resources, but obtained them by other means. Lower status persons, on the other hand obtained their food resources through the utilization of the agricultural implements found in association with them. Thus the distribution of productive tools at the site is indicative of differential access to basic food resources between low status groups who had to produce their own food, and high status groups who did not.

... FOR THE PREPARATION OF FOOD

Tools for the preparation of food include those items necessary for cooking, processing, eating, and storing foodstuffs. As with tools for food acquisition and production, differences in access to tools for food preparation may arise in situations where superior technology is available, or where there is specialization of labor. Unequal access to technologically superior tools may be manifested either directly in the distribution of those tools, or in the more intense utilization and re-utilization of such tools by those persons with restricted access to them. In the latter situation, all segments of a society may have the full range of preparative tools; however, those with increased access may readily dispose of the tools after minimal use, while those with reduced access strive to exploit the full use-value of the tools. This pattern would show up archaeologically in the amount of wear and repair on the pertinent objects in the assemblages of the different segments of the society. In situations where craft specialists are responsible for the production of preparation tools, differential access to the labor of those specialists would constitute a form of stratification. Archaeologically, the tools crafted by the specialists would be found in greater abundance in the assemblages of those persons with increased access. Also, the crafted preparative tools may be used as sumptuary goods, rather than as strictly utilitarian items, by those with increased access.

Since tools for preparation occur in greater abundance and in more circumstances than do tools for acquisition and production, there is slightly more archaeological information about relative access to the former than the latter. In China there is evidence that, in the Shang Period, bronze, ceramic, and bone preparative tools were produced by craftsmen. All of these types of items show markedly unequal distribution in both burial and residential contexts in Shang sites (Chang

1977:218–58). While some houses and burials completely lack bronze tools and have but small quantities of ceramic and bone tools, other houses and burials have an abundance of ceramic, bone and bronze preparative tools (Chang 1977, 1980; Kao 1959; Shih 1959 and *K'ao-ku Hsueh Pao* 1957, both cited in Chang 1977:231–36).

In South America, evidence of differing access to preparative tools is present in the Early Intermediate Period. Again at the site of Pampa Grande, preparative tools have a similar distribution as productive tools. The tools are found in abundant association with lower status residences, but are absent from a high status residence. It can be inferred that the occupants of a high status residence did not prepare their own food, and had privileged access to the preparative labor of others (Haas 1975, n.d.). In other areas and earlier time periods in South America the relative intrasite distribution of tools has not been examined, or at least it has not been reported.

In Mesoamerica, there is evidence that obsidian, a common medium used for preparative tools, was distributed equally in residences in the Valley of Oaxaca during the Early and Middle Formative periods (Winter and Pires-Ferreira 1976). However, there is no data from the same area on obsidian distribution from later periods, when archaeologists believe the state first emerged in the area (Flannery and Marcus 1976; Blanton 1976). Consequently, the earlier data have no bearing on the possible role of stratification in state formation. At the Formative site of Tlatilco in the Valley of Mexico, where several hundred burials have been excavated, some of the graves have few or no offerings of any kind, while others had abundant sumptuary goods as well as different kinds of stone tools and ceramic vessels (Porter 1953).

Similarly, in Classic Period Maya sites there is evidence of distinctly unequal distribution of specially crafted preparative tools in different burial assemblages. Higher status burials had more tools and tools of a higher quality than did lower status burials (Rathje 1970). At the city of Teotihuacán in the Classic Period, preparative tools were produced on such a large scale by craft specialists, that unequal access to those tools can be indirectly inferred. With virtual monopolization of certain types of preparative tools, specifically obsidian blades, non-craft specialists would have had to have gained access to those tools by voluntarily or involuntarily contributing goods or services (Spence 1967, 1973). Unfortunately, there has been insufficient (or at least published) work done at Teotihuacán to indicate the context of preparative tools in residences or trash deposits (Millon 1973, 1976).

Protective Devices

. . . FOR COPING WITH THE PHYSICAL ENVIRONMENT

Protective devices for coping with the physical environment consist predominantly of artifacts of clothing and of housing. As in the case of preparative and productive tools, stratification may be exhibited in unequal access to clothing items, resulting from craft or labor specialization. If clothing materials are produced by only one segment of the population, or if clothes are manufactured by only one segment of the population, then those persons outside the production and manufacture process have restricted access to those necessary resources. Archaeologically, the people with limited access would be expected to extract the full use out of available clothes and materials, while those with greater access would be expected to have more of the items and to utilize them less intensively. One methodological problem in regard to clothing is that cloth and clothing materials, because of poor preservation, are poorly represented in the material record.

The other main type of environmentally protective device, housing, is much more adequately represented archaeologically. With housing, stratification would be marked by unequal access to the materials and/or labor necessary for construction of residential architecture. This difference in access would be most directly reflected in more spacious and technically superior houses for the upper strata than for the lower. However, there is a problem with testing this proposition empirically. It is of relatively little significance to state that larger and better houses characterize the upper levels of a stratified society, without specifying how much larger and better they are. In a ranked society and chiefdom, it is not unexpectable that the leader may have a larger and better house than anyone else. But since all members of the society have equal access to the necessary materials and labor of housing construction, there should not be a marked disjuncture between the size and quality of the leader's house and the houses of the other members of the society. Conversely, in a society in which the system of stratification includes unequal access to housing materials and labor, the housing of upper level individuals should be qualitatively distinct from that of lower level individuals, in terms of the amount of labor invested in construction, size and number of rooms, and quality or type of building material. In other words, in a stratified society there should be "palatial" architecture clearly different from other low status residential architecture of the society.

Empirically, relative access to materials and labor necessary for housing construction is more adequately represented in the available archaeological record than is access to other types of consumer resources. In China, South America, and Mesoamerica, there have been sufficient studies to indicate clearly that all three areas are characterized by the qualitative differences in residential architecture which is expectable with stratification. At the major Shang cities of Cheng-chou, Erh-li-t'ou, and Hsiao-t'un in northern China, there are large houses, ranging from several hundred to several thousand square meters in area, built on stamped earth platforms up to three meters high (Shih 1954, 1959 and Kao-ku 1974a, all cited in Chang 1977:23–50). There are some smaller houses, located in areas of craft specialization (associated with pottery kilns, bronze foundries and other craft tools), which are also built on stamped earth platforms (Chang 1977:236). In sharp contrast are numerous semi-subterranean pit houses, located both inside and outside the cities (Cheng 1960; Chang 1977; Shih 1959). These pit houses are up to 4 m deep and less than 100 sq m in area. The differences in size and building material in Shang residences are thus of a qualitative nature, indicating similar differences in relative access to the materials and labor necessary for housing construction.

The site of Pampa Grande can again be used to illustrate differences in access to housing resources in South America. At the site, there is one high status residence with over 1000 sq m of floor space, built completely of adobes. While adobes are also used in building storehouses, warehouses, compound walls, and ceremonial structures, there have been no other adobe residences positively identified at the site (Day 1975; Anders n.d.; Haas 1975, n.d.). The other known residences at the site are all much smaller in size and have walls built of river cobbles with a trash-filled core (Shimada 1976, 1977). A similar pattern is found at the roughly contemporaneous site of Galindo and the earlier site of Moche (Bawden 1977; Topic 1977). At both sites there are large, formally laid-out adobe residences contemporaneous with numerous smaller houses with stone and trash filled walls.

In Mesoamerica, there is evidence of stratification based on access to housing resources at Teotihuacán, at different sites in the valley of Oaxaca, and at the Mayan site of Tikal. At Teotihuacán there are large, open, and elaborate palatial residences in compounds in the center of the city, and a range of smaller, more crowded, and simpler dwelling complexes in a wide belt around the center (Millon 1973; Millon et al. 1973). In Oaxaca, where housing has been subjected to a more intensive statistical analysis than in any other area in Mesoamerica, Marcus Winter (1974, 1976) has found that there are qualitative intrasite differences between houses at the beginning of the Classic Period. There are three general types of houses in the valley, with a clear difference in size, arrangement, and number of rooms between the largest and most formal type and the other two. High status burials (measured in terms of luxury goods) are found in association with the larger houses, further supplementing the inference that differential access to housing labor and materials is at least one element in some form of economic stratification in Oaxaca. At Tikal, there is evidence of high status stone masonry residences in the area of the ceremonial center of the site, which are contemporaneous with lower status masonry and thatch residences in the surrounding area (Haviland 1970; W. Coe 1965).

. . . FOR COPING WITH AN AGGRESSIVE SOCIAL ENVIRONMENT

Protective devices for coping with aggression include both physical items such as weapons and defensive architecture, and social features such as protective residential units. Stratification, as manifested in unequal access to weapons and, concomitantly, ability to defend against of attack, may be seen in the distribution of either all types of weapons or technologically superior weapons (again, for example, metal versus stone). This distribution should be directly observable in the artifactual assemblages associated with different segments of the society. Stratification may also be seen where there is unequal access to architecture, which bestows an advantage in the event of external aggression. Walled, moated, or otherwise inaccessible compounds or fortifications would be examples of such defensive architecture. Archaeologically, unequal access to such architecture would be observed in residential and settlement patterns. Residences immediately inside such structures or compounds would have a defensive tactical advantage over outside residences; similarly, residences in close proximity would have an advantage over those located at some distance away.

In the absence of specific defensive architecture, the relative size of residential units may also be indicative of a form of stratification. Assuming some truth in the adage that there is strength in numbers, larger residential units would have a tactical defensive advantage over smaller units, given relatively similar geographical position. As in the case of housing size and quality, it can be expected that in nonstratified societies, there will be some variation in the size of residential units. However, stratification should be marked by qualitatively different-sized units. Examples would be the differences between an urban city and a small rural community, or between a village and an isolated single-family household. It is also possible that in a single large community, there may be some consolidated residence units that are qualitatively larger than contemporaneous units in the same community. In such cases, it can be inferred that the larger unit has an advantage not only in the face of external aggression, but also in the event of internal disputes. It should be noted that differential size of residential units can be used as an indicator of stratification only when it can be established that warfare or intrasocietal competition is an important element bearing on the survival at that point in time.

In Mesopotamia, the clearest evidence of differential access to defensive resources is in settlement patterns. In terms of settlement size, there are urban centers of hundreds of thousands of square meters in area contemporaneous with small villages of less than 1,000 sq m in area in the Early Uruk Period (Adams and Nissen 1972; Johnson 1973). While there is some pictographic evidence of warfare (Porada 1965), the lack of substantial fortifications throws some doubt on the importance of warfare at this time (Johnson 1973; Redman 1978). Therefore, although the defensive advantage of a large site over a small site might constitute a "basic" resource, the presence and importance of warfare needs to be clarified before any inferences can be made. More work also needs to be done on the possible presence and distribution of weapons during the Uruk period as well.

Evidence of unequal access to defensive mechanisms in Shang China is exhibited in weaponry, settlement pattern, and fortifications. Weapons, ranging from halberds to spears to chariots, have been encountered extensively in the context of burials, where they are found in a small minority of "royal graves (Kao 1959; Shih 1950; 1959 (cited in Chang 1977); Cheng 1960). Furthermore, the large majority of weapons come from sacrificial burials associated with individual high-status persons (Chang 1980:196). In other words, the distribution of weapons indicates that a minority of persons had such items, and this minority, in turn, was at the disposal of an even smaller number of elite individuals.

While survey has not been as extensive in China as in Mesopotamia, there appears to be a similar distinction between large and tactically more defensive urban centers such as Hsiao-t'un and Cheng-chou, and much smaller outlying villages located at variable distances away from the urban centers (Chang 1977). The only fortification yet clearly identified for the Shang Period is a massive wall aroung the city of Cheng-chou. Inside this wall have been found high status residences as well as specialized craft workshops (*Wen-wu* 1974b, cited in Chang 1977:234). At Hsiao-t'un remnants of a major ditch, 7–21 m wide and 5–10 m deep have been found near the palace area, and it has been argued that there was originally a moat around the palace structures (Chang 1980:110). Thus unequal access to the defensive advantages of a city wall in one city and a possible moat in a second constitute potential elements of social stratification in Shang China.

In South America, there are qualitatively larger settlements in evidence as early as the Cotton Pre-Ceramic Period (c.1500–1800 B.C.) (Mosley 1975a; Engel 1966). However, the absence of evidence of warfare precludes the inference that site size was an exploitable basic resource at that early time period. The combination of site size differentials and warfare first occurs toward the end of the Early Horizon and continues into the Early Intermediate Period. There are a number of residential sites with occupation areas of hundreds of thousands of square meters, contemporaneous with sites of several thousand square meters (Rowe 21963; Lumbreras 1974; Willey 1953). The presence of warfare during this entire time period can be inferred from the discovery of a number of fortified sites in different areas (Willey 1953; Patterson 1971:45; Topic and Topic 1978). Warfare is also vividly depicted on ceramic vessels and murals on the north Peruvian coast during the Early Intermediate Period. Aside from site size differentials, more direct evidence of unequal access to defensive architecture can be seen at the sites of Pampa Grande and Galindo. Neither site is situated for particular defensive advantage, but both contain a limited number of high status residences located inside large, defensible adobe compounds, while the lower status residential areas lie open. Whether or not the compound walls were erected specifically to provide the high status occupants with defense in times of war, they nevertheless would have served that function. It is also of interest to note that inside one of the compounds at Pampa Grande there is a mural depicting warriors which demonstrates a regard for warfare at the site (Anders n.d.).

In Mesoamerica, evidence of relative access to protective mechanisms is slight. There have been no studies delimiting the distribution of weapons in any of the early complex societies in the area. Surveys in Oaxaca, the Valley of Mexico and the Mayan highlands and lowlands indicate that there were sites of qualitatively different size in all these areas by the beginning of the Classic Period (Flannery 1976; Parsons 1976; Millon 1973; Puleston 1974; Bullard 1960). Also at the lowland Maya site of Tikal there is evidence that the ceremonial center and residences near it were surrounded by a large defensive earth wall, while houses further away had no such protection (Puleston and Callender 1967). At Teotihuacán residential complexes in the center of the city were surrounded by large defensible walls, though some lower status complexes lacked such defensive devices (Millon 1973; Millon et al. 1973).

There have been few specific archaeological studies dealing with prehistoric stratification, and most of the general survey and excavation projects have either not collected or reported the kinds of data needed to ascertain the presence or absence of stratification. However, when the relevant data have been reported, they consistently indicate that in the areas of initial state development, some people had qualitatively greater access to certain basic resources that did other people. In other words, some members of the first archaic civilizations had significantly higher standards of living than other members in terms of food, housing, tools, craft items, and mechanisms of defense. Thus, stratification, which is the basic element in the conflict model, can be tentatively confirmed with available archaeological evidence. With some empirical confirmation of stratification, the next step subject to empirical testing in the conflict model is the proposition that the qualitative differences in access to resources and standards of living will lead to conflict between social groups. Testing for something as incorporeal as conflict in the archaeological record is difficult, but not impossible.

Conflict: Haves vs. Have Nots

In a situation of unequal access to basic resources, the relationship between unequal social groups is predicted to be one of conflict, expressed in some degree of sustained hostility and antagonism within the society. Persons with restricted or lesser access to basic resources would contest, rather than simply accept, the unequal distribution of those resources, or the benefits reaped from greater access to them (Fried 1978). On the other hand, those persons with unrestricted or greater access would protect or defend their privileged access and social position in the face of such contestation. This on-going antagonistic relationship between social groups within a society could be expected to lead to the separation and relative isolation of the groups from one another. The groups with greater access and a favored position would also be expected to institute defensive mechanisms to physically protect their position in the face of prolonged internal aggression or hostility.

In the archaeological record, therefore, it may be predicted that conflict between unequal social groups would be materially manifested in the segregation of residences or residence groups. The persons with greater access to basic resources would reside apart or isolated from the persons with restricted access. It may be further predicted that in circumstances of internal conflict, the residences of the privileged group would be safeguarded against possible aggressive measures which might be taken by the unprivileged group in attempting to equalize the distribution of resources. Types of specific safeguards would include defensive walls surrounding the residences, or location of the residences in naturally defensible or inaccessible positions. Turning to the available archaeological data, the clearest evidence of separation, isolation, and internally oriented defense of upper strata residences in the first civilizations is found in South America and China, with somewhat less clear evidence from Mesoamerica.

In South America the most definite indications of internal conflict between groups come during the Early Intermediate Period on the North Coast of Peru. The expected separation and relative isolation of high-status residences from other residences is found at a number of sites in the Viru and Moche valleys. In the Viru Valley, Willey found that at the cluster of sites known as the "Gallinazo Group," there were very large stone-floored houses separated by several hundred meters from contemporaneous village aggregations of from twenty to one hundred small rooms or houses (1953:347–48; see also Bennett 1950). At the later site of Galindo in the Moche Valley, lower status stone masonry houses are clustered on the hillslopes to the rear of the site, while the higher status adobe houses are down below on a flat plain area (Bawden 1977). In addition to this relative isolation, the high and low status residential areas are separated by a massive stone wall. Furthermore, the higher status residences at the site are also surrounded by large defensible compound walls. At the site of Moche, the high status houses are clustered together between two huge pyramid structures in relative isolation from the lower status residences at the edges of the site. Topic (1977) also found some evidence of a possible compound wall around portions of the central part of the site, though confirmation of this wall was hampered by the presence of several meters of windblown sand over the site.

At Pampa Grande in the Lambayeque Valley, separation and isolation of high and low status groups is extreme. The site is not located in a particularly advantageous military position, and there are no indications of protective mechanisms or fortifications erected to defend the immediate avenues of approach. Consequently, it can be inferred that defense was not a primary variable in the determination of the location and layout of the site. However, within the 4 sq kms of the occupied site area, there is one enormous walled compound, and several comparatively smaller walled compounds. The wall around the single main compound is roughly rectangular, measuring 600 m along the long axis and 400 m along the short. It is constructed entirely of adobe, with an original height of at least 4 m and a width of more than 2 m.

Within this compound, architecture is sparse and most of it is arranged in a formal pattern. The dominant architectural feature inside is a massive platform or truncated pyramid. The structure is composed of a series of stepped terraces and platforms. The height above ground level of the various floors on this structure ranges from 10 to 55 m. The only means of access up onto any of the upper levels is by way of a walled corridor/ramp. Access is further restricted by a number of cross walls or checkpoints along this ramp. To gain access onto the uppermost level of the structure required that a person pass through an additional baffled or zigzagging entry and another walled ramp. Located on the summit of the structure is an elaborate, multi-roomed residential complex (Haas n.d.). This high status residence is thus not only separated and isolated from other residences at the site, but it is also a highly defensible stronghold against any possible internal acts of aggression or hostility. The indications that the site itself is not fortified or defensively located support the inference that the elaborate defensive measures surrounding the single high status residence are addressed to internally rather than externally originating aggression.

Below the large platform, there is another large and formally arranged complex of rooms inside the compound walls. On the basis of surface indications this complex also appears to be high status residences, but confirmatory excavations have not been conducted. There is another complex of rooms at the rear of the compound which appears to be residential as well, but is definitely not high status. These rooms are small, have rock and rubble walls, and are randomly arranged. However, while these rooms are within the compound and afforded the protection of the surrounding wall, equally massive walls separate and isolate this lower-status complex from the probable residential complex at the front of the compound and from an access ramp leading up to the platform complex. In other words, the compound walls serve to isolate the interior residences from the majority of the site, and subdividing walls further isolate the higher status residences from the few lower status residences within the compound.

Work on the other, smaller compounds at the site has not been focused on residential architecture; thus, the extent of isolation and separation of residences cannot be determined at present. The investigations which have been carried out in these smaller enclosures have revealed structures associated with warehousing and storing certain agricultural resources such as maize and cotton (Day 1976). The walls around storage and warehousing areas may be interpreted as preventative mechanisms against possible usurpation or theft.

A pattern similar to that found at Pampa Grande is found at the Shang site of Cheng-chou in North China, where there is an earthen wall, over 7000 m in total length, 9 m in height, with an average width of 20 m. Within the wall are administrative, ceremonial, and residential complexes (Chang 1977:233–34). While there has been very limited work within this enclosed area, excavations have revealed numerous "palatial" type houses on stamped earth platforms, and one house with a lime-plastered, burned-hard floor (Chang 1977:234). Houses of this type and magnitude have not been found outside the walled compound, where residences were predominantly dirt-floored, semi-subterranean pit house structures (Cheng 1960; An 1957). A similar pattern has been found at the smaller site of Pan-lung-ch'eng, where a major wall (290 by 260 m) surround a single large palace" (Chang 1980:161). Thus, again there is a situation in which higher status residences are isolated and separated from lower status residences by a defensive wall.

In the region of An-yang high status, elevated residences, located at the site of Hsiao-t'un, are geographically segregated from the concentration of lower status residences in the region. While there is no definite wall recorded around this site, there is the possible moat. Chang (1977:248) also believes the lack of a wall may be an artifact of limited excavation rather than a reflection of the absence of a wall. The reason given for proposing a possible wall at Hsiao-t'un is that Cheng-chou, which precedes Hsiao-t'un chronologically, has a wall as do virtually all the cities associated with the following Chou Period. For example, the Chou cities of Lo-yang, Han-tan, Hsin-t'ien, and Hsia-tu all have interior walled areas containing "palatial" type residences on raised platforms (Chang 1976:66–69; 1977:322–38; Wheatley 1971: 136–46). (See also Fei 1953 for a discussion of the historical role of the walled inner city as a tool for the protection and maintenance of the Chinese ruling class.)

Data pertinent to intrasocietal conflict in Mesoamerica are somewhat less conclusive than those from South America and China. At the Classic Mayan site of Tikal, the wall around the site circumscribes both high and low status residences. Within this walled area, the former appear to be somewhat separated from the latter in that they are clustered around the ceremonial architecture at the center of the site (W. Coe 1965). In the Valley of Oaxaca high status and low status residences are both found in the city of Monte Albán and in smaller rural communities (Winter 1974). However, information on relative distribution and concentrations of different house types in the area is not presently available.

Teotihuacán provides the best residential evidence of probable intrasocietal conflict in Mosoamerica. At Teotihuacán, the vast majority of all the residences are artificially isolated from one another by being enclosed in large compound walls (Millon 1973, 1976). The city, in other words, is composed of a series of separate walled compounds of both high and low status residences. However, the highest status residential compounds are aggregated at the center of the city, and these also appear to have been the first walled compounds built. In discussing the compartmentalization of Teotihuacán, Millon maintains that the division of the city into walled compounds was associated with "major conflicts, antagonisms, and tensions" (1976:224). Thus, internal conflict between social groups at Teotihuacán seems to have been a dominant element from the beginning of the site's occupation.

In addition to separation, isolation, and internally oriented defense mechanisms, intragroup conflict may be exhibited in the form of revolution or rebellion. The lower status group or groups may take physical or violent measures to depose the upper status group from their privileged position. While such a rebellious action should have some material manifestations, for a number of reasons, it may be difficult to discern in the archaeological record. If the rebellion were short-lived and unsuccessful, it could be expected to have minimal impact on the makeup and distribution of material artifacts that can be recovered archaeologically. Similarly, if the rebellion was successful, but did not result in the dissolution of the system of stratification, but with the preemption of those positions of high status or privileged access by a group which formally had lower status and restricted access, then again the impact on the archaeological record would be minimal.

On the other hand, if the rebellion was successful and did result in the dissolution of stratification, the resultant material could bear some similarities to a situation in which a high status ruling elite is deposed by a foreign power through warfare. In both situations, violence aimed at the upper class group or at the residences or material goods associated with that elite group, might be expected. Internal rebellion would thus have to be independently distinguished from external defeat and subjugation. Methodologically, deposition of a high status ruling group at the hands of a foreign power should be distinguishable by the presence of intrusive foreign elements in the defeated area subsequent to its defeat. The exact nature of the intrusive elements may range from the wholesale occupation of the original area by the victors to the presence of small quantities of foreign goods or products brought in by the invaders. To fully determine whether or not there were internal rebellions in the first states, it would be necessary to design and implement a highly specific research project addressed directly to the question. Since such projects have yet to be carried out by archaeologists there is little available evidence that is strongly indicative of either the presence or absence of prehistoric rebellions.

In spite of the lack of appropriately oriented research, there are possible indications of internal rebellion in South America, Mesoamerica, and Mesopotamia. All the data, however, are somewhat equivocal. The single instance in Mesoamerica comes from the Formative Period Olmec site of La Venta in the southeastern Mexican lowlands. In the course of excavations at La Venta a total of forty large stone monuments were uncovered. These monuments, predominantly religious or political in nature, ranged from large slabs or stelae carved with different scenes or figures, to life-size representations of priests carrying babies, to the colossal stone portrait heads for which the Olmec are famous (Drucker et al. 1959:197–209; Stirling 1943; Drucker 1952). Of the forty monuments found at the site at least twenty-four of them had been deliberately mutilated or destroyed (a number of the monuments had been too badly eroded to determine whether or not they had been mutilated) (Drucker et al. 1959:229–30). Furthermore, the mutilation or destruction of the monuments took place during the final phase of occupation at the site, either at or close to the time of abandonment.

Similar data to those from La Venta have been recovered from the Olmec site of San Lorenzo, as reported by Coe and Diehl (1980:297–98). At San Lorenzo, again, tremendous energy was expended on the mutilation, destruction, and burial of numerous stone monuments. In this case, however, there is continued occupation after the monuments were destroyed, and while previous ceramic types continue, two new utilitarian wares also appear (Coe and Diehl 1980:188).

At both sites the deliberate destruction of monuments has been interpreted as resulting either from conquest or internal revolt (Drucker et al. 1959:230; Heizer 1960:220; Coe 1968a:72; Coe and Diehl 1980:188). Both alternatives are feasible; however, there are no signs of foreign intrusion at La Venta and only minimal signs at San Lorenzo. Also, it is not unwarranted to expect that if conquerors went to such considerable trouble to mutilate or ruin the religious monuments at La Venta and San Lorenzo, they would have substituted religious elements of their own. (Witness, for example, the Spanish conquest of Mexico and the destruction of native religious iconography by the missionizing priests.) No such new elements have been found in the area, and at least at San Lorenzo life continued much the same as before only without mound building and monumental sculpture.

An additional factor which points to internal revolt as the source of the monument destruction at La Venta concerns an increase in labor output during the final occupation period at the site. Throughout the occupation of La Venta the population contributed labor in transporting and carving stone monuments, in burying massive quantities of imported stone as religious offerings, and in building large ceremonial structures. During the final occupation period at the site, the additional burden was placed on the population of quarrying and transporting, from a source over fifty linear miles away, over two hundred basalt columns, each weighing approximately two tons (Drucker et al. 1959:126). These columns were used to build an elaborate tomb and a wall around one of the ceremonial areas of the site. While numerous columns were stockpiled nearby, the enclosure wall was never completed. As one possible explanation of why the wall was not completed, Drucker et al. offer the hypothesis that the additional burden of bringing in and erecting the columns was too much for the La Venta population, and they rebelled (1959:126–27).

Ethnographic support for this interpretation may be found in much smaller scale but analogous circumstances in Polynesia. Specifically in Hawaii, the ruling chiefs were able to extract some goods and labor from their subordinate population. However, as chiefdoms grew quantitatively, the demands made by the chiefs grew qualitatively. When their demands placed too great a strain on the populace, and they were also unable to meet increased expectations of the populace, unrest developed and often resulted in the overthrow of the chief and the dissolution of the chiefdom (Sahlins 1968:92–93). While the Olmec situation may not be fully analogous to the Polynesian (see chapter 8), the pattern of rebellion in the latter area is fully consistent with the body of data recovered from the former area. Overall, revolution or rebellion at La Venta and San Lorenzo cannot be firmly established, but it would appear to be the most parsimonious explanation to account for a number of different artifactual patterns found at the site.

The site of Pampa Grande in Peru provides another case of site abandonment accompanied by violence directed at the internal authority structure. Almost all of the ceremonial platforms at the site,

including the massive central structure and the high status reside
on top of it, were burned and never reoccupied or utilized. Again, i
pattern may be alternately explained as either the result of forei,
invasion or internal revolt. Since there have been absolutely no foreig
elements found in the upper occupation layers of the lower statu:
residences or on the top of the burned ceremonial structures, interna'
revolt is slightly more consistent with the available evidence than is
foreign invasion. Without attaching undue significance, it is also of
interest to note that at least the concept of rebellion was not unknown
on the north coast during the Early Intermediate Period. At the si+
of Moche there is a mural on one of the two large pyramids whic
depicts an assortment of ceramic vessels and other artifacts apparently
rising up and actively rebelling against their users (Lumbreras 1974:102).
Whether this mural is a symbolic representation of human rebellion
is certainly open to question, but it offers a tantalizing possibility
nevertheless.

The only possible example of internal revolt in Mesopotamia is even
more equivocal than the examples in Mesoamerica and South America. At the site of al-U'baid, the central temple utilized during the
Early Dynastic has been violently dismantled piece by piece (Wooley
1956). After the destruction, the temple was abandoned, with no material indications of foreign intrusion. Unfortunately, the excavation
record is insufficient to allow the extraction of any further information
to infer whether the destruction was due to warfare or revolt.

Positive indications of revolution in the first states must be considered inconclusive based on the present corpus of available data. Additional information is needed to determine whether the limited cases
sketched above did result from revolutions, and whether other areas
or sites may have experienced short-lived and unsuccessful revolutions—a question that has not been specifically addressed by archaeologists. However, it should also be mentioned at this point, that while
revolution or rebellion may be considered indicative of internal conflict within a society, it cannot be inferred conversely that the absence
of revolution is equally indicative of the absence of conflict. In fact,
one of the fundamental premises of the basic conflict model is that
the assumed conflict between economically unequal groups is resolved
by the active repression of those persons with restricted access to basic
resources. Consequently, through the application of physically and
economically coercive sanctions, the economically favored upper class

precludes any rebellious actions by the economically disenfranchised lower class. In reviewing the archaeological record of the first states, therefore, the paucity of evidence of revolutions is as logically consistent with the premises of the conflict model, as it is with those of the integrative model. Thus, the comparative evaluation of the alternative explanations requires the determination of whether or not the lower classes were subjected to coercive sanctions, which would act as a physical deterrent to revolution.

Force: The Ultimate Arbiter

The application of forceful coercive sanctions in support of a system of stratification is the final basic element in the conflict model. Force may be manifested either in direct physical violence or, as was argued in chapter 3, in the withholding of certain necessary goods and services. While it is possible to confirm whether or not some form of direct or indirect force was systematically applied internally in the early state societies, it must be recognized that in circumstances of forceful repression, actual coercive sanctions may be applied with relative infrequency. If a ruler is able to physically demonstrate the ability to apply such sanctions, then the threat of applying them may be used as an effective mechanism for maintaining the subordinate position of the lower status portion of the population (cf. Bierstedt 1950:73; Dahl 1969:86; for a more detailed explication of the relationship between the ability to apply sanctions and the threat of applying them, see chapter 6 below). In other words, if there is forceful resolution of conflict between unequal social groups in the first states, it is not to be expected that the application of force will be omnipresent, nor will it be the only means used to govern the population. Considerable insight into the way in which the rulers of the first states could have utilized coercive sanctions to maintain the system of stratification may be gained from ethnohistoric examples of complex societies at or approaching statehood.

Two societies in particular, the Hawaiians of Polynesia and the Zulu of South Africa, provide examples of highly complex political forms that developed without overriding influence from outside state societies. While neither may be considered a pristine state, both experienced internal development relatively independent of the states they were in contact with. Service (1975:116, 285) treats both societies as primitive states, and asserts that force or coercive sanctions were not used in either of them as a successful means of governing or maintaining a system of stratification. However, upon examining both of these cases, it is apparent that coercive sanctions were actively and regularly applied against the lower status portions of the population as a highly successful means of maintaining social control.

In Hawaii at the time of contact, the paramount chiefs had managerial control over the distribution of land and water rights. They also served as the foci for the collection and redistribution of certain kinds of resources. They used this economic control and central position in a number of ways. They personally subsidized specialized craftsmen, enjoyed qualitatively greater consumption of numerous luxury goods, employed personal litter bearers, and lived in superior housing (Sahlins 1958:15–18). They also monopolized certain kinds of foods, though their food consumption was not greatly different from that of the rest of the population. Moreover, to maintain their position, they were obligated to justly distribute the foodstuffs they collected. According to Malo, the redistribution of food was a positive means of governing the population and of keeping the people "contented" (1951:62). However, the chiefs were not totally dependent on positive means of governing. Rather, they used their control over land and water to dispossess from the means of subsistence those persons who failed to contribute labor demanded of them, who failed to produce sufficient resources, or who secretly accumulated resources (Malo 1951; Sahlins 1958:14–16). More direct physically coercive sanctions were applied against commoners who committed criminal acts or misdeeds. Particularly severe sanctions were applied when the misdeeds affected the paramount chiefs. According to Sahlins:

> Punishment varied according to the status of the parties. Within this framework, coercive force was applied by the chief in punishing those who infringed his rights, especially if the transgressors were low in status.
> According to Ellis, Handy, Malo, and others, *people were slain by a high chief if they violated his economic or personal tabus, stole from him, or committed adultery with his wife.* (1958:19, emphasis added)

Thus, Hawaii clearly demonstrates how coercive sanctions can be and are applied in the maintenance of a system of qualitatively different statuses.

The Zulu offer an example of secondary state formation in which the application and threat of violent coercive sanctions played a paramount role. The initial formation of the Zulu state came about as a result of the conquest and subordination of several hundred chiefdoms in southern Africa by the combined Mthethwa and Zulu chiefdoms (Walter 1969; Morris 1965). Once formed, the subsequent development of the Zulu state was characterized by widespread terror and wholesale slaughter of thousands of people at the instigation of the first two rulers, Shaka and Dingane. People were publicly executed for relatively minor criminal acts, and at times for apparently arbitrary reasons. Both of these rulers governed for approximately ten years before being assassinated. With the ascent of the third ruler, Mpande, the volume of slaughter decreased markedly, and the Zulu lived in relative internal peace for the more than thirty years of Mpande's rule (Walter 1969: ch. 6; Gluckman 1940; Morris 1965).

Service asserts that this basic sequence of events illustrates that government by force is highly inefficient and ultimately unsuccessful (1975:111–16). He also cites Walter (1969) to support the assertion that the mass slaughter instigated by Shaka and Dingane was not aimed at coercing the populace, but at impressing potentially rival chiefs (1975:116, 285). However, an examination of the data and Walter's analysis reveals a markedly different picture from that painted by Service.

On an absolute scale, it may in fact be true that Shaka and Dingane both ruled for relatively short periods of time. However, their combined despotic rule resulted in the population experiencing over twenty years of mass executions. In other words, the initial Zulu reign of terror lasted a full generation. Given a span of twenty years of terror, it would seem difficult to support a claim that the government of the first two Zulu rulers did not have a lasting coercive effect on the Zulu population. Walter makes this point very clearly:

> In the despotic system beginning with Shaka, as the intermediate authorities—fathers, elders, headmen, chieftains, chiefs—lost their autonomy, they were still respected, but the ruler became a magnified center of fear and awe. As the frequency of violence increased beyond measure, the people's fear not only augmented in degree but also changed qualitatively—the emotional climate was a compound of servile, inhibiting fear, preventing the desire to resist or even the thought of doing anything new (1969:188–89).

Walter does demonstrate that the violence of the first Zulu rulers was a political device aimed at their subordinate chiefs. But he never underestimates the tremendous effectiveness of that violence in maintaining the subservient position of the rest of the population. The application of violent sanctions was by no means aimed strictly at impressing potential rival leaders as claimed by Service.

Furthermore, the data also show that the application of violent sanctions did not come to an end with the assassination of Dingane. There are numerous examples of the succeeding ruler, Mpande, ordering executions for offenses ranging from conspiracy to thievery to wearing one's hair too long (Walter 1969:211–17; Gluckman 1955:40). According to early observers, the primary reason Mpande did not employ even greater violence is that he was prevented from doing so by the Boers and British, who by this time exercised a degree of colonial control in the area (Walter 1969:214–15). Walter points out that under Mpande:

> The despotic system had contracted, but terroristic rule, considerably limited in scope, remained. Generally regarded as the mildest of Zulu rulers, Mpande still declared flatly to Sir Theophilus Shepstone, Chief Native Affairs Commissioner of Natal, *"The Zulus are only ruled by being killed."* (1969:218, emphasis added)

Walter also states that while at no time was violence the only means used by the Zulu rulers to govern the population, it was always a critical component of the governing process, even under Mpande.

> The system of power included other methods as well—authority, economic redistribution, rewards, persuasion, magic, and other techniques familiar to legitimate rulers. The pattern of violence, however, reacted to fundamental conflicts and it inhibited resistance. It made government possible. (1969:218)

As a whole, the development of the Zulu state serves to illustrate how violent coercive sanctions are used to keep the majority of a population in a position of subordination. The rule of Mpande also illustrates how the threat of violence, accompanied by limited application, is an effective element in long term stable government.

Turning to the archaeological record of the first prehistoric state developments, it is possible to make a limited empirical investigation to determine whether or not the rulers in those first states used forceful sanctions in governing their respective populations. Archaeological manifestations of coercion potentially may be exhibited in skeletal materials and/or in iconographic representations. Skeletally, physically coercive sanctions may be seen in consistent patterns of violence inflicted on persons of lower social or economic status. Economically coercive sanctions may be seen in the deprivation of some individuals of nutritionally adequate subsistence resources. In other words, coercion may be manifested in the physical or nutritional disorders concentrated in the skeletal remains of the lower socioeconomic groups within the population. Artistic evidence of coercion might include actual representation of the application of sanctions, or the results of such application.

The clearest direct evidence of significant coercive sanctions being applied to a lower class population is found in China. In one case, mentioned earlier, a number of the retainers, who were sacrificed and buried with the royal personages at the Hsi-pei-kang burial site, were suffering from malnutrition (Mao and Yen 1959; Chang 1976:55). It may also be considered that all the sacrificial burials at Hsi-pei-kang, at nearby Hsiao-t'un, and at other Shang sites are evidence that coercive sanctions were at the disposal of and exercised by the upper strata of the Shang society. The Shang royalty had the ability to exact the slaughter of hundreds of people, ranging from probable slaves to servants to warriors. As many as 164 people were sacrificed for one royal burial and over 600 met their deaths in the commemoration of a single house at Hsiao-t'un (Shih 1970, cited in Chang 1976:52).

This would appear to be a clear case of extensive physical violence being applied in the reinforcement of the superior position of royalty over lower status groups. While it might conceivably be argued that these servants went willingly to their deaths, Chang points out that this was definitely not the case in later historic times in similar cases of sacrifice at the time of the ruler's death (1976:52–53).

Another instance of coercive physical force comes from the site of Erh-li-t'ou, where a number of persons, buried in low status housing areas, were found to have been decapitated. Others had parts of limbs missing, while still others were found with their hands tied, apparently having been buried alive (Chang 1977:225). This material evidence is supplemented by oracle bone records that detail a wide variety of physical punishments meted out for crimes committed by subjects of the Shang kings (Chang 1980:201).

In other areas of early state development evidence of the use of coercion is primarily pictographic rather than skeletal. In Mesoamerica, there is some indication of decapitation among the burials at the late Formative site of Chupicuaro (Porter 1956). However, there is not sufficient information available to rule out the possibility that these persons were beheaded in a context of warfare. This pictographic evidence is also highly ambiguous. There are Olmec artworks which show elaborately clad invididuals holding other unclad or semiclad individuals by a tether around the neck (Gay 1967; Covarrubias 1957 fig. 29). There is also an Olmec carving which depicts a nude man tied, and being confronted by masked individuals bearing clubs (Wicke 1971:18–19). The latter carving is interpreted as representing a sacrifice. From the Formative occupation of the Mayan site of Kaminaljuyú there have been stone sculptures recovered depicting kneeling male figures, with ropes around their necks and their hands and ankles tied behind their backs (Borhegyi 1965). Again, these appear to be sacrificial victims, who are not particularly willing to participate in the upcoming event. From such limited kinds of pictorial evidence, it cannot be concluded that physical sanctions were being regularly and widely applied in the early states of Mesoamerica.

In South America, evidence for the application of violent coercive sanctions is found exclusively in art. No substantial skeletal populations recovered from Early Horizon or Early Intermediate sites have been subjected to intensive analysis. South American art, however, provides a more fertile data base.

Of particular importance is the highly realistic Moche ceramic art from the Peruvian north coast. Art work on Moche ceramic vessels shows a number of different coercive sanctions being applied in circumstances which do not appear to be related to warfare. A number of individuals are depicted whose noses and/or lips have been cut off in a consistent pattern of mutilation (Benson 1972; Larco Hoyle 1938; 1945; Kosok 1965:112). On other vessels, individuals are shown bound to a stake or in stockades. In some cases these bound individuals are being attacked by carnivorous birds; in others they have been partially flayed (Donnan 1978: figs. 137, 147, 148; Larco Hoyle 1945; Kutscher 1950:200; Lanning 1967:123). Others are shown with amputated limbs or genitals (Larco Hoyle 1945; Kosok 1965: plate 42). Direct representation of coercion is manifested in scenes in which scantily clad individuals are herded in a line by others brandishing whips (Lumbreras 1974:103).

The inference that these different depictions of coercive sanctions do not represent the treatment of prisoners of war is based on other scenes that explicitly depict the capture and treatment of such prisoners. In these scense, prisoners are shown being exchanged for other prisoners (Lumbreras 1974:105), or they are shown being sacrificed. In the latter cases, the sacrifice consists of either the prisoner being decapitated or having his throat slit and heart removed (Kutscher 1950:199–201). Thus, the disfigurement, mutilation, and torture of individuals in some ceramics does not appear to be analogous to the treatment of prisoners of war shown in other ceramics. While it cannot be ruled out that these persons were war captives, the alternate interpretation, that they were local natives subjected to physical punishment for misdeeds is more consistent with the available data.

In Mesopotamia, there is presently insufficient evidence to test for the presence or absence of the application of coercive sanctions in the early stages of state development. No skeletal populations have been adequately analyzed, and there are minimal artistic works relevant to the problem. The few pictographic representations of men being killed or tortured all appear to be within the context of warfare and the victims are war captives (Woolley 1928; Porada 1965). The only positive evidence of coercion in the area comes from historic materials of a relatively late date. In examining the legal codes from the second millennium B.C., Fried (1978) finds a consistent pattern of laws which dictated economic and/or severe physical sanctions for offenses committed against either the state of individual property owners (see also Prichard 1950). Unfortunately, there is no data on how frequently the sanctions were carried out. Realizing that these data do not necessarily pertain to the states of a millennium earlier, they do still indicate that the application of coercive sanctions in later periods was an established and codified governmental practice in the Mesopotamian area.

Taken as a whole, the archaeological record from the early periods of state development does not overwhelming demonstrate that coercion or physical violence was being systematically applied to the lower status portions of the populations. However, there are indications that the rulers in the first civilizations had the option of applying coercive sanctions, and at times they exercised that option. It also may be inferred that the threat of applying physically coercive sanctions must have accompanied the actual application of such sanctions, as an alternative mechanism for maintaining the subordinate position of the lower status groups. By combining the limited archaeological evidence with the ethnohistoric Hawaiian and Zulu data, there is much greater empirical confirmation for the conflict hypothesis that forceful coercive sanctions were used to maintain a system of stratification, than for Service's integration hypothesis that such sanctions were not an integral part of the first formal governments or primitive states. A more conclusive test of the conflict and integration positions will require new data, the collection of which is specifically directed to the problem.

When the basic premises of the conflict position—stratification, conflict, and force—are examined in the light of the available material record of the archaic civilizations, the position can be at best only partially confirmed. In none of the world areas where initial state development has been best documented is there solid, unequivocal evidence supporting all the major contentions of the conflict model. The heartland of the Shang Dynasty in North China offers the best archaeological evidence of a conflict-based state, and Chang (1980) presents extensive data derived from oracle bones which supports all three of the conflict components. There is less distinct evidence from the North Coast of Peru and positive but ambiguous evidence from the Mesoamerican lowlands and the Valley of Mexico. The highly restricted research carried out in Mesopotamia provides even less support for the conflict model. However, the lack of strong supporting evidence alone cannot be considered a refutation of the model. Rather, the situation encountered in the archaeological literature is that the types of data needed to test the model more fully have not been collected or recorded (see, for example Redman 1978:277–78).

With few exceptions, archaeologists have not formulated research designs aimed at elucidating the nature of prehistoric political organization. At the same time, while the conflict model cannot yet be adequately tested or confirmed, neither can the integrative model. When critically examined, the archaeological record simply provides no support for the strong positive or negative conclusions made by Service. As was argued earlier, many of Service's conclusions are derived from untestable intuitive inferences about what went on in the minds of prehistoric peasants and have no logical base. Much of the rest of his argument is based primarily on a refutation of the premises of the conflict model. While the data supporting the premises of the conflict model are meager, there is no corresponding body of data which specifically refutes those premises. In assessing the comparative validity of the opposing models, therefore, there is relatively greater empirical confirmation of the conflict model than of the integration model.

Conflict/Integration: A Comparison of Explanatory Power

While testing for the presence of stratification, conflict, and forceful repression in the archaeological record is one means of empirically evaluating both the conflict and integration models, it is not the only means of carrying out such an evaluation. Another avenue open for comparing the opposing positions lies in assessing the relative ability of each to provide explanatory insight into empirically verifiable patterns of material development characteristic of all the first prehistoric states. There are a number of specific patterns of development, such as the rise of regional art styles or urbanism, which could be used to test the explanatory value of the two theoretical models. A more general and inclusive pattern, however, provides a more comprehensive grounds for comparing the two. Briefly, the initial developmental stage in all the areas of pristine state formation is characterized by a distinct cultural efflorescence. There are major innovations and additions not only in art styles and settlement patterns, but also in monumental architecture and other labor projects, in recording and calendrical systems, and in religion. This broadly observed pattern of major material and organizational change provides a general data base for cross-culturally comparing the relative explanatory value of the conflict and integration models.

As was noted in chapter 3, Service assigns the label of "archaic civilization" to that period of initial development characterized by the rapid development of art styles, architecture, etc. He also asserts that the transition from the preceding chiefdom stage to the archaic civilization stage was a quantitative rather than qualitative evolutionary process. He states:

> Civilizations of the classical type were not created *de novo;* their basic characteristics were all foreshadowed in earlier stages of society. The term

civilization is thus a relative concept and should not be defined in terms of the appearance of some single attribute; not violence certainly, nor even writing, or fine arts. From an evolutionary standpoint, the relativity is achieved by thinking not in terms of arbitrary demarking points but of a continuum of directional change. (1975:305-6)

This quantitative rather than qualitative assessment is based on his conclusion that the material and organizational characteristics of the archaic civilization stage are quantitative elaborations of similar characteristics found in chiefdom level societies. Specifically, Service asserts that the rulers of the archaic civilizations used essentially the same positive and supernatural means of governing the population as did their chiefly predecessors (1975:290-308). They did not use negative coercive sanctions, or force, to gain the compliance of their respective populations. Service is basically using "archaic civilization" as a replacement term for "state" which carries the implication of forceful repression. He employs the label to distinguish "advanced stages of primitive development" (1975:305), which are characterized by complex administrative bureaucracies. Furthermore, he claims empirical validation for the term by appealing to the ability of archaeologists to recognize a civilization when they see one:

> There seems to be no practical difficulty in the archaeological discrimination of the original archaic civilizations from the previous developments. At least, there seems to be no fundamental disagreement among archaeologists and historians as to the identity of the full-fledged developments, with only a few arguments about whether to include early forms such as the Olmec or Chavín. (1975:305)

He does not say exactly how archaeologists accomplish this feat, and when an answer is sought in the archaeological literature, Service's conclusions about the quantitative evolution of civilizations are brought into question.

In examining the literature, there does in fact seem to be little disagreement over the identification of civilizations in the archaeological record. However, the reason for the relative lack of disagreement is that civilizations appear as qualitatively distinct from preceding cultural developments. In his analysis of the evolution of urban society, Robert Adams (1966) eschews the use of the term "civilization" for most purposes because it is too general to be methodologically useful. However, he does specify one situation in which "civilization" has some methodological validity:

> This is not to deny that the term "civilization" has advantages for other purposes, and in particular for characterizing *state societies* as they are distinguished from societies of lesser degrees of complexity. As Morgan already saw, *civilizations are associated with qualitatively greater scale and internal differentiation than other societies or cultures*, and it is entirely proper to set them aside as a class under this term. (1966:13, emphasis added)

Adams thus defends the use of the term "civilization" for circumstances outwardly similar to those for which Service uses it. The fundamental difference between Adams and Service is that Adams considers "civilization" to denote the *qualitative* material and organizational differences that distinguish a *state* from a prestate form of political organization. Furthermore, according to Adams, the cultural efflorescence seen in civilizations is a result of the increased power afforded to the state governing body through the monopolization of "the use of force for the preservation of order" (1966:14; see also Redman 1978:5).

Sanders and Price (1968) draw a similar conclusion in discussing the evolution of civilization in Mesoamerica. They assert that it is difficult to distinguish chiefdoms from early nonurban civilizations in the archaeological record; but their overall analysis clearly indicates that the cultural achievements of developed civilizations are qualitatively above those of the preceding chiefdoms (1968:227–32). They also conclude that the tremendous labor projects and increases in occupational specialization witnessed in Mesoamerican civilization cannot be attributed solely to population increase or increase in organizational complexity. Rather, they must be attributed to a qualitative change in the nature of the political and economic organization (1968:227). Like Adams, Sanders and Price maintain that it is the state, based on a system of stratification and forceful repression, that is responsible for the monumental accomplishments of the Mesoamerican civilization (1968:227–32; see also Millon 1976; Coe 1968b).

Chang presents a similar argument for the development of the Shang civilization in China. According to Chang, the greatest qualitative marker of civilization is seen in the elevation of the position of the ruling elite:

The transitions from the Neolithic Lung-shan Culture, which is the culture immediately antecendent in western and northern Honan, to the
Shang civilization is a quantum jump of the highest order in the quality
of life for the elite, yet there is no discernible corresponding change in
the technology of food production. (1976:56)

In searching for an explanation of this quantum leap, Chang independently arrives at the coercive sanctions of the state as the primary
causal variable:

The Shang period witnessed the beginning in this part of the world of
organized large-scale exploitation of one group of people by another
within the same society, and the beginning of an oppressive governmental
system to make such exploitation possible. (1976:57)

Based on these syntheses of Adams, Sanders and Price, and Chang,
it is apparent that civilizations *are* readily recognized archaeologically.
This recognizability is essentially based on the qualitatively distinct
material and organizational characteristics of civilizations. Also apparent is the consensus among these synthesizers in the conclusion
that the observed efflorescence characteristic of civilizations is due to
the introduction of coercive sanctions into the process of governing.
Each of them proposes a basic conflict model, and maintains that the
force-backed power of the state is behind the qualitative development
of the early civilizations.

Service, in contrast, wants to have one without the other. While he
accepts the archaeologist's identification of civilizations as social types,
recognizably distinct from their antecedents, he rejects the arguments
of Adams and others who see *state* institutions as playing a primary
causal role in the distinctive accomplishments of civilizations. (As we
have seen above, there is little if any solid empirical support for this
rejection.) However, in rejecting these arguments, Service is left without a viable explanation of why the cultural achievements—monumental architecture, water control systems, calendrical systems, long
distance trade networks, craft specialization—in the "non-state civilizations" were qualitatively greater than either their immediate evolutionary antecedents or any ethnographically known chiefdom. He
is unable to explain why the rulers in prehistoric civilizations appear
to have exercised a virtually unlimited amount of power, while chiefs
have definite limitations on the amount of power they can exercise.

For example, in societies Service identifies as archaic civilizations there are abundant examples of monumental labor projects that required hundreds of thousands or even millions of person-days of labor (e.g., Coe and Diehl 1980; Heizer 1960; Redman 1978; Chang 1977; Moseley 1975a; Hastings and Moseley 1975; Haas 1975). While Service cites Kaplan (1963) and Erasmus (1965) in arguing that monumental buildings of considerable size could conceivably be built voluntarily without the application of coercive sanctions, neither he nor they present any ethnographic documentation to support this argument. They offer no examples from any of the largest ethnographically or ethnohistorically known chiefdoms of Polynesia, South America, Africa, or the northwest coast of North America of labor projects of the same magnitude as are found in *all* of the archaic civilizations. In general, the available data strongly suggest that the rulers in the archaic civilizations were able to command far greater quantities of labor and services per capita from their subordinate populations than any of the chiefs in ethnographically or ethnohistorically known chiefdoms (see Sahlins 1958; Goldman 1970; Jennings 1979; Nadel 1942; Drucker 1965; also chapters 6 and 7).

In conflict theory the qualitative difference between the relative ability of rulers and chiefs to extract labor from their respective populations is explained as being due to the application of coercive sanctions by the former but not by the latter. In Service's integration theory there is no comparable explanation of the observed phenomena. Both rulers and chiefs are asserted to rely on positive sanctions and the "right of authority" in governing their respective populations. In comparing the two theories, therefore, conflict theory can be judged the more powerful, since it provides a parsimonious and logically sound explanation of the qualitative empirical differences between known chiefdoms and civilizations, while integration theory does not.

Conclusion

In attempting to test empirically the conflict and integration positions, it has been apparent in this chapter that there is inadequate data from the early states to definitively confirm or refute either one. The kinds of information needed to more fully test the positions simply have not been collected by archaeologists working in areas of initial state development. The problem is particularly acute with regard to the earliest stages of state emergence. With the exception of the Olmec of Mesoamerica there is almost no available relevant data from the first states in the different world areas that have been considered here. In spite of this dearth of evidence, however, there are some reasons for accepting the basic premises of the conflict theory over the integration theory presented by Service. First, in the few cases where relevant kinds of data *have* been collected and analyzed, they correspond to the conflict rather than the integration position. While this does not constitute positive confirmation, it does provide limited empirical support for the basic premises of the conflict position at the expense of integration. Second, the conflict theory appears to have greater explanatory power than does the integration theory in accounting for the initial efflorescence characteristic of the early civilizations.

At the same time, tentative acceptance of the basic conflict premises for either or both of these reasons does not necessarily entail the concomitant rejection of all the premises of the integration position. It is possible to accommodate certain aspects of the integration theory within the theoretical confines of the conflict theory, without comprising the integrity of the latter. The most well-argued and strongest premise in Service's thesis is that there are beneficial integrative advantages in the concentration of power and authority in a centralized governmental apparatus. He presents a logically sound argument that a large-scale society stands to gain such advantages in the waging of warfare, trading, and efficiently producing and distributing resources (1975:297–303). Conditionally accepting this proposal on the basis of Service's logical argument, it can be incorporated easily into the conflict model.

Retaining the proposition that the first step in the development of the state is the rise of economic stratification, it may be argued that such stratification results from the adaptive process of centralization. (A more detailed discussion of how stratification and centralization may develop together under different material circumstances will be presented in the following chapter.) Also retaining the proposition that coercive sanctions were used to resolve conflict arising in conditions of stratification, it may be further argued that the material benefits gained through centralization would have been used by the rulers of the first civilizations as positive mechanisms to govern their respective populations. Service provides ethnographic support for this argument (1975: chs. 6–9). However in incorporating the use of such benefits into the conflict model, they are not considered to be the only means of governing the population, but as a means of supplementing and reinforcing the application of coercive sanctions. There is nothing inherent in the conflict model as presented by Fried, White, Childe, or Engels, which says that state government exercise only repressive force and never apply positive sanctions. Actually, Service's integrative model also does not necessarily exclude some conflict and coercion. He simply stresses integrative variables while the conflict theories stress other variables. By taking Service's strong points and combining them with the major premises of the conflict model, a stronger and more productive theoretical position arises. Thus, while the major thrust of the conflict and integration models represents a complete opposition, a significant synthesis can be effected by introducing major integration elements directly into a broadened conflict model.

[Chapter 5]

Alternative Routes to Statehood

Having incorporated integrative elements into the basic outline of the conflict model, it is possible to turn to a more detailed discussion of how stratification and the state may have originally developed. A number of specific theories have been offered to explain the emergence of state societies in prehistory. Some of these attempt to explain the general process of pristine state formation, while others focus only on specific states. Most of the theories appear to adequately explain the development of particular states, but none of them are broad enough to explain the development of the full range of initial states that is manifested in the archaeological record. The purpose of the present chapter is to examine the major theories offered and to point out their similarities, differences, and deficiences. An attempt is also made to demonstrate the relationship between each of the theories and the basic principles of the conflict model. By extracting elements from each of the theories and generalizing from their specific arguments, a broader explanatory framework can be formulated for dealing with the development of all pristine states.

Background

Throughout most of the last century the archaeological study of the state has been indirectly subsumed under general descriptions of events associated with the development of "civilization." While "civilization" has been defined in myriad ways, it has been used in an archaeological context primarily to refer to the elaborate and large-scale societies that appeared in different parts of the world after the agricultural revolution. It has usually been identified on the basis of a number of material traits, all of which are readily recognized in the archaeological record. Among the traits most commonly cited as hallmarks of civilization are: urban settlements, monumental architecture, regional art styles, long distance trading networks, writing, calendrical systems, metallurgy, large-scale irrigation, and agricultural surplus. The state has often been tacked onto this list, as pointed out above, because most researchers have concluded that the achievements of civilizations could have been accomplished only through the coordinating and/or coercive efforts of a formal institution of government.

Descriptive analysis of the prehistoric development of civilization began with John Lubbock (1870) in the latter part of the nineteenth century (Daniel 1968:16). As increasing amounts of archaeological data were recovered in the nineteenth and twentieth centuries, subsequent scholars progressively updated the chronological events accompanying the emergence of civilizations. Emphasis was on filling out the details of a time-space framework. Some scholars tried to elucidate patterns in the developmental history of a number of civilizations. Others focused on the development of a single society or world area.

As a whole, there has been a considerable bias toward the Old World civilizations in the broader analyses, almost to the exclusion of the New World completely. This is probably due to the fact that large-scale excavations were more numerous in the Old World during the late nineteenth and early twentieth centuries, and possibly to the fact that the Old World civilizations had written languages that proved to be more amenable to deciphering. Consequently, the time-space frameworks could be more easily and fully filled out for the Old World than for the New. Regardless of the scope of study or amount of material available, however, almost all of these studies were concerned only with artifact descriptions, site lists and stratigraphic sequences. In most cases where sociocultural interpretations of the data are made, they are based on intuition and have no logical foundation (Redman 1978 and Chang 1976 being notable exceptions).

With a very few exceptions, it has not been until the last decade that any archaeological studies of cultural evolution have moved beyond the stagnating description of cultural sequences to the explanation of cultural processes. Although this shift in emphasis from description to explanation is occurring in almost all branches of archaeology, it is especially prominent in studies of the development of civilization and the state. The primary goal of these explanatory studies is to determine why the state developed in different parts of the world, and under what material circumstances the state form of political organization has arisen. There are also increasing efforts to operationalize the concept of the state in material terms and to identify indirect manifestations of it in the ground. In contrast to the descriptive studies, the explanatory studies also tend to place state organization in a central role in the evolution of civilization, with the material characteristics of civilizations representing either causes of effects of state formation.

Processual analyses of state development exhibit a great deal of diversity in the theories they offer and the conclusions they reach. Despite their inherent differences, however, there are certain basic points of agreement. First, state formation is seen as a highly complex process involving a large number of variables systemically interrelated (for the ultimate vision of complexity, see Flannery 1972). Single prime movers and simplistic explanations, such as Oppenheimer's speculations on the juxtaposition of herdsmen and agriculturalists, have either been discounted or reformulated into more sophisticated multi-component models. In a sense, prime movers, such as irrigation or warfare, are still utilized, but primarily as catalysts of the process of state development, not as independent causes of the state. This point will be addressed more extensively below. Other areas of agreement concern the general correlation between the state and relatively high population density, warfare, and extended trade systems. However, as will be shown, there is major debate over the role each of these correlates may play in the process of state formation.

Beyond general agreement on certain correlates of the state and on the complexity of state formation process, most specific theories of state development differ from one another at a number of critical junctures. The major divergence appears in the use of different institutional complexes as primary vehicles for the initial emergence of formal governments in prehistoric societies. Based on the type of complex used, there are three different groups of theories: warfare theories, trade theories, and an irrigation theory. Within the first two groups there are also different specific theories. Although most of the individual theories have been comprehensively applied to only one or two prehistoric societies, they all contain nomothetic statements about the material conditions under which states should emerge in any area. To the extent that different theories argue that the state could emerge *only* under certain conditions, they may be in conflict with one another. However, it is possible to view each of the theories as an alternate explanation of how societies could evolve along different trajectories and still arrive at the same state level of organization.

Before turning to a review of the specific theories, there is one major problem that must be considered. Although each theory gives the appearance of dealing with the same phenomenon, the state, many of them operate under widely variant definitions of what the state is. Furthermore, even when the same basic definition is employed, there is little agreement among scholars as to how the state is to be recognized archaeologically. For example, in Mesoamerica Rathje (1972), using Fried's basic concept of the state as an institution maintaining a system of stratification, sees the Olmec culture of 1200 B.C. as the first state in the area; on the other hand, Sanders and Price (1968; see also Price 1977), also using Fried's concept of the state, see Teotihuacán at about the time of Christ as the first state in Mesoamerica. The question of how the state might be identified archaeologically was partially answered in chapter 4. It was pointed out that the kinds of information necessary to make such an identification have not been systematically collected in any of the areas of initial state development. Available information does provide some indication of what were and were not states in prehistory, and additional criteria will be given in the following chapter for distinguishing between state societies and their prestate antecedents. However, empirical questions about what may have been the first state in any region would be premature at this juncture. In the meantime, the conceptions of the state incorporated within each of the different theories of state formation will be taken into consideration in evaluating them and attempting to resolve some of their differences.

Warfare

The warfare theories that have recently been offered to explain the origin of the state are direct descendents of the nineteenth-century theories of Herbert Spencer. Recalling Spencer's ideas about warfare, we know that he saw it as a mechanism both for the endogenous development of government and for the external imposition of government by one group on another. The two alternative modern theories reflect Spencer's two evolutionary lines. They have been considerably updated, and the variables have been refined, but the underlying premises of the arguments remain the same.

Robert Carneiro

The first revitalization of Spencer came with the theory of state origins offered by Robert Carneiro. Carneiro observes that prehistoric civilizations in all parts of the world have been shown archaeologically to have engaged in intensive warfare (1970:734). Taking this observation as a starting point, he constructs a theory explaining how warfare can provide the mechanism for the emergence of state-level societies. He argues that the specific conditions of circumscription and demographic pressures lead to the formation of the state through warfare. Circumscription may be either environmental, as when an agriculturally productive area is surrounded by unproductive land or natural barriers, or social, as when an area is surrounded by densely inhabited lands that preclude peaceful expansion (1970:734, 737; see also Chagnon 1968:249–51). Under such circumscribed conditions, any population growth would eventually lead to a strain on available resources. From this point, Carneiro succinctly states the crux of his theory as follows:

> As population density in such [circumscribed] areas increased and arable land came into short supply, competition over land ensued. This competition took the form of war, and those villagers vanquished in war, being unable to flee as they might have done in areas of uncircumscribed land, had to remain in place and be subjugated by the victors (1978:207).

Thus, he sees circumscription and population pressures as resulting in warfare and subsequent conquest of weaker groups by stronger. He then argues that the process of political evolution involves the uniting of increasingly larger social units. The state arises when all the communities in a circumscribed area become subordinate to a single polity: "Finally, an entire circumscribed valley was unified under a single banner. The political unit thus formed, so much larger, stronger and more highly organized than the small chiefdoms out of which it had arisen, warranted being called a state" (1978:208). It can be seen from this statement that Carneiro conceptualizes the state as simply a circumscribed population unified under a militarily dominant governing authority.

There is a certain elegance in Carneiro's theory that makes it difficult to resist. It is logically sound and concise. Unfortunately, it does not seem to work. There are data from a number of areas that overtly contradict the implications and conclusions of his model. Carneiro does not attempt to document his argument in detail, but he does use the coastal valleys of Peru as a generalized illustration. Each valley is tightly circumscribed by desert, mountains, and the ocean. They all exhibit population growth in the course of their prehistoric occupation, and extensive warfare on the coast can be amply documented. However, in the only published account of an intensive survey of one of the coastal valleys, the evidence presented by Willey (1953) does not support Carneiro's thesis.

Willey's data indicate that in the occupational sequence of the valley the first rapid increase in population is indeed accompanied by indications of intensive warfare. But these indications point to *inter*-valley warfare, not *intra*-valley warfare. The individual villages are not fortified, but there are communal fortifications located at the side of the valley (Willey 1953:375–76). There were numerous clusters of villages in other parts of the valley with no indication of internal conflict between them. Later fortifications were also located at either the edges or the head of the valley, sometimes in relative isolation from any contemporaneous villages. Thus the general hypothesis that population growth in a circumscribed area leads to competition and internal warfare appears to be disconfirmed by the evidence from at least one Peruvian valley. Similar evidence of inter- but not intra- valley warfare in another valley has also just been published in preliminary form (Topic and Topic 1978).

Unification of a circumscribed area through warfare is also brought into question by evidence from another part of the world. In an intensive survey of the Susiana Plain in southwestern Iran, an area circumscribed by mountains and desert, Johnson (1973) clearly demonstrates that there was unification under a central polity at a time of increased population density (1973:101–41). However, there is no evidence for warfare or conflict either prior to or during this period of unification. There were no fortifications, no weapons, and no artistic representations of warfare found on the Plain from this period of time. In fact, the only evidence of warfare occurs after the unified polity began to break apart (1973:152).

The evidence from Peru and Iran does not invalidate all parts of Carneiro's theory, but it does specifically refute the theory as presently formulated. Circumscription and population growth do not necessarily lead to intra-regional warfare and conquest; and intra-regional unification, as he appears to define the state, may come about through other mechanisms than warfare. Aside from these empirical problems with Carneiro's thesis, there is a logical inconsistency as well. If warfare arises in a circumscribed area as a result of competition over scarce resources, conquest of all the people within that area does not improve the situation at all. The same demographic pressures remain, and no new resources have been introduced into the system. Intra-regional conquest, therefore, accomplishes nothing. Thus, additional conditions must be specified if warfare is to be shown to have a causal role in the origin of state societies. A second type of warfare theory has been presented, which borrows heavily from Carneiro, but also rectifies some of the problems inherent in his formulation.

Malcolm Webb and David Webster

This second theory is similar to Spencer's endogenous line of evolution. Slightly different variations of the theory have been presented most comprehensively by Malcolm Webb (1975) and David Webster (1975). Both theorists follow Carneiro in ascribing intensified warfare to conditions of circumscription and population growth. Unlike Carneiro, however, they view the state as developing, not through a process of increasingly larger-scale conquests, but through a process of increasing solidification of the power of a society's war leaders. They both acknowledge that militarily stronger societies will subjugate weaker ones in a circumscribed environment, but such subjugation is not the primary basis of stratification in the emergent state. Their common argument is that under conditions of inter-societal competition over limited resources, the war leaders in a ranked society are in an advantageous position to gain control over resources. That control then provides the primary basis of stratification and enables the war leaders to exert coercive state-level controls over their subordinate populations. This process is stated by Webb and by Webster in slightly different forms as follows:

The war chief, who would have the right to divide spoils, would be able to take the surplus of defeated groups, who could not resist and would be absolutely tied down by the environment. Because the land, while limited, was so very highly productive, this loot would provide the chief with a source of wealth unparalled in quantity and in freedom from internal tribal controls. Even after the customary ceremonial and redistributive obligations had been met, enough would be left over to enable him to overcome local and kin loyalties and to gather about him a group of retainers or a war band large enough to keep in check all other groups in the society. . . . With his new following, the chief now would enforce decisions, collect taxes, undertake public works, and mobilize the society for external defense—in a word, subvert the tribal constitution and establish the state. (Webb 1975:185)

Constant warfare not only provided an important and highly adaptive managerial function for emergent elite segments of society, but it also stimulated the acquisition of small amounts of "wealth" (i.e., basic resources) which were external to the traditional system and could be manipulated in various self-serving ways by these same groups to dampen internal dissention and attract supporters. Out of this milieu developed political and economic special interest groups which ultimately provided the basis for social stratification. (Webster 1975:469)

In both theories the state is conceptualized as an economically stratified society with coercive control mechanisms applied to insure the obedience of the subordinate portion of the population.

While Webb's and Webster's arguments have the same general thrust, there are differences in the specific conditions each outlines as being conducive to the development of the warfare-state. Webb's model is the simpler of the two and follows Carneiro's more closely. He basically argues that the conditions necessary for the development of the state are environmental circumscription, highly productive land within the circumscribed area, population pressure, and an existing ranked or chiefdom level of sociopolitical organization (Webb 1975:172, 189). Briefly, his argument is that population pressure and a strain on local resources results from population growth in a circumscribed area, and leads to intensified warfare. Warfare, in combination with highly productive land and an existing ranked social structure, then results in economic stratification and ultimately the state. The presence of the four basic conditions is both necessary and sufficient for the origin of the state through warfare according to Webb.

Webster's model is somewhat more complex. The conditions he

considers necessary for state formation are: juxtaposition of environmental zones of markedly different productive potential, sufficient
agricultural potential to generate surpluses, local variability of basic
resources within environmental zones, rapid population growth, and
social circumscription. He argues that rapid population growth results
in the occupation of agriculturally marginal zones surrounding a zone
of high agricultural productivity. The central zone thus becomes socially circumscribed. With continued population growth, the resources
become limited in the circumscribed zone, and warfare is the most
immediate solution to the problem. Concurrent with the rise of warfare, an incipient hierarchy develops within the circumscribed area
due to local variability in the distribution of resources or productivity
of land. The combination of warfare with this incipient hierarchy leads
to the accumulation of wealth by the societal leaders and economic
stratification. The wealth is used, in turn, to maintain the system of
stratification. Webster considers the environmental and demographic
variables to be necessary but not sufficient for formation of a warfare-
based state. He argues that rather than engaging in warfare in the face
of limited resources and circumscription, populations could have chosen one of several alternative solutions to the problem (reduced standard of living, agricultural intensification, etc.) (1975:467). While he
maintains that warfare was the most likely choice, there is still an
ideological escape valve built into his model (cf. Wittfogel's "open
historical situation" 1957:15–17).

   As presently formulated, the two endogenous theories are again
contradicted by Willey's data from Peru. They both argue that warfare
takes place *within* a circumscribed zone, while the data indicate that
warfare took place *between* such zones. However, a minor modification
may be made in both theories, such that this contradiction is elimi-
nated. Unlike Carneiro's theory, the endogenous theories see warfare
primarily as a mechanism for obtaining supplementary basic resources,
not as a mechanism of conquest. Since resources may be obtained
through externally oriented warfare (directed against marginal zones
around a circumscribed core, or against neighboring circumscribed
areas), it is unnecessary to stipulate that the warfare must be intra-
regional in nature. By leaving out this stipulation, the central argument
of the endogenous theories remains intact, and they are no longer in
conflict with the body of data from Peru. In regard to the data from
Iran, neither of the theories argues that all states must come about

through the forcible unification of a region, nor do they argue that the state is synonymous with regional unification. Thus, while they do not explain the Iranian data, they are also not in conflict with that data.

Positive empirical confirmation of either or both of the endogenous theories is difficult for a number of reasons. There is, in fact, empirical evidence of intensive warfare, population growth, some form of circumscription, early ranked societies and high agricultural productivity in all the world areas of initial state development. However, there is insufficient data to confirm the specific sequence of events in either Webb's or Webster's model. Both of them argue that the correlation between prehistoric states and warfare and the other variables constitutes confirmation of their theories; but simply demonstrating a correlation does not establish a definite causal relationship between elements of a system. There are equally plausible theories which argue that the emergence of stratification and the state is conducive to the intensification of warfare, thus reversing the proposed causal arrow between them (Fried 1961, 1967:213–16). Consequently, confirmation of either endogenous warfare theory must await additional data which will illuminate the relative order of state emergence and intensification of warfare in any particular area.

Despite this general caveat, it should still be possible to assess the relative validity of Webb's and of Webster's theories, since differences do exist in the variables each employs. The major variation concerns the type of circumscription seen as leading to an intensification of warfare: Webb argues for environmental circumscription, while Webster posits the importance of social circumscription. Yet, because of disagreements over the archaeological recognition of statehood, both theories may find support in different societies in the same world area. Using Mesoamerica as an example again, possible states in the Olmec area may be considered to be socially circumscribed and otherwise fit Webster's environmental criteria (Coe 1968b; Drucker et al. 1959; Rathje 1972); while the Teotihuacán state in the topographically circumscribed Valley of Mexico fits the environmental criteria of Webb's model (Sanders and Price 1968; Wolf 1976). The problem again becomes one of identifying what is a state, with the distinct possibility that different kinds, or levels, of pristine states may have emerged under different conditions within a large geographical area such as Mesoamerica.

Summarizing the warfare theories as a group, they all follow the basic argument that population growth and circumscription lead to intensification of warfare and consolidation of social units into state societies. The specific notion that the state arises through expansive conquest and forcible unification of large circumscribed areas does not appear to be consistent with presently available bodies of archaeological data. The notion that warfare leads to the internal consolidation of power and the state, on the other hand, is consistent with available evidence. The specific conditions under which warfare may produce the state and the relationship of warfare to other variables in the state formation process, are still open to debate, however. One factor deserving emphasis is that in both of the internal-development theories, warfare is seen as a mechanism through which a society's leadership gains independent control over basic resources; thus establishing the basis of economic stratification. Both theories, then, while emphasizing warfare as an integrative mechanism, can be subsumed under the overarching framework of the conflict model.

Trade

The two alternative trade theories in current anthropological literature exhibit greater disparity than is seen in the warfare theories. One sees inter-regional trade as the vehicle for the initial rise of state society based on stratification. The other views intra-regional trade and exchange as the vehicle for the rise of state society based on integration. There is agreement between them, however, that the consolidation of power on a state level is achieved through the management of a large-scale trade system involving basic resources.

William Rathje

The first theory, related to inter-regional trade, is an outgrowth of an argument first presented by Childe. Childe (1936) notes that in the areas of initial state development in Mesopotamia and Egypt, a number of necessary resources are unavailable locally, and must be imported through trade. In fact, he postulated that the primary reason a surplus is first produced in these areas is to obtain these basic resources. William Rathje (1971, 1972) takes Childe's idea of resource deficiencies and expands it into a general model of state formation.

Rathje's theory is framed within the specific context of the lowlands of Mesoamerica. Salt, obsidian, and stone for grinding corn—all basic resources in prehistoric Mesoamerica—are lacking in large parts of these areas. To obtain these resources, the occupants of the lowlands had to engage in trade with adjacent highland regions where the resources occur naturally. In this situation, Rathje argues that the lowlands can be divided into two zones, which are similar in terms of agricultural potential and general environment, but nevertheless experience differing environmental pressures. He refers to the areas in closest proximity to the highlands as "buffer" zones, while the areas removed from the highlands at the interior of the lowlands are "core" zones. He maintains that the buffer zone has an immediate advantage over the core, since its occupants can trade directly with the highlands, and are in a better position to exchange surplus foodstuffs for the needed resources. The core occupants are in a more difficult position. They not only have to organize long-distance trade networks to obtain the resources, but since the buffer zone already supplies foodstuffs, they also must find other goods or services to offer in exchange. It is this set of circumstances that Rathje sees as conducive to the development of state societies in the lowland core areas:

> The ecology and geographic position of the core area select for the development of a complex organization capable of maximizing resources to compete with the buffer zone for highland commodities. This includes the ability to mount large trading expeditions, maintain open trade routes, support factories, schedule efforts to deal with numerous resource areas, and manufacture commodities desired in both resource and buffer zones. (1972:373)

Up to this juncture in Rathje's analysis, his argument is logical and theoretically tight; however, his next step seems to involve circular reasoning. He states: "If complex organization is necessary to obtain resources, then community ceremonial interaction and luxury paraphernalia are equally necessary to maintain stratification and organization" (1972:373). He then continues that it is the ceremonial complexes and luxury paraphernalia, developed to support the trade hierarchy, that are the commodities exchanges to the highlands for basic resources: "Core exports will therefore be the byproducts of community stratification" (1972:373). What he fails to explain is how the stratified trading complex is initially established if there are no existing export commodities. He also does not explain why the highlanders would accept the ceremonial complexes of another society in exchange for material resources extracted from the earth. I do not think these problems in his analysis are irresolvable, however, and corrective modification can be made without compromising the integrity of his overall argument.

Since Rathje argues that luxury goods, such as cacao, cotton, decorated textiles, ceramics and possibly wood products, as well as foodstuffs are exported from the lowland regions, it can be hypothesized that the disadvantaged position of the core would select for specialization in the production of these items. Such specialization would result in high quality commodities, and/or the more efficient production of them. The increased quality and efficiency would then give the core area the necessary edge in trading with the highlands. This hypothesis is supported by considerable evidence of craft specialization in the core zones of the Mesoamerican lowlands (see, for example, Bernal 1968, 1976; Coe and Diehl 1980; Weaver 1972), and it rectifies a critical problem in Rathje's model without contradicting his major conclusions.

Continuing with his model from this point, Rathje argues that once a centralized trade system is established in the core zone, the necessary conditions for stratification and the state are met. Those persons in managerial control of the long-distance trading system have differential access to the basic resources being imported, and they can use that access to enforce their demands on the population. It can also be used to support an elaborate ceremonial complex to legitimize the stratified hierarchy (see Webster 1976 and chapter 6 below). The widespread distribution of important goods in the lowland areas supports Rathje's predictions of an extensive trade system. The fact that the most elaborate lowland cultures are located in the core zones also supports his inferences about the interaction between political and environmental variables (1972:375–79). The model cannot be considered to be adequately confirmed, however. The centralization of lowland trade and its correspondence to the initial efflorescence of cultures in the lowland core zones are yet to be established. Both of these elements can be examined archaeologically, but appropriate data are not currently available from the Mesoamerican lowlands.

It must also be pointed out that Rathje's model is not intended as a universal theory of state formation. It is nomothetic in the sense that it can be applied cross-culturally to explain the development of specific states under a given set of environmental circumstances, but it does not purport to specify the conditions under which all pristine states must have arisen. There are areas of pristine state formation, for example, which do not lack significant basic resources, and thus do not fit into Rathje's model. The coastal valleys of Peru and the Yellow River area of northern China are cases in point (Moseley 1975a; Lumbreras 1974; Chang 1977, 1980). Rathje thus presents a lower level theory which may be applicable to specific states, but not to all states.

Henry Wright and Gregory Johnson

The second trade theory is also aimed at explaining the development of specific states but not all states. Henry Wright and Gregory Johnson (Wright and Johnson 1975; Johnson 1973; Wright 1977a, 1977b) first formulated the argument that intra-regional trade or exchange provides a vehicle for the emergence of the state, to explain the development of complex polities in southwestern Iran. The basic theory has subsequently been applied to the formation of states in Peru and Mesoamerica (Isbell and Schreiber 1978; Marcus 1975), and therefore may have wider applicability outside the specific context of southwestern Iran.

The basic argument is that labor specialization results from increased demands, brought about by demographic and environmental fluctuations, for goods and food. This, in turn, produces administrative problems in managing the exchange of specialized resources. Such problems are resolved by the gradual centralization of administrative responsibilities into the hands of a specialized administrative hierarchy. When this hierarchy develops to a point with three distinct levels of administrative responsibility, Wright and Johnson claim that the society is at a state level of organization (Johnson 1973:3, 141; Wright and Johnson 1975:272).

In the specific case of southwest Iran, they hypothesize that an unexplained influx of herders into the area creates increased demands for agricultural products and goods, such as ceramics. In response to these demands, different communities within the area begin to specialize in the production of particular kinds of resources. To manage the intra-regional distribution of these resources, administrative nodes develop to serve as exchange centers. Over time, higher order nodes emerge, until the entire system is integrated into a hierarchical system with a single city at the apex.

This system is represented archaeologically by a four-tiered site-size hierarchy, with material evidence of administrative responsibility (recordkeeping seals and stamps) in the upper three tiers. The distribution of sites also generally corresponds to the predictions of a Central Place Theory of economic geography (Johnson 1973:101–13, 1977:494–501). In support of their argument for labor specialization they point to the centralized production and distribution of ceramics in the area (Johnson 1973:113–39).

Despite the general correspondence between Wright and Johnson's model and the Iranian data, there are certain problems with using it as a general theory of state formation. They are unable to specify the conditions under which intra-regional specialization and its incumbent administrative hierarchy will emerge. They hypothesize an increase in nomadic herding without offering an explanation for that increase and without citing any archaeological evidence of it. Even with evidence of an increase in herding, unless it can be shown to have distinct temporal priority, it seems equally reasonable to argue that specialization in herding was part of, and not the cause of, a general trend toward increasing labor specialization. Without firmly defining initial causal factors, Wright and Johnson's analysis remains at the level of description rather than explanation.

Another problem with their model concerns their conception of how the state is to be recognized archaeologically. Their basic definition of the state is "a society with specialized administrative activities" (Wright and Johnson 1975:267). They then qualify this definition by asserting that a state level of administrative specialization is to be recognized by the presence of three or more levels of a decision-making hierarchy. While their basic definition is in line with the general political science and anthropological conception of the state as a society with a formalized institution of government, their reliance on a three-tiered hierarchy as a definitive characteristic would appear to be a theoretically unfounded decision. Their primary reason for making such a decision appears to be their perceived need for a convenient way to recognize the state archaeologically. They provide no reasons why a two-tiered hierarchy can not perform the same decision-making and information-processing activities as a three-tiered hierarchy, nor why the addition of a third tier suddenly transforms a society from one level of political development to a new higher level. There is validity in an emphasis on the emergence of specialized administrative apparatuses, but Wright and Johnson's use of arbitrary definitive characteristics tends to obscure rather than elucidate critical questions of how and why such apparatuses originally developed (see Yoffee 1979:20).

There is also a danger of focusing on site-size hierarchy and losing sight of the central importance of administrative specialization. Johnson himself falls into this trap. He infers that a three-level site-size hierarchy in the Early Uruk Period probably represents the first emergence of the state, even though the complex administrative technology did not appear until the later Middle Uruk Period (1973:139–41). Thus, the evidence of three levels of sizes is given precedence over evidence of administration.

The problem is also illustrated in the application of Wright and Johnson's model in other areas. Isbell and Schreiber (1978), in trying to determine whether Huari (a city in the central Peruvian highlands) represents a state capital, make direct use of Wright and Johnson's model. In their analysis, however, they give precedence to the site-size hierarchy without giving full consideration to other manifestations of an administrative hierarchy. They find a four-tiered site hierarchy, but cannot confirm an administrative relationship between the third and fourth order sites and the first and second order sites. On this basis alone they leave the question of Huari statehood open to question (1978:386). What they do not consider is the probability that *within* Huari there are multiple levels of highly developed administrative specialization. The site is huge, covering over 300 hectares, and contains a number of large and small compounds that Isbell and Schreiber interpret as having administrative functions. By focusing only on site size, they ignore such possible alternative manifestations of *intra-site* administrative specialization. Site-size hierarchies provide a neat way of pigeonholing societies in an ordinal sequence, but by themselves, they provide little help in understanding the evolutionary process of state formation.

Neither the inter-regional trade theory of Rathje, nor the intra-regional trade theory of Wright and Johnson provides a satisfactory general explanation of the origin of the state. They are each confined to particular circumstances (in the latter case these are undefined), which are not found in all areas of initial state formation. However, as in the case of the warfare theories, the basic elements of the two trade theories can be incorporated into the general framework of the conflict model. Whereas in the warfare theories the war leaders of a society gain increased access to basic resources through seizure, in the trade theories, the administrative leaders of the society gain increased access through managerial control over imported or exchanged basic resources. This control can then be used to provide ideological and physical reinforcement of the leaders' superior position in the society. In this sense, the management of trade in basic resources advocated in both theories provides another avenue for the rise of stratification and the state as outlined by the conflict theorists.

Irrigation

Karl August Wittfogel

In *Oriental Despotism*, Karl August Wittfogel offers a comprehensive analysis of the causal relationship between irrigation forms of agriculture and the organization of societies. Contained within this analysis is a general theory of the formation and development of the state. Wittfogel defines the state as "government by professionals" (1957:239), and argues that it arises as an organizational concomitant of the development of large-scale irrigation systems. While he does not maintain that the first states necessarily arose because of irrigation, he does point out that irrigation played a major role in all the world areas of initial state development.

The conditions Wittfogel argues are necessary for the pristine development of the irrigation-based state are potentially arable land juxtaposed to a major supply of water and agriculturalists who are above an extractive subsistence economy and "beyond the influence of strong centers of rainfall agriculture" (1957:12). When such conditions are met, the agriculturalists are faced with "an open historical situation" and may choose to engage in irrigation (1957:15–17). Once this "choice" has been made, irrigation requires certain organizational changes in the structure of society:

> A large quantity of water can be channeled and kept within bounds only by the use of mass labor; and this mass labor must be coordinated, dis-

ciplined, and led. Thus a number of farmers eager to conquer arid lowlands and plains are forced to invoke the organizational devices which—
on the basis of premachine technology—offer the one chance of success:
they must work in cooperation with their fellows and subordinate themselves to a directing authority. (1957:18)

Large-scale irrigation, specifically, requires that a large labor force be
organized under a specialized managerial hierarchy. Furthermore,
once this hierarchy develops, Wittfogel argues that it assumes responsibility for overseeing other activities, such as time-keeping (calen-
drics), other types of construction projects, establishment of communication systems, and the military defense of the society (1957:29–43).
The leaders of this multi-functional hierarchy then represent the governmental professionals of a state level society.

In their specific role as managers of the entire subsistence system,
these leaders exercise considerable control over the population. Such
economically based control is further reinforced by their monopolization of the military, and by attaching to themselves the symbols of
supreme religious authority (1957:59–67, 87–100). This combination
of economic military and ideological control gives the state government near total power over the subordinate population. While Wittfogel emphasizes the importance of integration and the necessity of
cooperation in the initial development of the irrigation-based state, he
also sees the state leaders as using their power for purposes of self-
aggradizement, maintenance of their position, and physical repression
of the population (1957:33, 128–34, 137–49). In short, irrigation government is despotic, not benevolent, in nature:

> The hydraulic state is a managerial state, and certain of its operations do
> indeed benefit the people. But since the rulers depend on these operations
> for their own maintenance and prosperity, their policies can hardly be
> considered benevolent. A pirate does not act benevolently when he keeps
> his ship afloat or feeds the slaves he plans to sell. . . . His behavior may
> temporarily benefit the persons in his power; but this is not its primary
> purpose. Given a choice, he will further his own interests, and not the
> interests of others (1957:126).

Because of its inherent conciseness, Wittfogel's basic argument can
be summarized without too much difficulty; however, to outline the
full ramifications and details of the argument would be almost im-

possible. His treatment of irrigation society is comprehensive, and involves arguments on many theoretical and empirical levels. Consequently, a full critique of his analysis will not be attempted here. But I will try to evaluate his general irrigation theory of state formation within an archaeological context.

While irrigation agriculture was practiced in all the major world areas of pristine state development, a number of scholars have raised questions about whether irrigation actually played a primary causal role in the formation of the state in those areas. Adams (1966:68–69), for example, argues that there is no evidence of large-scale irrigation in southern Mesopotamia until *after* the Early Dynastic Period—well beyond the time of initial state development in the area. Johnson (1973:157) also finds no evidence of large-scale irrigation systems on the Susiana Plain either before or during what he considers to be the initial period of state development. Chang (1977) argues that while there are ditches for purposes of water control in Shang China, they are not tied to an irrigation system. He states that true evidence of intensive irrigation does not appear until the Chou Period (1977:289, 356–57). Lanning (1967) also argues against the causal importance of irrigation in Peru, and Millon (1973, 1976) says that it is not of critical importance in the development of the state at Teotihuacán.

In each of these areas, however, there are counter arguments to the effect that irrigation may in fact play a causal role in the initial formation of the state. For example, Harris (1968:686) maintains that there is insufficient evidence to definitely conclude what role irrigation played in prehistoric Mesopotamia, but that what little there is indicates a positive correlation between increasing cultural complexity and intensification of irrigation systems. Moseley (1975a:104–5) points to a similar pattern in the coastal valleys of Peru. The most comprehensive analysis of irrigation's causal role in the development of a particular state society has been offered by William Sanders and Barbara Price for Mesoamerica (Sanders and Price 1968; Price 1973; Sanders 1976b; Sanders et al. 1979:387–403).

William Sanders and Barbara Price

The basic argument of Sanders and Price is that irrigation had a causal role in combination with other variables in the development of the state in the Valley of Mexico. The Valley is characterized by a number of diverse environmental zones, each of which offers different resource potential and requires different systems of resource exploitation (Sanders 1976a; 1976b; Sanders et al. 1979). Some zones require irrigation for the reliable production of agricultural resources. Other zones have the potential for irrigation and also permit greater agricultural productivity and population density. A third type of zone is not amenable to irrigation in any significant form. With population growth in this heterogeneous environment, Sanders and Price argue there is a centralization of authority and control over resources through the interrelationship of two ecological processes: symbiosis and irrigation (1968:175–93). In regard to the former they maintain that a symbiotic regional exchange network develops to procure raw materials and finished products from the different environmental zones and distribute them throughout the Valley. The specific vehicle for the exchange network is a system of centralized regional markets. Accompanying this symbiosis and providing the mechanism for the ultimate unification of the Valley into a single state polity is the development of irrigation agriculture:

> The complex interdigiting of hydraulic and nonhydraulic zones with their consequent variations in population density, the short distances between hydraulic zones, and the dramatic contrast in productivity between hydraulic and nonhydraulic agriculture in a sharply circumscribed environment would provide an extremely competitive social environment. The combination of a system of agriculture that requires cooperation, the consequent uneven distribution of population, and a competitive social environment would all act to stimulate the development of highly organized, centralized political systems. Once the communities of a hydraulic zone were organized in this fashion the resultant state would enjoy an obvious competitive advantage over neighboring nonhydraulic zones and more distant hydraulic zones of smaller size or less efficient organization. (1968:186–87).

The site of Teotihuacán is strategically located in one of the zones of high hydraulic productivity, which (in combination with other factors, such as being located at the Valley's narrowest point and near critical obsidian resources) gave it the competitive advantage to eventually assume hegemony over the entire Valley (Sanders et al. 1979:394; Price 1973). It also serves as a major market center for the regional symbiotic network.

Sanders and Price's explanation of state development in the Valley of Mexico is not universally accepted (cf. Millon 1973), but their empirical analysis lucidly illustrates how irrigation may provide an avenue to stratification and the state in prehistoric societies. In general, it may be found that some pristine states arose without irrigation, but the close correlation between hydraulic systems and the most complex and elaborate prehistoric states would indicate that there is a causal interrelationship between them (see Steward 1955:178–209). This interrelationship will be treated more extensively in the following chapters.

Summary and Conclusions

There are three general types of theories offered to explain the development of pristine states: 1) The state evolves under conditions of circumscribed and intensified warfare; 2) The state evolves when material conditions demand extensive importation or exchange of basic resources; 3) The state evolves when a society initiates irrigation agriculture on a large scale. Within each of these types, specific theories offer potentially viable explanations of the development of highly complex societies in one or more parts of the world. However, none of the individual theories offers a universal explanation of what have been considered in the archaeological literature to be state societies. This may be due to a lack of clarity in the archaeological definition of the state and/or to the possibility that none of the theories is broad enough to encompass the full range of pristine states. There is also the problem that insufficient data have been collected to adequately test the relative validity of the theories in each of the world areas of initial state development. Despite deficiencies in definition, theory and data, there are, nevertheless, patterns of similarity and diversity in the diffent theories that offer valuable insight into the process of state formation.

While emphasis is on a wide range of different variables in the three types of theories, they all conform to certain general patterns. Furthermore, these patterns tend to confirm the notion offered in chapter 4 that basic premises of Service's integration model can be successfully incorporated into the outline of Fried's conflict model. All the theories begin with stratification and outline alternate ways by which certain members of a society may gain differential access to basic resources.

In the case of warfare, the war leaders have increased access to captured land or conquered territory or other forms of booty; and in the cases of trade and irrigation, the managerial leaders have greater access to the resources under their administrative purview. In all three cases, this differential access is based on *control over the production or procurement* of the resources in question.

With one exception, all the theories also view the state as developing through the internal specialization and elaboration of a hierarchical bureaucracy. In warfare, it is the military bureaucracy; in trade and irrigation, it is the economic bureaucracy. However, even when the bureaucracy is military, the initial state-level control exercised by the leaders is based on access to resources not military might. The single exception to this general pattern is the revitalization of the conquest theory by Carneiro. But this is also the only theory for which there is definite refutatory evidence that cannot be resolved through minor reformulation of the theory, and no confirmatory evidence. In light of this lack of support, the deviation of Carneiro's theory does not justify amending the generalizations derived from the other theories. With this tentative exclusion of Carneiro, it may be concluded on the basis of the other theories that the development of the state involved the specialization of a governing bureaucracy, as argued by Service, *and* the emergence of stratification based on access to basic resources, as argued by Fried. The two factors are not mutually exclusive; rather, they must be considered together to adequately explain the origin of the state.

Beyond patterns of similarity, there are fundamental differences between all of the viable theories which should not be underestimated. One of the major areas of dissimilarity lies in the type and importance of basic resources controlled by the leaders of an emergent state. In the warfare theories, basic resources external to the system are monopolized by the leaders and then used to initiate more efficient social control mechanisms and to generally support their own position. In the trade theories, basic nonsubsistence resources are controlled by the leaders and could be used in a similar fashion. The irrigation theory suggests that the entire subsistence system is under the command of the leaders, and can be used independently as a powerful control mechanism. Thus, the different theories have significant implications concerning the relative power of leaders in emergent state societies. This point will be addressed more fully in chapter 7.

Another major area of dissimilarity lies in the material conditions under which the state may emerge. Different necessary conditions hypothesized in specific theories carry definite implications concerning the developmental potential of various states. For example, the irrigation and warfare theories argue that the state develops in areas where major agricultural intensification is possible. The trade theories do not insist on this condition. Therefore, if there is any validity to the trade theories, it could be expected that trade-based states in areas of limited agricultural potential might not develop at the same rate or to the same level as states in areas without such agricultural limitations. Similarly, warfare-based states initially evolving under socially circumscribed conditions may have greater potential for expansion than states evolving in environmentally circumscribed areas. The only theory in which the developmental potential of different states is taken into consideration is Wittfogel's. He argues that different types of environmentally determined irrigation systems will lead to considerable variability in the potential economic power of state leaders in different societies (1957:163–66). If the other theories similarly are considered in the context of the developmental potential of different state societies, a major step may be taken toward explaining the wide variation in prehistoric societies that appear to have been at a state level of political organization.

Taking the individual theories as alternative routes by which states, or particular kinds of states, may emerge, the similarities and differences between theories may provide insight into both the universal process of state formation, and into the diversity of prehistoric states. In the following chapters a framework will be presented for incorporating the individual theories into a broader theory of state formation, and for explaining and measuring some of the differences observed in prehistoric state societies.

[Part 2]

POWER AND THE STATE

[Chapter 6]

Power and Archaeology

In this chapter I want to focus on an analysis of the processes of state formation and development in terms of the exercise of *power* by rulers over their populations. A broad framework, oriented around the exercise of power, will be offered in chapter 7 to explain some of the major similarities and dissimilarities that are observed in prehistoric states in different areas and over long periods of time.

The concept of power is widely recognized in political science and anthropology as a critical element in understanding political processes and evolution (see Adams 1975; Fogelson and Adams 1977; Lenski 1966; Bell et al. 1969; Dahl 1968, etc.), but it has rarely been used by archaeologists. It is not that archaeologists have failed to recognize the importance of power as a central variable in state evolution (see, for example, Hill 1977:304–13), but they have not attempted to operationalize and use it in their theoretical and empirical research.

As a foundation for the analysis of the role of power in prehistoric societies, the concept will first be defined in terms relevant to the relationship between rulers and their populations. It will also be broken down into a number of interdependent variables, each of which has direct or indirect material manifestations that can be recognized in the archaeological record. With power defined and broken down into component parts, a series of predictive logical arguments will be offered to explain different aspects of the processes of state formation and development. These arguments will be based on the conditional acceptance of an expanded conflict model as argued in chapter 4, and the different specific theories of state formation discussed in chapter 5. To illustrate the specific and general applicability of the logical arguments, empirical examples of state formation and development in the New World will be examined with reference to manifestations of power (chapter 8).

Power

· Power has been considered in most basic terms to be "a capacity to get things done" (Stinchcombe 1968:157; Parsons 1960:181; also Emmett 1954). While this gives the essence of the concept, we need to distinguish the power exerted specifically in social situations from other types of power (e.g., horsepower, electric power, etc.). Most power analyses in the social sciences today use a definition derived ultimately from that of Max Weber. Weber states: "Power is the probability that one actor within a social relationship will be in a position to carry out his own will despite resistance, regardless of the basis on which this probability rests" (1947:152). By specifying that a person has power when he/she can carry out his/her own will despite resistance, Weber goes a long way toward clarifying how the concept of power may be applied in social situations. However, his definition cannot deal in any depth with the nature of interaction between actors in a power relationship. It focuses primarily on the power holder, treating only by implication the role of the other actors in the relationship. It is not clear whether resistance on the part of other actors is always necessary in a power relationship, or whether it may be absent in some power relationships. Resolution of some of the problems in Weber's definition is provided by the political scientist Robert Dahl.

Dahl defines power in a way that retains the essence of Weber's definition, but clarifies the relationship between actors. According to Dahl, "A has power over B to the extent that he can get B to do something that B would not otherwise do" (1969:80). This definition provides a more explicit means for distinguishing between those social relationships in which power is exerted from those in which it is not. There is specific emphasis on the ability of a power-holding actor to change or modify the behavior of another actor, and the definition thus avoids the ambiguity inherent in Weber's reference to "despite resistance." There is still a problem with Dahl's definition, however, in that it includes such a wide range of types of social relationships, that it limits the use of power as a specific concept per se. Dahl himself seems to recognize this problem when he states:

> Power terms evidently cover a very broad category of human relations.
> Considerable effort and ingenuity have gone into schemes for classifying

these relations into various types, labeled power, influence, authority, persuasion, dissuasion, inducement, coercion, compulsion, force, and so on, all of which we shall subsume under the collective label power terms. The great variety and heterogeneity of these relations may, in fact, make it impossible—or at any rate not very fruitful—to develop general theories of power intended to cover them all. (1968:407)

However, since the intent here is not to develop a general theory of all "power terms," but to arrive at a definition of power that will distinguish it from these other terms, Dahl's definition must be further refined. Such a refinement may be accomplished by adding that a power-holding actor affects changes in the behavior of other actors by applying or being able to apply some form of sanctions. The sociologist Robert Bierstedt argues for the inclusion of sanctions as a central element in a definition of power as follows.

Power itself is the predisposition or prior capacity which makes the application of force [sanctions] possible. Only groups which have power can threaten to use force and the threat itself is power. Power is the ability to employ force, not its actual employment, the ability to apply sanctions, not their actual application. Power is the ability to introduce force into a social situation; it is the presentation of force. . . . Power symbolizes the force which *may* be applied in any social situation and supports the authority which *is* applied. Power is thus neither force nor authority but, in a sense, their synthesis. (1950:733)

While Bierstedt emphasizes "force" in this statement, he earlier equates the application of force with the application of sanctions and states that sanctions may be either positive or negative and either require or prohibit a social act (1950:733).

Taking this sanction oriented conception of power and integrating it with Dahl's analysis, the concept can be defined so as to be clearly distinguished from other "power terms," such as influence, authority, or persuasion. For the present purposes, I would define power as the ability of an actor, A, to get another actor(s), B, to do something B would not otherwise do, through the application, threat, or promise of sanctions. This definition is not radically different from other power definitions used in recent anthropological studies of the state, but I believe it is somewhat more explicit. As defined, power can be seen as playing a role in only certain types of social situations, and involving a distinct vertical relationship between two or more social actors. The definition thus narrows the field of interest by excluding: 1) those situations in which sanctions are not manifest in some form; 2) strictly egalitarian relationships; and 3) cases in which the actions of one actor (B) are determined by something other than the commands, demands, threats, or promises of another actor (A).

Nevertheless, there is still a wide range of social interactions—from a parent giving candy to an obedient child to a judge sentencing a convicted criminal—which would be considered power relationships under this definition. To clarify and distinguish differences in the nature of particular power relationships, the concept of power can be broken down into a series of different variables. Each of these pertain to different aspects of power relationships, and can be used to measure the variability in power exerted in diverse relationships.

Dahl's analysis again provides a valuable starting point for measuring power variability. He considers all power relationships to have four basic elements: a power *base*, a *means* of exerting power, the *scope* of power being exerted, and the *amount* of power being exerted (1969:80–81). A similar breakdown of the concept of power has been made by Lasswell and Kaplan (1950:74–83), who refer to the base, weight, scope, domain, and coerciveness of power; however, Dahl's elements are more clearly defined and consistent with the definition of power used here.

In addition to the basic list of variables outlined by Dahl, there are several other elements which can be considered in examining power relationships. John Harsanyi (1969) amends Dahl's list by adding the *extension* of power, the costs to the power holder of exerting power (*power costs*), and the costs to the respondent of refusing to comply with the demands of the power holder (*refusal costs*). I would further amend it by adding the costs to the respondent of actually complying with the demands of the power holder (*compliance costs*), and the *gains* to the respondent in complying with the power holder's demands. Thus, there are nine potential variables which can be used in measuring the variability of power in social relationships. Each of these variables and the interplay between them will now be discussed in greater detail. Examples will also be given to illustrate how the variables, as expressed in a power relationship between societal leaders and their populations, can be recognized in the archaeological record.

Base

According to Dahl (1969:81), a power base consists of all those resources which a power holder, A, can exploit in order to effect changes
in the behavior of a respondent, B. Thus, the power base is a critical
factor in understanding *how* A is able to get B to do something B would
not otherwise do. It is substantively as well as figuratively the bottom
line in a power relationship.

For greater insight into the abstract nature of a power base, Richard
N. Adams' analysis of social power is helpful in the present context.

> In dealing with social power, we are concerned not so much with the rate
> of flow or conversion [of energy] as with *the control that one actor, or
> party, or operating unit exercises over some set of energy forms or flows*
> and, most specifically, over some set of energy forms or flows *that con-
> stitute part of the meaningful environment of another actor* (1975:12, em-
> phasis in original).

Adams uses environment here in the broadest terms to refer to "the
material, physical, or energy-form-and-flow aspect of man's social and
physical habitat" (1975:13), and to include everything from topography,
climate, and natural resources to other human beings, speech and
symbols (e.g., an examination grade or a religious icon) (1975:13, 24).
Extrapolating from Adams' analysis, a power base then can be seen
as a portion of the environment controlled by a power holder and of
importance to a respondent.

In complex prehistoric societies there are three general portions of
the total environment which may serve as potential bases of power for
societal leaders: economic, ideological, and physical.

1. Leaders may exercise economic power based on control over the
production or procurement and distribution of subsistence and/or nonsubsistence resources. Such control may be either managerial or physical. Evidence of centralized irrigation or trade systems in the archaeological record, for example, can be seen as manifestations of
potential economic power bases for the managers of the systems.
(Whether or not potential bases of power are exploited must be determined from evidence of other aspects of a power relationship.)
Evidence of physical control over resources as another form of potential economic power base, may be manifested in the occupation of

a critical location in the production or procurement of economic resources. Physical control may also be seen in the monopolization of quantities of resources in large-scale centralized storage facilities. A good example of combined physical and managerial economic bases of power can be seen at the site of Pampa Grande on the north coast of Peru. The site, which has been interpreted as a kind of political capital (Day 1976; Shimada 1976, 1978), is located at the neck (the narrowest part) of the Lambayeque Valley. It is immediately adjacent to the headgate for the single main irrigation canal that provided water for forming the entire lower portion of the valley. Thus, the presence of a centralized irrigation system and the location of the site would have provided the leaders at the site with the potential for both physical and managerial control over the production system in the valley as a potential economic power base.

2. Leaders may exercise ideological power based on control over symbols which have religious or supernatural significance to the general population. Such control may be manifested archaeologically in the concentration or centralization of religious symbols in particular sites or portions of sites. It may also be manifested in artistic representations. A clear illustration of control over religious symbols is to be found at the Olmec site of La Venta in the Mexican Gulf lowlands. At La Venta there is a major concentration of religious iconography manifested in numerous large stone sculptures and enormous ceremonial offerings. There are also particular carvings at the site which show individuals holding werejaguar babies that have been interpreted as having central ceremonial significance in the Olmec religion (Joralemon 1971; Drucker et al. 1959; Coe 1968b). The concentration of symbols and the artistic representations can be interpreted as indicating that at least some occupants of La Venta controlled symbols that would have provided them with a potential ideological power base.

3. A physical power base may be derived from managerial control over the personnel in a military or police force. In other words, the physical strength of specialized warriors or policemen represents a potential power base that may be exploited by the leaders who command the military or police force. The presence of such a potential physical base can be inferred archaeologically from pictographic or mortuary evidence of specialized warriors or policemen. For example, at Pampa Grande there is a mural depicting elaborately garbed warriors

appear to represent a specialized military (Anders n.d.). Similar representations are common in Moche ceramics and murals her parts of the north coast of Peru, which indicates the wide-spread presence of military forces and potential physical bases of power.

Except in the few cases of physical control over some portion of the environment (as in the juxtaposition of Pampa Grande with an irrigation headgate), direct evidence of bases of power is generally difficult to find in the archaeological record. Managerial control over economic, ideological, and physical portions of the environment will often have few explicit material manifestations and be detected only through highly specific field research. However, it is less difficult to demonstrate the presence of a centralized economic, religious, or military system archaeologically, and the leaders at the apex of such a system can be inferred to have had a potential power base in their managerial control over resources, symbols or personnel.

Means

The actual exploitation of a power base by a power holder in order to affect changes in the behavior of a respondent constitutes the means of exerting power. In the context of the definition of power being used here, the means are the sanctions that are applied, threatened, or promised by the power holder (Dahl 1969:81). The means or sanctions may be either positive or negative and could include anything from physical violence to a failing grade to promised salvation.

The potential types of means exerted by a power holder are dependent on the nature of the power base of that actor. If the power base consists of control over major substantive portions of the environment, such as a police force, subsistence resources, or an exchange medium, then the potential means of exerting power will also be substantive. A police force can apply very real sanctions, and food or gold can be very effective direct inducements to get respondents to do something they would not otherwise do. On the other hand, if the power base consists of control over essentially symbolic portions of the environment, such as religious paraphernalia or academic grades, then the potential means of exerting power will be less direct and substantive and more on the level of threats and promises. A priest can promise heaven, but deliverance cannot be immediately supplied. Thus, the nature of a power base, in terms of the portion of the environment controlled by a power holder, dictates the kind and strength of the means that may be applied in any social situation.

Direct evidence of the means of exerting power is again difficult, if not impossible, to find in the archaeological record. As was argued in chapter 4, sanctions may be applied only infrequently and still be effective in eliciting desired changes in the behavior of a respondent population. Furthermore, in terms of the three types of power bases that may be found in a prehistoric society, only the application of sanctions associated with the exploitation of a physical base is likely to be manifested archaeologically. There are few direct behavioral correlates connected to the application of economic and ideological sanctions; accordingly, such sanctions will rarely be reflected in material remains. The application of physical sanctions, on the other hand, should be reflected in skeletal remains. Although I can find no cases of prehistoric skeletal populations that have been adequately analyzed to detect the possible application of physical sanctions, the Moslem practice of cutting off thieves' fingers or hands and the Western practice of hanging are ethnographic examples of physical sanctions that would be reflected in skeletal remains.

Aside from actual application, the threat or promise of some sanctions, particularly ideological or physical, may be materially manifested in various art media. A drawing or sculpture that depicts the application of a sanction can be seen as a threat or promise of that sanction. The frequent depiction of racks and individuals tied on racks in Moche ceramic art (Donnan 1978:80–81, 95), for example, can be interpreted as representing the threat of physical sanctions. At the same time, however, while there is little direct evidence of the application, threat, or promise of sanctions, potential means of exerting power can be inferred along with potential power bases. If there is evidence of a centralized irrigation system, then withholding or threatening to withhold water are inferable negative means of exerting power, and providing and promising adequate water are inferable positive means of exerting power. Similar arguments can be made about the application, threat, or promise of other types of economic sanctions as well as ideological and physical sanctions. Generally, if observations can be made on potential bases, the potential means of exerting power can also be logically deduced.

Scope

A direct measure of the strength of the power base and effectiveness of the means is the scope of power being exerted. The scope consists of the type of responses a power holder is able to elicit from a respondent. In other words, what a power holder is able to get a respondent to do that the respondent would not otherwise do. A child going to bed early, a man going to prison, or the citizens of New Jersey paying income taxes would be examples of the scope of power exercised in different situations. The scope of an actor's power is dependent on the base and means, such that the stronger the power base and more effective the means of exerting power, the greater the scope of power. For example, there will be marked differences expected in the scope of power exercised by a teacher who controls grades and can pass and fail students, and by a ruler who controls a police force and can impose direct physical sanctions on members of a society.

It is nevertheless possible that two actors may have similar scopes of power but widely variant bases and means of exerting power. The priest promising heaven may be able to get his constituency to build a church of a given size, while a ruler using a police force may be able to get a population to build a palace of a similar size. In terms of total energy expended, the scope of power may be the same, but the substantive portions of the environment controlled by the power holders and the sanctions that may be applied are quite different.

It should also be pointed out that the ultimate limits on the scope of power exercised are determined not by the base and means of the power holder, but by the capabilities of the respondent. A child cannot build a pyramid, and a population cannot pay unlimited taxes, no matter what sanctions may be applied to them. However, observing the scope of power in terms of the actual behavior of a respondent or group of respondents *does* provide considerable insight into the base and means of a power holder.

The scope of power will also be more clearly reflected in the archaeological record than will the base and means. Behavior in response to the exercise of power, particularly the behavior of a number of individuals, is more likely to leave material remains than is control over portions of the environment or the use of sanctions. Generally, in a power relationship between leaders and their populations, the scope of power can be seen in communal labor projects instigated and directed by the former and carried out by the latter. Centrally planned and coordinated projects, unrelated to subsistence, constitute some of the clearest material evidence of the scope of power that is exerted in prehistoric societies. At the Olmec site of La Venta, for example, the main pyramid, subsidiary platform mounds, huge monolithic sculptures, and quantities of imported stone slabs and columns all reflect communal activities that would have been instigated and directed by some central leadership group. They can thus be interpreted as material evidence of the scope of power exerted by Olmec leaders.

Because scope of power is more readily manifested in the archaeological record, it can be used as an indication of whether or not potential bases and means were actually exploited by power holders in prehistoric societies. If potential bases and means are found in the absence of material evidence of a concomitant scope of power, it can be inferred that the bases and means probably were not exploited; conversely, if a scope of power is manifest, then the bases and means probably were exploited.

Amount

A fourth power variable, which further clarifies the relationship between the base and means of the power holder and the actions of the respondent is the amount of power being exercised. The amount of power represents the probability that a respondent will comply with the demands of a power holder (Dahl 1969:81–83). The amount is dependent upon the means of exerting power and the scope of demands being made by a power holder. Holding the scope constant, the amount of power increases with increases in the effectiveness of the means. Holding the means constant, the amount of power decreases with increases in the scope of demands.

The amount of power can be assessed by observing the relative frequency with which a respondent complies with the demands of a power holder. A constituency may build a church in response to the promises of their priest, but refuse to financially support or participate in a proselytizing mission. On the other hand, a population not only may build a palace in response to the coercive sanctions of their ruler, but also pay taxes and serve as soldiers in a foreign war they do not believe in. The ability of the ruler to enforce his demands with physical sanctions may thus be interpreted as giving him a greater amount of power than the priest who can only threaten and promise religious sanctions.

Archaeologically, the actual amount of power that was exercised by prehistoric leaders over their populations may be impossible to determine. The relative probability that a population would positively comply with any given demand has no direct material manifestations. However, the communal labor projects that reflect scope of power also reflect specific instances of positive compliance by the population. By observing the frequency of such projects in a particular society, inferences can be made about the relative amount of power that was exercised in that society. Again using La Venta as an example, there is evidence that over time the population contributed more labor to more projects of different kinds. At the time of abandonment, there is also evidence that the population refused to comply with a specific demand, and thereafter complied with no demands (construction of a series of enclosure walls was interrupted before completion, and there is no evidence of communal labor projects after this time) (Drucker et al. 1959:126–27). This evidence indicates a gradual increase in the amount of power exercised by Olmec leaders, followed by an abrupt decrease.

Extension

The fifth power variable, extension, is simply the number of respondents in a power relationship (Harsanyi 1969:226; Dahl 1969:83). A power holder may exercise power over one person, several persons, or an entire population. The extension is dependent upon the base, in that the portion of the environment controlled by a power holder will be of importance to a variable number of people. The religious symbols controlled by a priest may be of importance to only a small number of people in a community, while the police force or subsistence system controlled by a ruler may be of importance to all the people in many communities. Extension may also vary in relation to the scope of demands made by a power holder, since different numbers of people may respond positively to different demands. The entire constituency may help build the church, but only some of them may support the mission. Thus, the manifest extension of an actor's power may not be the same in different situations.

The extension of power may be assessed in two ways in the archaeological record. The *potential* extension may be estimated on the basis of the total population that resides in a geographic area or within identifiable political boundaries. Heizer (1960), for example, estimates that a population of 18,000 contributed to the construction and other labor projects observed at La Venta. He uses the carrying capacity of the land, current population levels, and environmental circumscription to arrive at this estimate. The *actual* extension in a particular instance of the exercise of power may be determined on the basis of the time and labor that went into a specific labor project. I can find no examples where actual time/labor calculations have been made for individual projects. (Pozorski (1980) recently tried this for an Early Horizon platform mound on the coast of Peru, but used unrelated labor figures derived from modern Mexican peasants. His time control was also less than optimal.)

Power Costs

Insight into another dimension of power relationships is gained by considering the costs to the power holder and the respondent(s). Harsanyi first considered costs in a specific attempt to measure social power using the theory of two-person bargaining games (1969:226–38). However, costs also may be considered in the broader context of a general discussion of the concept of power. The costs of exerting power—power costs—represent the monetary or physical units or energy that are expended by the power holder in attempting to elicit changes in the behavior of a respondent. The power costs are dependent on the particular means of exerting power. In other words, how much does it cost the power holder to apply sanctions or to effectively threaten or promise to apply sanctions? There are many possible sources of cost to the power holder. For example, a ruler, using a police force as a means of exercising his power, may personally expend very little in applying or threatening sanctions, but expend a great deal in maintaining the police force and supporting judicial and penal systems. Likewise, a priest, promising heaven as a means of exercising power, may expend little energy in making the promise, but expend substantial energy and resources in inculcating the belief in heaven among his constituency.

Differences in the cost to the power holder may depend on the compliance of the respondent. Withholding a threatened negative sanction in exchange for compliance will normally cost less than applying it for noncompliance; and providing a promised positive sanction will normally cost more than withholding it. When a power holder's base precludes the actual application of sanctions, there is obviously no way to calculate the costs of applying versus threatening or promising sanctions. Generally, the costs of exercising power can be used to assess the overall efficiency of the means available to a power holder.

In the archaeologtical record, power costs can be inferred from the evidence for potential bases of power. Maintaining and exploiting an irrigation or trade system as an economic power base, for example, can be inferred to entail costs in terms of the physical operation and administration of the system as well as providing the system with protection from disruption by potential enemies. In the case of the Olmec, it can be inferred from Rathje's argument that the leaders' primary economic power base was derived from control of a long-distance trade network (Rathje 1972). Exploitation of this base would have involved support of the traders and transporters, support of a military force to protect the traders, and possible support of trading outposts in areas removed from the Olmec heartland. Chalcatzingo, a Formative highland site, may have contained such an Olmec trading outpost (Grove et al. 1976).

In addition to the power costs, there are potential costs to the respondent in either complying or not complying with the demands of the power holder. Harsanyi considers only the costs of refusing to comply, and sees this as a measure of the "strength" of the power holder's power over the respondent (1969:227). However, even in the classic case of the gunman demanding "your money or your life!", the respondent always has at least two options, and the costs for each will often be quite different. Thus, I would argue that both the compliance costs and the refusal costs of the respondent should be considered in evaluating different power relationships.

Compliance Costs

Compliance costs are basically a supplementary measure of the scope of power exercised in a power relationship. Whereas the scope of power represents the type of responses that may be elicited by a power holder, the compliance costs represent a quantification of those responses. If the scope of power consists of labor, money or agricultural products contributed by a group of respondents, then the compliance costs measure how much and when the labor, money, or agricultural products are contributed. The priest may be able to elicit 5,000 person-days per year for ten years from his constituency to build a church, while the ruler may be able to elicit 50,000 person-days per year for a year from his population to build his palace. Holding the extension constant, the scope of power may be similar in both cases, but the immediate compliance costs of the two groups of respondents are quite different. If the extension of the ruler's power is ten times that of the priest, the compliance costs to the respective populations may be very similar. The compliance costs thus provide additional information on the intensity of a power relationship between leaders and their populations.

Compliance costs can be directly measured in the archaeological record by calculating the amount of labor and time contributed to a particular project, and dividing that figure by the size of the respondent population. Unfortunately, this is easier said than done. Measuring compliance costs requires addressing the very sticky issues of population size and length of time involved in constructing a mound or producing a monolithic sculpture (see Kaplan 1963; Erasmus 1965; Sanders and Price 1968). Since these issues are addressed gingerly below, they will not be discussed at length here. To simply illustrate the possibility of calculating prehistoric compliance costs, Heizer's (1960) figures for the construction of the main pyramid at La Venta can be used. He estimates the population at 18,000, and figures that the pyramid would have required 800,000 person-days of labor, which was broken up into eight labor periods spread over 400 years. With an average family size of five persons, construction of the pyramid would have entailed each of 3,600 families contributing one laborer for approximately one month of labor once a generation. This calculation then represents the compliance costs to members of the La Venta population for responding to their leaders' demands to build a pyramid.

Refusal Costs

While the compliance costs serve to quantify the scope of power, the refusal costs serve to measure the impact of negative sanctions on a respondent. The refusal costs basically refer to what will happen if demands are made of a respondent and the person refuses to comply. Depending on the base of the power holder, threatened sanctions may be applied, promised sanctions may be withheld, or there may be no consequences at all. The refusal costs are thus directly tied to the base and means, since the stronger the base and more substantive the means, the higher will be the refusal costs.

They cannot be as easily quantified as the compliance costs, since they do not necessarily involve changes in the behavior of the respondent; rather, they involve qualitative changes in the environment or personal well-being of the nonrespondent. The holdup victim may choose to be shot, the church constituent may choose to take his chances with Hell, or the subject may choose to be flogged or imprisoned. Each of these represents a refusal cost which is not readily quantifiable in terms of labor, time, money or other physical units.

Refusal costs can again be inferred archaeologically from the evidence of potential bases of power. Refusal to comply with the demands of a leader who controls the production or procurement of economic resources will result in being deprived of those resources. Likewise, refusal may entail the risk of religious or physical sanctions if the leader has an ideological or physical power base. Following Rathje's argument again, the Olmec leaders controlled trade in certain basic resources (salt, obsidian, and grinding stone) (Rathje 1972). Refusal to comply with the demands of these leaders thus would have resulted in not having access to the resources and would have led to a nutritional imbalance and decrease in standard of living for recalcitrant members of the population.

The compliance and refusal costs both have an effect on the amount of power being exerted, since they will usually influence to some degree the process of decision making by the respondent in a power relationship (Wagner 1969; Harsanyi 1969). The choice of compliance or noncompliance is ultimately up to the respondent, and both compliance and refusal costs are likely to be considered in making that choice. Generally, when the refusal costs outweigh the compliance costs there is a higher probability that the respondent will comply with the demands of the power holder, and a lower probability when the cost of compliance is greater than that of refusal. However, another factor which must be considered in assessing the relative amount of power is the potential gain to the respondent in complying with the demands of the power holder.

Gains

The gains to the respondent complement the compliance and refusal costs and reflect the impact of positive sanctions on a respondent. In other words, what benefits, if any, are there to be gained by a respondent in complying with the demands of a power holder? It might be argued that a respondent does gain something if a threatened negative sanction is not applied in exchange for compliance; but it is substantively more meaningful to consider gains in terms of the application of promised positive sanctions. In the case of "your money or your life!", consideration of the refusal costs provides far greater insight into the probable choice of the respondent than does a consideration of the possible gains. However, the choice of a factory worker to work the night shift in exchange for greater pay may be better understood in terms of gains than in terms of refusal costs.

Returning to the priest and the ruler, the constituency of the former may build the church because of the gains to be had in using it, but the subjects of the latter may build the palace strictly because of the high refusal costs that may be applied by the police force. Thus, by considering gains to the respondent in addition to the compliance costs and refusal costs, it is possible to arrive at a more comprehensive explanation or prediction of the actions of a respondent or group of respondents in a power relationship.

The immediate function of a communal labor project provides the clearest means of assessing potential gains to a prehistoric population. If a project has a direct economic function, those contributing to the project stand to gain economically from the fruits of their labor. Ceremonial projects may offer religious or perhaps socially integrative gains, while military projects, such as fortifications, may offer gains in terms of protection from enemies. In the case of the Olmec, the communal labor projects at La Venta appear to have strictly ceremonial functions and probably would have provided only religious or ideological gains to the population. On the other hand, participation in the trade system, in terms of contributing labor or exportable goods, would have provided economic gains in the form of the imported goods. Whether or not goods were actually distributed among members of the population (which would constitute direct empirical evidence of gains) cannot be determined from the available Olmec data base.

With nine such major sources of potential variation as just described, a power relationship can be seen to be highly complex, yet still open to direct investigation. Additional complexity might also be added to a discussion of power if such things as scope of demands (versus scope of responses) or gains to the power holder were considered; however, the nine variables stated here are adequate for measuring and understanding most of the variability in power relationships.

Thus, the concept of power can be used to provide a theoretical baseline for examining the evolution of the prehistoric state. The present definition of power and the different power variables, while derived from political science, sociology, and anthropology, are amenable to an archaeological analysis. They involve actions of individuals and control and use of portions of the environment, and so will tend to be manifested in some form in the material record of prehistoric societies. That they may be manifested archaeologically, however, does not mean that the appropriate kinds of data have been collected by archaeologists. Although it is possible to glimpse different variables related to the exercise of power by prehistoric leaders over their populations, direct measurement of these variables is not often possible. Nevertheless, by making maximum use of available data, the variables can be used in a general analysis of the evolution of the prehistoric state, and many of the similarities and differences observed between states can be shown to represent similarities and differences in the power relationships between particular state leaders and their respondent populations.

[Chapter 7]

A Framework for Studying
State Evolution

To begin an analysis of state evolution, the state can be redefined in terms of power. The initial definition of the state offered in the introduction was "a society in which there is a centralized and specialized institution of government." However, this was not offered as a final definition, but rather as a means of delimiting the general field of interest. It was also intended to provide a common base for comparing and evaluating the opposing conflict and integration models of state formation. In the subsequent critique and empirical test of these two models, it has been shown that the preponderance of *available* archaeological evidence tends to support the outline of the conflict position as well as elements of the integration position. Consequently, a more specific and useful definition of the state framed in terms of power should also be consistent with an expanded conflict model. Toward this end, I would redefine the state as a stratified society in which a governing body exercises control over the production or procurement of basic resources, and thus necessarily exercises coercive power over the remainder of the population.

In making this redefinition, three factors have been taken into consideration: First, in the critique of Fried's conflict theory of state formation, it was argued that stratification and the state should not be separated as different stages of political evolution; rather, stratification and the state come into existence simultaneously. Specialized institutions will probably develop to maintain a system of stratification; however, their development may be better viewed as an expansion of the power exercised by the leaders of any stratified society, rather than as a separate evolutionary process that is distinguished from that of stratification itself.

Second, in all the specific theories of state formation discussed in the preceding chapter, it is argued that the group initially gaining increased access to basic resources in an emergent state is also the governing body of the society. There is no separate propertied class that uses the governing bureaucracy as a means of maintaining its privileged position. In other words, the governors of the society also constituted the upper stratum of the society, and the intrasocietal conflict that arises out of stratification is between the governors and the governed.

The third factor, related to the second, is that the governing body, through centralization and specialization, ultimately gains increased access to basic resources by controlling the production or procurement of those resources. It is at this juncture that power can be seen to be a critical factor in understanding the evolution of the state. The control gained by the governing body over the production or procurement of basic resources provides it with a substantive base and coercive economic means of exerting power over the rest of the population.

These three factors, in addition to influencing the redefinition of the state in terms of power, also provide a foundation for making a general argument about the probable formation and development of leader/population power relationships in prehistoric states. The argument, as presented below, is intended to be used as a logical framework for predicting some of the major similarities and differences that can be expected to be found in prehistoric states and for explaining similarities and differences that are found. The relative lack of empirical evidence of the different power variables precludes a detailed test of the argument, but there is enough relevant data to conduct a more general test of its basic thrust. Therefore, following the abstract presentation of the argument itself, empirical cases of prehistoric state formation and development will be analyzed in terms of manifestations of power relationships that existed between leaders and their populations (chapter 8).

Since there are a number of parts to the argument, and the parts are interrelated, an outline can be given to provide a perspective of the whole.

1. From the different theories of state formation, it can be inferred that the evolutionary process of stratification provides the leaders of a complex society with a new form of economic power based on control over the production or procurement of basic resources. This new economic power base enables them to apply coercive sanctions as a means of gaining the compliance of the population.

2. Differences in the type of resources controlled by the leaders of different states produce differences in the scope and amount of power they may exercise. Specifically, control of basic subsistence resources provides greater power than control of basic nonsubsistence resources.

3. The initial economic power base also allows the leaders to accumulate additional economic bases of power when environmental circumstances permit.

4. Development of the initial economic power base provides the leaders with the potential and need for developing a police force as an independent physical power base.

5. To protect their economic power base from external threat, the leaders of a state society need to support a military force, which provides them with another form of physical power base. The police force and the military force may be one and the same.

6. To legitimize their exercise of power and thus decrease the costs of exerting power, the leaders may also be expected to initiate or exploit an existing ideological power base. This ideological base is derived from control over religious symbols and iconography.

7. An additional function of the ideological power base is to balance the physical strength of the military and police forces. By attempting to legitimize their superior position in the eyes of the population, leaders holding ideological power can use the physical plurality of the population as a balance against the physical strength of the military and police. In other words, ideology can be expected to be used in an attempt to prevent a coup d'etat.

Keeping in mind this general outline of the different parts of the whole argument, they can each be discussed at greater length.

1. In each of the different types of theories of state formation, it is argued that stratification involves the leaders of a society gaining control over a strategic portion of the economic environment. This control can be seen as constituting a new economic power base that qualitatively distinguishes the state society from its prestratified evolutionary antecedents. Reformulated in terms of power relationships and the development of a new economic power base, the different theories can be briefly reviewed: in the warfare theories, a military leadership gains power over the population by controlling the distribution of limited goods, land, and slaves seized in warfare; in the trade theories, a managerial leadership gains power over the population by controlling the inter-regional trade or intra-regional exchange of basic resources;

in the irrigation theory, a managerial leadership gains power over the population by controlling the means of production of subsistence resources. In each case, production or procurement of basic resources is centralized in the hands of the societal leaders, and all members of the society no longer have equal access to those resources. It is this differential access that makes the new economic power base of the leaders in an emergent stratified society markedly different from the power base of leaders in prestratified societies. The critical difference lies in the ability of the state leaders to withhold basic resources as a coercive means of enforcing their demands on the population.

Prior to stratification, it is to be expected that the leaders in any complex society will exercise some power over the population. However, since all members of such a society have relatively equal access to those resources necessary for subsistence and reproduction, the leaders have no substantive economic means to compel the obedience of the population. They may *threaten* negative economic sanctions, but lacking actual control over the production or procurement of basic resources, they cannot consistently *apply* those sanctions. Furthermore, without increased access to basic resources, they cannot support a specialized police force as a physical means of compelling obedience. Consequently, the possible refusal costs to a respondent population in a prestratified society do not normally include the loss of life, liberty, or the pursuit of reproduction.

With the emergence of stratification, through either warfare, trade, or irrigation, the societal leaders can go beyond threatening coercive economic sanctions and can apply them. Their power base enables them to withhold basic resources, thus raising considerably the cost to the population of refusing to comply with their demands. Depending on the type of resources controlled by the leaders, refusal to comply with their demands will have a direct impact on the physical well-being of disobedient members of the population.

2. If the leaders control basic nonsubsistence resources, the refusal costs to the population may not be loss of life, but rather a decrease in standard of living or probability of survival or reproduction. For example, salt may be considered a basic nonsubsistence resource in some areas, such as the lowlands of Mesoamerica, where there is insufficient salt in locally occurring foodstuffs for proper nutrition (Rathje 1972:390–91). In such areas, persons deprived of salt by a leader who controlled its procurement would not have their immediate sur-

vival threatened, but their health would deteriorate progressively over time. On the other hand, if a leader controls basic subsistence resources, the refusal costs to the population are more immediate and threatening to life itself. For example, persons deprived of food or the means of procuring food face starvation in the immediate or not too distant future. The difference in refusal costs between control over subsistence versus nonsubsistence resources should be reflected in differences in the scope and amount of power exercised. Leaders who control subsistence resources thus can be expected to have a greater scope and amount of power than leaders who control other types of basic resources.

3. A similar kind of argument can be made to the effect that the more types of resources controlled by the leaders, the greater will be their scope and amount of economic power. A leader who controls subsistence and nonsubsistence resources can be expected to exercise greater economic power than a leader who controls only one or the other. In developing state societies the leaders may gain control over multiple kinds of resources by playing a central role in more than one type of economic system. While the leaders of an emergent state may have a power base in only one system, continued growth in societal size and complexity may select for increasing centralization in other systems.

For example, the initial system of production or procurement may prove inadequate to meet the increased resource needs of a growing population, and another system would have to be initiated. (The resources that may be procured through warfare in particular are limited by the productive capacity and military capabilities of one's neighbors.) In another example, centralization of control may prove adaptively advantageous in additional economic systems other than the one that provided the initial vehicle for the emergence of stratification. (An irrigation system may provide the initial basis for centralization in a society, but the importation of technologically superior tools also may be most efficiently accomplished through the organizing efforts of a centralized leadership.) In either situation, the initial leaders of the society are already in a central economic position, and may be expected to assume a similar position in the newly initiated or centralized economic system. Thus, through a process of positive feedback the leaders of a military apparatus may come to play a central role in an irrigation system, or the managerial leaders of an irrigation system may come to play a central role in trade or economic warfare.

The range of economic systems and incumbent resources that may come to be controlled by the leaders of a developing state society will depend to a great degree on their surrounding environment. Irrigation is impractical in some parts of the world where states otherwise may emerge through trade or warfare (e.g., lowland Mesoamerica). Warfare is impractical (economically) when neighboring societies have military parity or superiority. Trade may also be impractical if there are no foreign sources of desirable resources, or if all one's neighbors are enemies (as well may be the case in a warfare-based state). However, in societies without such environmental limitations, continued growth in societal size and complexity after the initial stages of state formation may be expected to result in a centralized leadership exercising combined forms of economic power based on control over different types of economic systems and resources.

4. In addition to providing the leaders of an emergent state with a substantive economic power base, their initial control over the production or procurement of basic resources can also be used to support a new physical power base. Specifically, the resources controlled by the leaders can be used to support a specialized police force, which would provide them with another coercive means of exerting power. Police can threaten and apply negative physical sanctions that directly compromise a person's physical well-being, thus again raising the refusal costs to the population to a level above that found in prestratified societies. It should be pointed out however, that the effectiveness of a police force as a physical power base does not stem from its inherent physical strength, since a population will always have physical superiority in terms of sheer numbers. Rather, its power is derived from its superior organization, technology, and/or specialization (Bierstedt 1950:736). A police force can focus superior physical strength on selected portions of a population, and thus effectively threaten an entire population with physical sanctions.

How a police force is initiated and the role it comes to play in a state society depends to some degree on the nature of the leader's economic power base. In states arising under conditions of warfare, the leaders already have a physical power base at their disposal in the form of the military apparatus developed to engage in offensive and defensive operations. Recalling the words of Adam Ferguson, "the sword which was whetted against foreign enemies, may be pointed at the bosom of fellow subjects" (1819:228). In other words, the army that initially provides a leader with increased access to basic resources may also be used as a police force to compel the obedience of the population to the leader's demands. When a state arises through trade or irrigation, however, there is no physical element built into the leader's economic power base.

In such states, the need for a relatively independent physical power base lies in an inherent weakness in the economic base. In both trade- and irrigation-based states, the leaders' control over the production or procurement of resources is not physical, but managerial; thus, it is actually the labor of the respondent population that provides them with their economic power base. If the majority of a population refuses to supply that labor, the leaders lose their economic power base and their only means of exerting coercive power. In other words, the economic power exerted by the leaders is directly dependent upon the cooperation of the people over whom the power is being exerted. By supporting a police force as an additional physical power base, the leaders would have a separate coercive means of exerting power that is not directly dependent on the actions of the respondent population. This police force could be used not only to insure the continuance of their economic power base, but also to exert power in areas unrelated to the production or procurement of resources. Thus, control over economic resources provides the leaders of an emergent state with both a reason and potential for developing a relatively independent physical power base.

5. Beyond the need to exercise independent physical power over a respondent population, state leaders have another reason for developing a physical power base. In this case, the power base is a military force serving to protect the entire society against the threat of external enemies. State leaders derive their economic power from control over the production or procurement of resources, but it is the labor of their population that actually produces or procures those resources. Thus, an external threat not only endangers the physical well-being of members of the population, it also endangers the base of the leaders' economic power. A military force, supported by the leaders, can be used to maintain the security of their economic base by protecting their respondent population. For example, if they control the importation of basic resources through a trade network, it is in their direct interest to provide protection for the trade network itself (i.e., the traders and transporters) and for the laborers and craftsmen who produce the goods that are being exported.

While a military force may serve to protect (in trade- and irrigation-based states) an economic power base, it may also play a role in the internal exercise of physical power over a population. It was pointed out above that a military force may serve a dual role as a police force, but it also may serve as a positive means of applying or promising sanctions. There are definite gains to a respondent population in being protected by a specialized military force. Additional gains to some members of the population may be manifested in the distribution of booty captured in offensive military operations. The potential negative *and* positive sanctions that may be applied by a military force thus would provide the leaders of a state with additional supplementary means of exerting power over the population.

It should be pointed out that the logical arguments for the probable development of police and military forces in emergent states do not carry the implication that two separate forces will probably develop. The arguments simply infer the potential and need for physical power bases to serve different types of functions. Since one specialized body can serve both functions, and since maintenance of two separate forces would be more costly to the power-holding leadership, it might be expected that in early states a physical power base would be manifested in a combined military and police force.

6. While economic and physical bases of power provide substantive means of gaining the compliance of a respondent population, their maintenance and exploitation by the societal leaders may require the expenditure of considerable energy and resources. The *costs* of exerting economic and physical power, in other words, may be high. As argued earlier, the control over resources exercised by state leaders is dependent upon the labor of the population. If a majority of the population refuses to supply that labor, the leaders lose their economic base and means of exerting power, as well as their privileged access to those resources. A police force can coerce members of a population into contributing their labor, but the more members that need coercing, the larger the police force needed to do the job. As the size of the police force rises, the costs to the leaders of maintaining that force obviously will increase accordingly. However, physical and economic sanctions are not the only means of inducing a population to comply with the labor demands of its leaders. If the population can be convinced of the legitimacy of the demands of its leaders, it may be more willing to comply voluntarily with those demands. Thus, to decrease

the overall costs of exerting power and increase the amount of their power, the leaders of an emergent state might be expected to attempt to legitimize their demands.

Such an attempt at legitimization of demands can be examined in terms of the exploitation of an ideological power base. In an early state society, an ideological power base may be derived from control over religious or supernatural symbols which have ideological significance to a respondent population. This control may be used to threaten or promise the population various religious or supernatural sanctions, and it may be used to manipulate changes in the ideology of the society. For example, a leader who controls the symbolic means of communicating with the gods, or who is a god, not only can claim that noncompliance with his demands will result in divine retribution, but also that the demands themselves represent the bidding of the gods. In this fashion, control over ideological symbols can be used to transform secular demands into sacred ones and assign a religious value to obedience. Wittfogel makes this point in his analysis of the role of religion in hydraulic society: "The agromanagerial sovereign cemented his secular position by attaching to himself in one form or another the symbols of supreme religious authority" (1957:92).

The leaders in most developing complex societies can be expected to have some form of ideological power base even prior to stratification. In most, if not all, ethnographically known chiefdoms or ranked societies, the leaders play a central role in the religious system and exercise some form of control over religious or supernatural symbols (e.g., Service 1971a:162; Fried 1967:137; Sahlins 1958; 1968; Mair 1962). In fact, these leaders are often considered sacred symbols themselves as direct descendants of gods. It would appear likely, therefore, that in most of the first state societies, the leaders would have had an existing ideological power base that might be exploited in an attempt to legitimize their exercise of other secular forms of power. If the leaders did not have such a base to begin with, as might be the case in a warfare based state, for example (see Gearing 1962), they might be expected to gain one, either by coopting the symbols and iconography of the religious system or by using their control over resources to support a group of religious specialists.

7. The reasons for having and exploiting an ideological power base in a state society, however, do not stem solely from the need to legitimize demands and decrease the costs of exerting power. An ideo-

logical base can also be needed to gain the support of a majority of the population as a balance against the physical strength of the specialized military/police force. In the trade and irrigation based states, it was argued that the leadership group would be expected to initiate a specialized group to carry out military and police functions. This group could be used to apply supplementary physical sanctions to gain the obedience of the population and maintain the economic power base of the leaders. However, this group, itself, would constitute a threat to that power base. The physical strength of the group, gained through specialization, organization, and/or technology, would enable it to usurp the resources controlled by the leaders. Economic sanctions cannot compare with physical sanctions in a one-on-one competition. Consequently, in states where the leaders gain control over resources through some mechanism other than military prowess, they would need a physical means to counter-balance the physical strength of a police/military group.

In a technologically simple society, the only portion of the environment that can be exploited to counter the physical strength of a specialized police/military force is the population itself. If a leadership group is recognized as the legitimate ruling body of a society, the leaders can use the numberical superiority of the population as a physical balance to the specialized strength of a military/police force. In this case, the leaders may attempt to exploit an ideological power base to legitimize their superior position and gain the support of the population. In other words, an ideological power base provides a potential instrument for the leaders of a state to establish a second, informal physical power base. This second base, the population, can be used to prevent usurpation of their position and resources by the specialized body that constitutes the first such base.

To briefly summarize, it has been argued that a central feature in all of the major theories of state formation is the development of a new economic power base by the society's leaders. This new base provides the leaders with economically coercive means of exerting power, although the impact of these means will vary depending on the resources controlled. At the same time, it also gives them a reason and the ability to develop and exploit additional physical and ideological bases of power. A physical base can be used as an independent coercive means of exerting power and as a means of securing the society and the economic power base of the leaders from external threat. An ideological power base can be used as a means of modifying a society's ideology in an attempt to legitimize the exercise of economic and physical power. It can also be used by a managerial economic leadership group to gain the support of the population and counter the potential threat of a military/police group.

This argument is not intended to have mechanical applicability in the sense that all states *must* have one form of economic power based on trade, warfare, or irrigation, that all states *must* develop a specialized police or military force, or that all state leaders *must* use some form of ideological power base to legitimize the power structure and balance the strength of a military/police force. Nor is it intended to provide great new revelations into the nature and operation of ruling power structures in state societies. Numerous scholars have noted that economic, ideological, and physical elements play critical interrelated roles in the exercise of power in state societies (see, for example, Wittfogel 1957; White 1959; Lenski 1966; Adams 1966; Fried 1967, 1968; Krader 1968; Balandier 1970; Wheatley 1971; Flannery 1972; Harris 1975, 1977; Webster 1976). Rather, the argument is intended to show how these elements can be expected to interact in a power structure within the specific context of state formation and development. It is intended to be used as a flexible framework for making predictions about the process of state evolution, for explaining some of the similarities and differences that are observed in prehistoric societies, and for integrating different kinds of archaeological research and theory into a broader analysis of political organization.

Chapter 8

Power and the State in the New World

The logical argument for using the exercise of power as a predictive, explanatory, and integrative framework for analyzing state evolution can be empirically evaluated and illustrated using archaeological data drawn from specific prehistoric states. There are three general areas where the argument is open to evaluation: 1) All states will share certain similar characteristics in terms of the power relationships between leaders and their populations; 2) Certain differences in the power bases of state leaders will lead to specific kinds of differences between states; 3) After the initial process of formation, there will be specific patterns evident in the process of state development. These three very general hypotheses will be evaluated here using data drawn from cases of New World state evolution. Specifically, the first two will be examined in light of evidence from Mesoamerica, and the third prediction will be examined using evidence from Peru.

There are several reasons for using these two areas to evaluate different aspects of the argument, not the least being related to the availability of data. Compared to other areas, more archaeological research has been oriented toward problems of economics, social and political organization, demography, and religion in these New World areas of state evolution. As a result, there is more relevant empirical evidence of power and power variables than in the Old World areas of Mesopotamia, Egypt, India, and China. Mesoamerica specifically is used as a testing ground for evaluating the predictions on similarities and differences between states to illustrate the utility of the power framework in providing potential solutions to major problems faced by archaeologists. In particular, there is an active debate in Mesoamerica over when the first state arose in the area. This debate can be directly addressed in terms of predicted similarities in the power exerted in all states and differences in the nature of power exerted in specific states. Peruvian data, in turn, can be analyzed in terms of the predictions about patterns of state development primarily for methodological reasons. The Peruvian coast is a large region of environmentally similar zones in which there is a long and reasonably well-documented sequence of prehistoric political evolution. This region thus offers an opportune data base for examining the progressive development of power relationships in prehistoric states.

The Formation of the State in Mesoamerica

Within the field of Mesoamerican archaeology, a number of scholars argue that the Olmec, an early complex culture on the Mexican Gulf Coast, was the first state to have arisen in the area (Heizer 1960; Coe 1968a; Bernal 1976; Rathje 1972; Tolstoy 1974; cf. Coe and Diehl 1980 2:147) while others reserve that honor for the much later and more complex culture centered at the site of Teotihuacán (Sanders and Price 1968; Price 1977; Webb 1975). On the one side the protagonists infer that the elaborateness and magnitude of Olmec art and architecture required a state level of organization. On the other, they infer that the Olmec accomplishments required only a chiefdom level of organization, and that the difference in scale between art and architecture observed at Olmec sites versus Teotihuacán is a manifestation of the difference between a chiefdom and a state. However, neither side offers a deductive logical argument that provides a satisfactory answer to the question of Olmec statehood. By examining the Olmec in terms of power relationships more conclusive inferences can be made about their level of political organization.

The initial premise of the logical argument presented in chapter 6 was that the initial stage in the formation of the state is the development of an economic power base derived from control over basic resources. This base provides the leaders with an economic means of applying coercive sanctions, as well as the potential for developing a physical power base to apply physically coercive sanctions. The ability to apply economic sanctions and potential for applying physical sanctions is predicted to increase the scope and amount of power exercised by a state leader to a level qualitatively above that of prestate leaders. Thus, there should be a qualitative difference observed in the scope and amount of power exercised in states versus prestates.

In the case of the Olmec, Rathje argues that trade in basic resources provided the initial economic power base of the Olmec leaders, and there is some evidence of this trade system. The posited basic resources—salt, obsidian, and grinding stones—do not occur locally, and at least the latter two can be demonstrated to have been imported into the Olmec area (Rathje 1972:387–89; Coe 1968b; Cobean et al. 1971; Drucker 1952). On a more general level, there is extensive evidence that the Olmec were engaged in a major long-distance trading network (Coe 1965; Grove 1968, 1974; Grennes-Ravitz 1974). Coe and Diehl (1980 2:147) also present a convincing argument that control over highly productive river levee lands would have provided an alternative strong economic power base to the Olmec leaders at San Lorenzo. Evidence of a physical power base in Olmec society is seen in numerous pictographic representations of warriors (Coe 1963, 1968a, 1968b; Gay 1972; Drucker et al. 1959). However, the evidence of these potential economic and physical power bases is highly inferential and far too weak to support substantially a conclusion that coercive power was being exerted in an Olmec state. On the other hand, the evidence of scope and amount of power exercises in Olmec society is quite direct and more conclusive of Olmec statehood.

Scope and amount of power exercised by Olmec leaders is clearly manifested in the results of communal construction and production activities. At the central Olmec site of La Venta, there is a large pyramidal mound of over 175,000 cu m, along with a number of other mounds of lesser magnitude. Huge quantities of volcanic and metamorphic stone, brought from sources more than 100 to 125 km away, have been found at the site. Forty stelae and other stone monuments, weighing up to fifty tons apiece have also been found, along with hundreds of large stone columns used for construction and other stone artifacts. Thousands of tons of worked serpentine blocks, transported from sources 100 km away, have been found at the site buried in massive offerings (Drucker et al. 1959). At a second Olmec center, San Lorenzo, there are a number of smaller mounds on one large artificially modified mound of 3 million cu m. More than sixty stelae and monuments have been found at this site as well, along with large quantities of other stone artifacts. Again, all the stone is from distant sources (Coe and Diehl 1980; Coe personal communication 1979). Numerous other monuments have been found at other Olmec sites (Stirling 1943, 1955). The carving of the stelae and monuments, as well as highly technical carving of other types of stone (jade, serpentine, and magnitite), and the production of specialized ceramics is also indicative of full-time Olmec craft specialists supported by an economic surplus (Coe 1965; Coe and Diehl 1980).

Taken as a whole the evidence of Olmec construction and production activities indicates that the Olmec leaders were able to gain the compliance of their populations to a wide range of demands and on a relatively frequent basis. The question then becomes, does this observed scope and amount of power exerted represent the expected qualitative increase that should be manifested in an emergent state society? Looking at the accomplishments of antecedent cultures in the Olmec area, and in other lowland areas of Mesoamerica, and at the accomplishments of ethnographically known prestate societies, that question would have to be answered positively.

Prior to the efflorescence of Olmec culture between 1200 and 100 B.C., there are no known communal labor projects of any kind in the Gulf Coast area (Coe 1968a, 1968b, personal communication 1979; Coe and Diehl 1980). While surveys in the area have not been intensive, enough work has been done to indicate with high probability that there is no antecedent culture of remotely the same magnitude as the Olmec. In other areas the picture is similar. In Oaxaca, for example, prior to the efflorescence at Monte Albán and other large sites at approximately 500 B.C., there is no evidence of major monumental architecture or public works (Flannery and Marcus 1976; Flannery 1976; Blanton 1976). (The largest architectural structure is a little over 1000 cu m, and several relatively small stone monuments have been found, all from a source no more than five km away.) In the Mayan lowland area, prior to the efflorescence at sites such as Tikal, Altar de Sacrificios, Uaxactún, and Becán, there is a similar pattern, with the largest public buildings being low mound structures (Hammond 1977a, 1977b; W. Coe 1965; Adams 1977). Thus, the empirical evidence from Mesoamerica does indicate that the scope and amount of power exercised by the Olmec leaders is qualitatively above any power exercised in pre-Olmec societies.

Sanders and Price's contention that the construction and production activities of the Olmec could have been accomplished by a ranked rather than a state organization still remains an issue. Aside from citing the difference in scale between the Olmec sites and Teotihuacán, they also argue that if Olmec leaders had coercive power they would have used it to coopt labor and resources for personal use. Since no Olmec "palaces" have been excavated they maintain that there is no evidence of such personal use of power by the Olmec leaders. In answering their argument, two questions can be raised: can the leaders of a ranked society induce their population to engage in communal labor and production activities of the magnitude observed in Olmec sites? and, was there personal use of power by the Olmec leaders?

In regard to the first question, Kaplan (1963) and Erasmus (1965) raise a similar issue in arguing that the monumental architecture throughout Mesoamerica could have been accomplished by a relatively small number of people working voluntarily over a long period of time, without the coercive power of a state. Erasmus points out that small groups of people have been known to build large churches in Colonial Mexico, and Kaplan estimates from ethnoarchaeological studies of modern labor that most monuments could have been built without taking time away from subsistence activities. Sanders and Price would seem to be making a similar kind of argument about the Olmec:

> Even the massive stone sculpture at La Venta would not have required a labor force beyond the size of a chiefdom. Stirling (1955) has suggested that the massive stone heads represent chieftains, possibly of a dynastic line, which means that only one would have been carved per generation of chiefs. All that was needed, therefore, was the manpower necessary to move a block of stone 20 to 30 tons in weight from the quarry to the site once a generation, plus a small corps of full-time craftsmen to work the stone into its final form. A chiefdom would easily be capable both of integrating populations of that size and of maintaining the Jade Route postulated by Coe. (1968:127)

Yet, elsewhere in the same book they criticize this exact type of argument. Refering to Kaplan and Erasmus' work:

> These studies in no way demonstrate the probability or even the possibility that civic centers of the size of Uxmal or Teotihuacan were in fact dependent upon the labor of so small a population. The question is not what *can* be done, but what is *normally* done by organized groups of humans in the way of cooperative building projects. We know of no ethnographic parallel of a center of the size of Uxmal being constructed by an organized society of only 1200 families. . . . Such calculations can be manipulated at the will of the researcher to "prove" that societies of

almost any size are capable of building any structure or group of structures. (1968:55–56, emphasis in original)

They would appear to engage in the same kind of manipulation of calculations in focusing only on the Olmec heads and arguing that they could have been produced by a small group of people cooperating once a generation. They ignore, for example, the synchronic burial of 1,000 tons of imported, worked serpentine blocks in massive pits at La Venta (Drucker et al. 1959:97)! Sanders and Price, like Kaplan and Erasmus, cite no cases of prestratified societies engaging in nonsubsistence labor of the same magnitude that was required in transporting the heads and *numerous* other stone monuments over 100 km to the Olmec sites, nor do they give examples of such societies building pyramids or carrying out other ceremonial projects of remotely the same scale as those found at La Venta and San Lorenzo. While not having carried out an intensive search of ethnographic and ethnohistoric literature on ranked societies, I know of no examples that would support their contention.

There are cases of large-scale subsistence-oriented labor, manifested primarily in irrigation system, in prestate societies, for example, among the Kalinga in the Philippines (Barton 1949), in Polynesia (Jennings 1979), or among the Hohokam of the American Southwest (Haury 1976). However, such subsistence-oriented labor can be explained in terms of demographic and environmental pressures on the population as a whole (see Boserup 1965) rather than the direct inducements of leaders.

The Olmec labor projects, whose only identifiable function is ideological (Heizer 1960; Coe 1968b; Joralemon 1971; Wicke 1971; Grove 1978), cannot be attributed to such independent material variables. A more viable alternative explanation is provided in the power argument. In state societies it is argued that there should be an attempt by leaders to legitimize their exercise of power. In the Olmec case, I believe the overwhelming orientation of the labor projects toward a centralized, unified religion (Joralemon 1971) is a manifestation of this expected attempt at legitimization.

Labor did not go into building a communal building for the use of the community, it went into building an impressive pyramid, into an enormous mound in the shape of a bird, into the burial of 1,000 tons of stone over a jaguar mask, into the creation of huge stelae depicting elaborately clad individuals or single priests holding werejaguar infants, into the construction of large cairn burials of individuals (Drucker et al. 1959; Coe and Diehl 1980). These projects had no direct benefit to the population other than to demonstrate to them the power and glory of their religion *and* their priests.

Another argument offered by Price against Olmec statehood is that there was no personal use of power by Olmec leaders (1977:213). In other words, if Olmec leaders did exert coercive state power over their populations, it is reasonable to assume that they would use some of it to increase their own status or personal well-being. Price bases this argument primarily on the observation that there are no known Olmec palaces. This observation is true. However, there are no known Olmec residences of any kind, palatial or otherwise! At the sites of La Venta and San Lorenzo, where the most extensive work has been carried out, excavations have been limited almost exclusively to the immediate vicinity around the actual ceremonial architecture. Large mound complexes adjacent to the ceremonial structures have not been examined at all. Since a palace may not leave obvious surface remains, particularly in a rainfall environment, (see also Chang 1977:223–24; Haas n.d.); there is no reason to conclude that there were no Olmec palaces. At the same time, the open possibility of Olmec palaces does not imply their existence. But another line of evidence does indicate that Olmec leaders used their power for personal purposes.

Other than the cairn graves mentioned above, the most obvious illustration of such personal use of power is manifested in the colossal Olmec heads. Blocks of stone, weighing twenty to thirty tons and transported over one hundred km across the jungle were sculpted into highly realistic human heads. Twelve such heads have been found to date, at three different sites (La Venta, San Lorenzo, and Tres Zapotes) (Wicke 1971). These sculptures do not depict abstract gods in the Olmec pantheon, or amorphous humans. They depict distinguishable individuals, right down to the protruding front teeth and double chin (Wicke 1971; Joralemon 1971). I would argue that this considerable expenditure of labor to produce massive stone portraits does not represent the cooperative labor of a population to glorify its chiefs, but the personal use of state power by individual Olmec rulers (see also Renfrew 1973a and Trigger 1978 for the distinction between group-oriented and individualizing communal activities). Without additional excavation in Olmec residential areas it is impossible to tell the extent to which labor and resources were coopted to increase the status or well-being of the leaders, but the heads mutely speak to the fact that there was such personal aggrandizement.

Overall, the contention of Sanders and Price and others that the Olmec labor projects could have been carried out by a prestate society without coercive sanctions must stand without empirical verification and contributes nothing toward answering the question of Olmec statehood and understanding the process of state evolution. On the other hand, the predicted attempt by a state leadership to legitimize its position does appear to be manifested in the Olmec archaeological record, and there is evidence of the personal use of power by Olmec leaders. The only remaining substantive argument against Olmec statehood is the comparison with Teotihuacán. Sanders and Price point out that the scale of architecture, public works, and craft specialization is far greater at Teotihuacán than at any of the Olmec centers. This difference in scale, they argue, represents the qualitative distinction between a state and a prestate. While their observation of a major difference in scale is indisputable, when Teotihuacán and the Olmec are compared in terms of the overall power relationships between their respective leaders and populations, the difference between them appears much more quantitative than qualitative.

The major apparent difference between the two is in the general scope of power manifested in the archaeological record. The same kinds of large-scale labor products are found at both locations (i.e., monumental architecture, public works, craft specialization), but everything at Teotihuacán is much bigger and more complex than anything found in the Olmec area. However, when the scope of power is broken down in terms of the actual compliance costs to members of the respective respondent populations, the difference is not that great. The critical variable here is the relative size of the populations or the potential *extension* of the leaders' power.

In the tropical lowland environment of the Olmec, with the exception of a few highly restricted river levee areas, the soil is highly acidic, heavy in clay, and poorly drained (Coe 1968b:107). The only practical means of cultivation in this environment is slash-and-burn, with three to twelve years of fallow required for every year of planting (Sanders and Price 1968:123). This type of system requires large areas of land for small numbers of people, leading to a dispersed settlement pattern and low population densities in localized areas (Coe 1968a:59; 1968b:107;

Rathje 1972; Heizer 1960). The area is also covered by a heavy tropical rainforest, laced with rivers and swamps, and communication between areas would have been relatively difficult prehistorically (Rathje 1972; Coe 1968a; Heizer 1966). This combination of environmental circumstances, given a simple level of technology, would have placed material limitations on the number of people who could be effectively coordinated and governed by a centralized Olmec leadership (see Logan and Sanders 1976:33). Heizer (1960), citing average population densities in the lowland area, estimates a potential population of 18,000 people occupying an environmentally circumscribed area around La Venta.

On the other hand, in the highland environment of the Valley of Mexico around Teotihuacán, there are large areas of fertile, well-drained soil that allow for intensification of agriculture through irrigation and subsequent high population densities in localized areas (Sanders et al. 1979). Furthermore, the area is not covered by heavy forests, and is relatively free of interior mountainous terrain (though the valley is circumscribed by mountains). Consequently, communication and transportation between areas in the Valley would have been relatively easy compared to the rainforest environment of the Olmec. Thus, given the same simple level of technology, there would have been far fewer material limitations on the relative number of people who could be effectively coordinated and governed by a centralized leadership at Teotihuacán (Logan and Sanders 1976:33–53). Millon (1973) estimates the population residing at Teotihuacán to have been approximately 125,000 people, and there were roughly the same number residing in other parts of the Valley of Mexico (Sanders 1972:112 Sanders et al. 1979:114).

With an estimate of 18,000 for the sustaining area around La Venta, and one of 250,000 for the area around Teotihuacán, there were over ten times more people available to carry out and support the construction and production activities at Teotihuacán than at La Venta. In terms of compliance costs, there could be more than ten times more labor expended at Teotihuacán than at La Venta, with no measurable difference in the relative scope of power exercised by the two groups of leaders. Furthermore, the length of occupation at Teotihuacán, estimated at 800 years (the first evidence of modest monumental architecture is at 100 B.C. and the dramatic collapse is at A.D. 700 (Millon 1973)), is twice as long as the occupation of La Venta, estimated at

400 years (1000 to 600 B.C.) (Heizer 1968). Thus, strictly in terms of compliance costs, there could be more than twenty times more labor manifested at Teotihuacán than at La Venta (ten times the number of people multiplied by twice the length of occupation), with no measurable difference in the *relative* scope of power exercised by the two groups of leaders over their populations.

In offering these population and time estimates, I am not claiming that the labor represented in the different monumental projects at either Teotihuacán or La Venta was evenly spread out during the entire length of occupation of the two sites (the trap of manipulating calculations). Rather, I want to point out that observed qualitative differences in labor output by two populations of different sizes and time span may not reflect a qualitative difference in the relative scope of power exercised by their leaders.

That there were major differences in the power exercised by Olmec and Teotihuacán leaders cannot be disputed, but the most obvious difference in scale can be explained in terms of extension of power rather than scope of power. The Teotihuacán leaders governed a population of 100,000 to 250,000 people, while the Olmec leaders governed a paltry 18,000. But a state is not characterized on the basis of the number of people governed. It is characterized by the coercive nature of the power relationship between the leaders and the members of the population. If the leaders of different-sized populations exert similar levels of power, in terms of relative scope and amount, I would argue that we must infer that the power relationships between those leaders and their populations are also similar.

In Mesoamerica, I find no convincing evidence or line of argumentation indicating that the tremendous scope and amount of power observed at *both* Teotihuacán *and* the Olmec centers reflects anything less than the coercive means of exerting power characteristic of a state power relationship. There are very real differences between these two societies, but they can be more fully explained in terms of differences between states, rather than differences between levels of political organization.

The Development of the State in Peru

While consideration of the different variables in a power relationship can help to resolve some of the archaelogical problems in recognizing prehistoric states and explaining some of the differences between states, such consideration can also contribute to a greater understanding of the sequential development of complex societies in a particular area. One area that offers an optimal setting for looking at this kind of sequential development is the coast of Peru. In Mesoamerica the major environmental differences between such areas as the tropical rain forest of the Olmec and the highland valley of Teotihuacán make it difficult to examine concisely the process of development in terms of earlier and later states. In Peru, however, there is a series of similar arid river valleys on the Pacific coast, which when taken together, exhibit an unbroken internal sequence of political development. Although the full sequence cannot presently be traced in any one valley, there are no major environmental differences to complicate a general comparison between early states in some valleys and later states in others.

Looking at the chronological process of political development on the Peruvian coast, there is a clear progression of increasing scope and amount of power being exerted by societal leaders. To analyze this progression in terms of the evolutionary development of power relationships, it can be broken down into a number of stages: In the Cotton Preceramic Period (c.2500 to 1750 B.C.) modest mounds and other forms of communal architecture are being erected at a small number of coastal sites (Moseley 1975a; Feldman 1977); in the Initial Period and Early Horizon (c.1750 to 100 B.C.) there is a major population movement inland into the river valleys, and much larger platform mounds ("huacas") and communal architecture are being erected (Moseley 1975a; Lumbreras 1974); in the Early Intermediate Period (c.100 B.C. to A.D. 900) occupation remains inland by and large, population appears to increase, and large-scale mounds and other construction projects are more abundant and of an even greater magnitude (Lumbreras 1974; Rowe and Menzel 1967); in the Late Intermediate Period (on the north coast, c.A.D. 900 to 1450), mounds decrease dramatically in size, but other forms of monumental construction projects show a substantial increase (Moseley 1975c; Moseley and Mackey 1974). A complete power analysis of this progression would be beyond the limits of this essay, if possible at all since much of the necessary data on different variables has not been collected. However, it is possible to offer a general reconstruction and tentative explanation of this sequence in terms of predictable patterns in the exercise of economic, physical, and ideological types of power.

The first documented appearance of complex political organization in some valleys on the Peruvian coast occurs in the Cotton Preceramic Period. At several sites on the central coast in particular there are platform mound structures or other forms of modest monumental architecture (Moseley 1975a), with published accounts on excavations at two of them, Aspero and El Paraiso. At Aspero in the Supe Valley there are six large mounds, with a range in size up to approximately 5,000 cu m, and twelve mounds of a smaller size (Moseley and Willey 1973; Feldman 1977). At El Paraiso in the Chillon Valley, there are fifty hectares of large masonry room complexes, with walls three to eight meters high and a meter thick, representing 100,000 tons of stone (Engel 1966; Patterson and Lanning 1964). Other sites of the same early time period on the central coast have been reported as having mounds or structures of a similar magnitude (Moseley 1975a:89–95), but the large majority of contemporaneous sites lack such manifestations of communal labor projects (Lanning 1967:59). These few cases of communal labor projects also seem to appear rather abruptly on the coast, with no known smaller-scale antecedents in earlier sites.

The fact that monumental architecture of a moderate scale (compared to the Olmec, for example) occurs in a minority of sites, and has no apparent antecedents of any scale, would indicate that there were power holders at these few sites who exercised a new form of power not manifested in earlier periods, and a greater level of power than is manifested at other sites of the same time period. I would not try and argue that this evidence of increased scope and amount of power being exerted is an indication of the emergence of the coercive power of a state, but I would argue that it indicates that some power holding groups have new bases and means of gaining the compliance of other portions of the population to an increased scope of demands. Without additional evidence it is presently impossible to determine the composition of the two sides of the inferred power relationship. There may have been a centralized leadership body in some sites exercising power over other members of the same site as well as occupants of other sites along the coast, or the entire community with monumental architecture may have been exercising power over other communities along the coast. In either case, for the two sites that have been excavated, the source of the new power being exerted can be found in their location and in the initial development of agriculture in the area.

In all of the coastal valleys of Peru, rainfall is insufficient to allow agriculture in the main bodies of the river valleys without some form of irrigation. Limited agriculture is possible, however, in the small areas of floodplains along the river and in the larger areas at the river mouth. The two reported sites with large-scale architecture, Aspero and El Paraiso, are located near such river mouths. The occupation of these sites also corresponds chronologically to the time when domesticated plants were first introduced into the area (Moseley 1975a). Domesticated cotton, manifested in clothing and cloth, has been found at most sites, along with small quantities of domesticated food plants, such as maize and beans. Since all the sedentary sites are located near the shore during this period, it can be inferred that the relatively sparse domesticated products found archaeologically, were grown locally at the river mouth floodplains, rather than through irrigation of the inland valley floors (Moseley 1975a; Lanning 1967; Lumbreras 1974).

The presence of the new plant domesticates and the strategic location of the two sites, both point to control over limited agricultural resources and/or arable land as the probable new base of power held by the leaders at these sites. Such control would have allowed them to provide and withold desirable nonsubsistence resources and supplementary subsistence resources as economic means of exerting power over those portions of the coastal population that did not have access to the arable lands. Such economic means may not have been coercive, however, in the sense that the resources in question were not necessary for survival. Cotton clothing has only limited survival value in a temperate zone such as the Peruvian coast, where there is no annual precipitation, and the average temperature is 18° to 22° C, with only 6° annual variation (Moseley 1975a:8). In regard to domesticated foodstuffs, while they may have improved the diet nutritionally, they are absent at many of the small *and* large sites. No maize, for example, has been found at El Paraiso (Engel 1966). The ocean provided the primary subsistence resources during this period, and various wild plant products could be gathered from different microenvironments along the coast (Lanning 1967:59).

Overall, in the Cotton Preceramic Period, the combination of newly introduced domesticated plants and limited naturally arable land provides a potential new economic base and means for exerting an increased scope and amount of power on the Peruvian coast. However, the temperate climate and relative abundance of nondomesticated subsistence resources also combined to limit the effectiveness of this potential base and means (i.e., lower refusal costs), and accordingly reduce the potential scope and amount of power that might be exerted. Empirically, the emergence of communal labor projects is indicative of an increased scope and amount of power on the coast, and the occurrence of such projects at sites strategically located near arable land indicates that the potential new economic base and means were being exploited by leaders at these sites. Furthermore, the limited effectiveness of the potential base and means is reflected in the relatively reduced scale of the labor projects in comparison to later projects on the coast. Thus, from the limited available evidence it can be inferred that in the Cotton Preceramic Period there was a simple, probably noncoercive power relationship between power holding leaders at certain sites and other portions of the population on the coast, and that this relationship was probably based on control over arable land and/or domesticated plant products.

In addition to a limited economic power base, there is also some evidence that an ideological base was being exploited in these early societies. All of the large-scale architecture in the Cotton Preceramic appears to be primarily ceremonial in nature, with no indications of an independent secular function (e.g., administration, storage, fortification) (Feldman 1977; Engel 1966; Lumbreras 1974). The heavy ceremonial orientation of these structures indicates that the increased power is being exercised within an ideological context. As in the case of the Olmec, I would argue that this ceremonial orientation can be explained most efficiently in terms of the exploitation of an ideological power base to legitimize the exercise of other forms of power. The construction of large ceremonial mounds and buildings cannot be accounted for strictly in terms of the exercise of either economic or ideological bases *alone*; rather it can only be accounted for in terms of the combination of *both* types of power.

Following these initial developments in the Cotton Preceramic Period, there is evidence of power relationships growing increasingly complex and coercive on the coast of Peru. In the Initial Period and ensuing Early Horizon, a major increase in scope of power being exercised and a potential new economic power base are both manifested in the inland construction of monumental architecture of a larger scale than anything found in the shore sites of the Cotton Preceramic. While this transition proceeded at different rates along the coast, it apparently took place relatively early and rapidly in two adjacent valleys on the central coast, the Rimac and the Chillon.

The large site of El Paraiso, located at the mouth of the Chillon River, was abandoned shortly before the advent of pottery at approximately 1750 B.C. (based on a radiocarbon date taken from the uppermost level of occupation—Lumbreras 1974:52; Engel 1966:5). At almost exactly the same time, Huaca La Florida (initial construction radiocarbon dated to between 1800 and 1600 B.C.), a huge pyramid structure, was erected at a pottery-bearing site immediately to the south of El Paraiso, but 14 km inland in the Rimac Valley (Kosok 1965:24; Lumbreras 1974:52; Lanning 1967:90; Moseley 1975a:105). While the architecture at El Paraiso is the largest among its contemporaries in the Cotton Preceramic, Huaca La Florida is described by Lanning as "the largest single pyramid ever built on the central coast" (1967:90). The exact size of La Florida is not reported in the literature, but Lanning's statement places it in relative perspective when it is considered that at a later site 5 km away there is a pyramid over 400,000 cu m in volume (Kosok 1965:24; Lumbreras 1974:120)! Thus in a short period of time, there is evidence of a tremendous increase in scope of power being exercised over a similar, if not the same, population on the central coast.

The inland location of La Florida is also significant since it implies the initiation of at least a minimal irrigation system. According to MacNeish, Patterson, and Browman,

La Florida, the largest settlement in the region, is located in a place where agriculture cannot be practiced without some form of water management system because of the amount of postglacial river-cutting occurring in this part of the valley. Without going into the specific details of the argument, it is highly likely that the La Florida population utilized a water-control system composed minimally of a single canal—four to six kilomenters in length—which would have roughly quadrupled the amount of arable land available. (1975:38; see also Moseley 1975a:105)

The movement away from the shoreline is also indicative of a decreased reliance on marine resources, and increased dependence on agricultural resources, a pattern that Lanning notes in general for the Initial Period:

There was a definite increase in the consumption of food crops on the coast during the Initial Period. The quantity of maize, peanuts, manioc, sweet potatoes, and lucuma found in Initial Period middens is much greater than that of cultivated plant foods in the typical Period VI [Cotton Preceramic] refuse deposit. (1967:89)

The inference of irrigation and greater dependence on agriculture is supported by a consideration of power. With no evidence of marked population growth between the construction of the Huaca at La Florida and the occupation of El Paraiso (thus no evidence of a greater potential extension of power), the increased scope of power manifested at the former site can only be accounted for in terms of a new or increased base of power. The development of an irrigation system and a greater subsistence role for agricultural products would provide the necessary foundation for the emergence of true economic stratification, and at the same time introduce a potential new economic base and coercive means of exerting power. In other words, as plant domesticates evolve from supplementary to basic resources and come to be produced through a centralized irrigation system, those in control of the system have new means of enforcing greater demands on a respondent population. While documentary evidence is admittedly sparse, the great magnitude of the pyramid at La Florida, its inland location, and the potential for irrigation would all tend to indicate that the coercive power relationship characteristic of a state had arisen on the central coast of Peru by the beginning of the Initial Period.

The combination of large-scale monumental architecture coupled with inland movement and increased dependence on domesticates is a pattern repeated in other valleys along the Peruvian coast during the Initial Period and Early Horizon. For example, between the Casma and Huarmey valley, a large Cotton Preceramic/Initial Period mound and room complex on the shore (at the site of Las Haldas) is followed by much larger Initial Period/Early Horizon pyramid and architectural complexes at the inland sites of Cerro Sechín and Sechín Alto in the Casma Valley (Moseley 1975a:107; Lumbreras 1974:43, 49). At Caballo Muerto, an Early Horizon site in the Moche Valley, Pozorski (1980) reports several large platform mounds. He roughly estimates that the largest of these, Huaca de los Reyes, required almost 350,000 person/days to complete.

Another possible pattern should be noted, though the empirical evidence is limited. In other valleys along the coast where there is no early coastal efflorescence, inland movement in the Initial Period and early part of the Early Horizon is not accompanied by the construction of monumental/communal architecture. In the Viru Valley, for instance, there are large coastal sites in the Cotton Preceramic, but no form of identifiable communal construction projects (Bird 1948). In the following Initial Period and Early Horizon, the coastline itself is abandoned, and occupation sites are found anywhere from five to forty-two km from the shore. The largest communal structures in any of these sites are stone foundations up to 156 m in circumference (Willey 1953:354). The inland location of these sites would again imply the presence of some form of irrigation systems, but the absence of monumental architecture or other types of communal labor projects also would indicate that irrigation probably was not exploited as an economic power base, at least initially, in these areas.

Moseley (1975a:5, 111–13) has argued that the mobilization of work forces for the construction of communal architecture on the early coastal sites "preadapted" the societies for the subsequent evolution of irrigation systems. However, the second pattern noted in some valleys would indicate that rather than being "preadapted" for irrigation, the early monument-building populations in some areas were "preadapted" to subordination and responding to the demands of a central power holding leadership. In other words, some members of the Cotton Preceramic population in some valleys were able to gain control over certain resources and exert limited power over other members. Once this power relationship was established, irrigation provided the vehicle for the power holders to gain a more effective base and means of exerting power over the existing respondent portion of the population. When an initial power relationship was not established in the Cotton Preceramic, the population still managed to carry out irrigation, but there was no existing central power-holding group to exploit immediately the potential of the irrigation system as an economic power base.

Whether or not irrigation was initially exploited as an economic power base, it would appear that the largest scale communal labor projects after the Cotton Preceramic are associated directly or indirectly with the operation of an irrigation system. In each of the valleys along the coast the reported cases of monumental architecture are contemporaneous with either substantial inland occupations and/or direct empirical evidence of canal systems (Lumbreras 1974; Kosok 1965; Willey 1953; Lanning 1967). I would argue this pattern indicates that irrigation did play a critical economic role in the exercise of power in the later societies along the Peruvian coast. However, economic power based on irrigation was not the only form of power exercised in these societies.

One additional economic power base may be found in trade. MacNeish, Patterson, and Browman (1975) have argued that resources, such as agricultural products, crafts, and luxury goods, were being exchanged between valleys and between the coast and the highlands in both the Initial Period and the Early Horizon. Keatinge (1979) has also suggested that the spread of the Chavin religion in the Early Horizon may be at least partially attributed to the widespread trading of certain types of nonbasic resources. If such trade or exchange of resources was organized and implemented by the leaders of the coastal populations, it would have provided them with additional means of exerting power. However, since these resources were not basic, control over their trade would have provided only a supplementary, noncoercive economic power base. Much more work needs to be done to understand the extent and role of trade in the earlier periods of Peruvian prehistory.

As was the case in the Cotton Preceramic, there is also evidence that the economic power exercised in the Initial Period and Early Horizon was accompanied by the exercise of ideological power. The known large-scale communal labor projects in the later periods have all been interpreted as having a central ceremonial function (Lumbreras 1974; Lanning 1967; Benson 1971). Again, I would maintain that this ceremonial orientation represents an attempt to legitimize the exercise of greater economic power by the societal leaders. In the Early Horizon, however, the nature of the ideological base that was being exploited is complex and somewhat problematical. During this period, most of the coastal valleys, as well as most other parts of Peru all seem to have shared a common religion, as manifested in the pervasive distribution of a single religious art style, the Chavín. In each valley Chavín designs and iconographic elements are found repeatedly in architectural decorations, stone carvings, ceramics, and textiles (Willey 1951; Patterson 1971; Kan 1972; Menzel et al. 1964; Moseley and Watanabe 1974; Pozorski 1980; Roe 1974; Sawyer 1961; Larco Hoyle 1941; Lumbreras 1974).

The center or geographical point of origin of the Chavín art style and religion has not been definitively established, but it is commonly believed to have been at the site of Chavín de Huantar, after which the style is named. This is an elaborate ceremonial center in the northern highlands, where monumental stone architecture is profusely decorated with Chavín iconography, and where Chavín stone sculpture and ceramics are found in abundance (Bennet 1944; Lumbreras 1971; Rowe 1967). The spread of the Chavín art style and religion, whether from this highland site or from a site or sites yet to be discovered or identified, has been most often attributed to the efforts of peaceful missionaries (Patterson 1971:42–45; Rowe 1967; Keatinge 1979). There is no evidence of military conquest or even regularized warfare until the very end of the Early Horizon, and no indication of any form of economic hegemony over the region.

In terms of power and the state, some tentative inferences can be made about the role of Chavín religion as an ideological power base in the Early Horizon. It should first be pointed out that a few elements of Chavín religion and art style are widespread in central and north-central Peru prior to the Early Horizon and construction of the ceremonial center at Chavín de Huantar (Patterson 1971:42). However, these elements are manifested exclusively in ceramics, and do not appear to be selectively correlated with monumental architecture or ceremonial centers. While data supporting this pattern are minimal, it nevertheless may be inferred that an initial form of Chavín religion was probably present in Peru before it became a dominant religion in later societies.

At the beginning of the Early Horizon, Chavín religion became much more widespread and visible throughout Peru. A number of different reasons might be offered to explain this spread of the Chavín. Patterson, for example, has suggested that a parallel may be drawn with the spread of Christianity in the Mediterranean and Near East after it became the state religion of the Roman empire in the fourth century.

> The spread of the religion was not associated with military conquest; the peoples outside of the core area accepted it either through a desire to imitate or to be in close contact with the adherents of the faith. This pattern also has analogies with the spread of Christianity after it became a state religion in the fourth century. Christianity spread outside of the Empire during this period, not so much by military conquest on the part of the Romans, but rather by its acceptance by peoples who were impressed with the grandeur of Rome or who wanted to establish trade or other sorts of relations with the state. (1971:43)

However, the example of Christianity presents another possible explanation of the spread of Chavín religion other than because of the desire to imitate or establish trade contact. Harris (1974:179–203, 1975:564) maintains that Christianity initially spread as a kind of passive revolutionary movement to free the peasantry of the poverty and labor incurred by the rule of the Roman state government. Along this same line, it might be equally argued that the Chavín religion was widely accepted by local populations in response to the repressive rule of their respective state governments.

Whether it was accepted initially to facilitate or as a means of passive revolution, it appears that during the early stages of the Early Horizon the Chavín religion was adopted by societal leaders in most of the coastal valleys as an ideological power base. This adoption and exploitation of the religion is most clearly manifested in the incorporation of Chavín elements into the external decoration of a variety of forms of monumental architecture (Moseley and Watanabe 1974; Pozorski 1980; Larco Hoyle 1941; Willey 1971:122–3; Kosok 1965:109). By providing large-scale communal labor projects with a religious front (both literally and figuratively), the power holding leaders in these societies can be seen as using religion in an attempt to legitimize their exercise of power.

The events that followed the initial spread and acceptance of the Chavín religion also support the idea that it was being used as a means of legitimizing local power structures. According to Patterson:

> The increasing regionalization of Peruvian cultures during Early Horizon 3 and 4 suggests that the Chavín cult was breaking up into a series of local cults, each of which may have emphasized different aspects of the ancient religion but still maintained contact with the principal centers. (1971:44)

This process of regionalization is to be expected if the independent leadership groups in the different valleys were using the Chavín religion to suit their own particular ends in exercising power.

Overall, there are few data from which inferences can be made about the exercise of power in the coastal valleys during the Early Horizon. The presence of substantial populations in inland locations indirectly indicates that irrigation was probably present and provided a potential economic power base. The presence of monumental architecture indicates that this potential base was probably being exploited in at least some of the valleys, though not necessarily in all of them. The pervasiveness of the Chavín religion and its association with the monumental architecture suggest that a supplementary ideological power base was also being exploited. The absence of evidence of regularized warfare until the very end of the Early Horizon indicates that for most of the period there was no specialized military to provide either a second economic base or a physical base for exerting power. There is also no immediate evidence of a police force or for the regularized application of physical sanctions in the Initial Period or Early Horizon; although, this may be more an artifact of selective excavation and analysis rather than a reflection of reality.

In the Early Intermediate Period (c.100 B.C. to A.D. 900) the economic and ideological power bases inferred for the Early Horizon continue, and there is evidence for the addition of a physical power base as well. The clearest manifestations of power are found in the Moche occupation of the north coast valleys. Extensive direct evidence of an economic power base in the Moche area can be seen in centralized systems of irrigation canals which water entire valleys (Willey 1953; Kosok 1965). (The expansion of canals in the Early Intermediate and later periods may be a major reason why no earlier canals have yet been found.) Indications of the ideological power base again can be seen in the ceremonially oriented monumental architecture, the construction of which reached a peak in the Early Intermediate Period (Lumbreras 1974; Kosok 1965; Willey 1953; Moseley 1975b; Haas 1975). The physical power base is indicated by the evidence for endemic warfare, manifested in fortifications and the frequent artistic representation of elaborately clad warriors (Willey 1953; Kosok 1965; Topic and Topic 1978; Donnan 1978; Anders n.d.). The direct exploitation of a physical power base by societal leaders is also to be seen in the representation of physical sanctions being applied in various Moche art media, as described in chapter 4.

In terms of the development of state power relationships from the Early Horizon to the Early Intermediate in the Moche area, the complex of economic, ideological, and physical elements provided the leaders with a stronger combined base and means of exerting power. This increase in power is directly reflected in the greater size and number of large-scale labor projects carried out by the respondent Moche populations. While survey in the individual valleys has been extremely limited, the relative number of examples of monumental architecture found dating to the Early Intermediate Period is much greater than the number found dating to the Early Horizon (the time span is roughly the same for both periods) (Lumbreras 1974:68–69, 99–102; Lanning 1967:117; Kosok 1965:101–8; Willey 1953:354–58). The architecture of the later period is also of a considerably greater magnitude. Platform mounds, such as Huaca del Sol at the site of Moche and Huaca Grande at Pampa Grande (Moseley 1975b; Haas 1975), constructed in the Early Intermediate, stand over 50 m high with volumes of 1–3,000,000 cu m. Furthermore, the large Moche mounds that have been examined in detail (particularly Sol and Grande) were constructed in a relatively few discrete periods of intensive labor. There is at least one Early Horizon mound of a similar magnitude (Sechin Alto), but it apparently was constructed over a long period of time through a gradual accretionary process (William Isbell, personal communication 1979; Richard Keatinge, personal communication 1979).

Whether the numerous examples of monumental Moche architecture reflect an increase in scope of power, an increase in extension of power, or a combination of both cannot be fully determined from available archaeological evidence. Such a determination would require knowing the number of people and the amount of time involved in the construction of individual platform mounds and the relative size of governed populations in individual polities in the coastal valleys. No systematic studies have yet been conducted to recover either of these types of information. However, some indirect evidence would indicate there probably was an increase in both scope and extension of power in the Early Intermediate Moche occupation of the north coast. An increase in scope is expected given the addition of a physical base to the Moche power structure that was absent throughout most of the Early Horizon. A greater extension of power is also to be expected since centralized irrigation systems in the Early Intermediate Period were expanded to cover much larger areas.

In addition to the monumental manifestations of increased power, there are indications of the interrelationship between bases of power in the Moche material culture. Warriors in Moche art are frequently depicted as having supernatural characteristics, and almost all of the warfare related scenes appear to have some form of religious significance (Donnan 1978:182). Prisoners of war are also repeatedly shown being sacrificed in a ceremonial context. Ideology is similarly incorporated in artistic representations of the application of coercive sanctions. The clearest example of this is in the depiction of individuals tied to racks which are decorated with supernatural symbols (Donnan 1978:95). This general pattern of ritual identification of warriors, warfare, and physical sanctions can be seen as the use of ideology in the legitimization of a physical power base or bases.

There are also scenes showing fishing, hunting, craft production, and other economic activities in a ceremonial context. In one particular case there is a highly ritualized presentation of large quantities of foodstuffs to elaborately clad individuals by less well-clad individuals. This may be seen as the attachment of ideological significance to a distinct pattern of economic behavior (Donnan 1978:105). Another example of the apparent use of ideology to legitimize the position of a power-holding elite is found at the site of Pampa Grande. As discussed earlier (chapter 4), there is a high status residence located on top of the central platform mound (Huaca Grande) at the site. Since large parts of this mound clearly served some form of ceremonial function (Haas n.d.), the immediate physical location of the ___ 'e places it in a direct ceremonial context. The front wall of the r is also decorated with supernatural symbols, and its constr marked by the dedicatory burial of a llama and a child. W presently impossible to determine the exact role of the occup the residence, it is clear that their high status position was pr with a cloak of ideological legitimacy. Furthermore, the presen an *in situ* stone mace in the residence can be tentatively interp as indicating that there may have been some form of associatior tween the occupants and a military or police organization of the P Grande polity.

Looking at the whole of the Moche occupation of the north c it can be inferred that there was probably a triadic integration of e nomic, physical, and ideological bases in a unified power structure. The different bases complemented each other, and provided the Moche leaders with alternative strong and effective means of exerting power over their respondent populations. Following an obscure "Middle Horizon" about which virtually nothing is known, the triad of bases continues in the Late Intermediate Period on the north coast, but there is a tendency toward the increasing secularization of the central power structure. In other words, the role of ideology in the power structure apparently is not as strong as it is in the preceding periods (Keatinge et al. 1975).

While the intricacies of the power relationships in the Late Intermediate are far too complex to be adequately summarized here, some general observations can be made to demonstrate and interpret the trend toward secularization. In terms of political organization, the Late Intermediate witnessed the rise of a single dominant polity, the empire of the Chimu. With its capital at the city of Chan Chan in the Moche Valley, the Chimu empire expanded through military conquest and eventually came to rule most of the Peruvian coast from the far north all the way down to the central valley of Chillon (Lumbreras 1974:180). A series of kings headed the power structure of the empire, each of whom resided at Chan Chan. The general nature of the power exercised by these kings can be abstracted from both ethnohistoric and archaeological records.

The presence of extensive irrigation systems in the Moche Valley and other parts of the Chimu empire again provided the foundation for an economic power base, but for the first time on the north coast there is also evidence of the accumulation of extensive economic wealth as at least a secondary power base. Each of the kings lived in an enormous walled compound at Chan Chan (Conrad 1981), and within each of these compounds large concentrations of storage facilities have been found (Moseley 1975c; Day 1974). While the contents of these storage facilities have yet to be determined archaeologically, their very presence indicates that tremendous quantities of goods were being collected, kept, and provided with physical protection by the Chimu kings.

The large Chimu army reported in ethnohistoric records was headed by the king (Rowe 1948), thus providing him with one form of strong physical power base. While there is no evidence of a specialized police force, the ethnohistoric record indicates that physical sanctions were applied for a variety of criminal offenses (Rowe 1948). Furthermore, as was indicated in Moche art, the application of sanctions is couched in religious terms:

> Religion served as an excellent mechanism of social control because behavior is subject to supernatural rewards and punishments. The beginnings of law and justice appear in the extensive regulations that are associated with the developing church structure. Among the Chimu, disrespect to the temples and disobedience to civil laws were both punished by burying the culprit alive. Sacrifices were made to Si (the Moon) and to Pata (Orion) to gain their assistance in finding a robber; when he was caught, he, as well as his father and brothers, were handed to the victim for execution. (Lumbreras 1974:187–88)

This ideological legitimization accorded to physical force is also extended to the economic wealth of the kings, as particularly manifested in the extensive use of supernatural symbols to decorate the interiors of the compounds and the administrative buildings associated with the interior storage facilities (Lumbreras 1974:185; Moseley and Mackey 1973; Moseley 1975c:8). However, while ideology can be seen here as being utilized to legitimize the power of the Chimu kings, its overall role in the exercise of power at Chan Chan appears to be considerably less than it was at preceding large Moche sites such as Pampa Grande and Moche.

The greatest scope of power expressed in construction of huge ceremonial mounds in the Early Intermediate sites is expressed in the construction of massive compound walls, burial platforms for the kings, and storage facilities at Chan Chan (Moseley and Mackey 1974). In other words, the primary exertion of power at Chan Chan was oriented toward the construction of architecture which had an overt secular rather than sacred function. Another manifestation of the shift toward secularization in the Late Intermediate can be seen in the administrative units associated with the storage facilities in the compounds. These units, called "audiencias," are distinctive U-shaped structures that are strategically located so as to control all access to the numerous storerooms (Day 1974; Keatinge and Day 1973, 1974; Andrews 1974). They are also found in other sites outside Chan Chan in the Late Intermediate, and are consistently in an administrative/economic context (Keatinge and Day 1973). Similar structures have recently been found in the Early Intermediate occupation of a large site to the north of Chan Chan (the site of Pacatanamu in the Jequetepeque Valley); however, in this case, the structures are on top of platform mounds in a clear ceremonial context (Keatinge et al. 1975). The shift over time from a ceremonial to an economic context for the audiencias has been interpreted as representing a transition from an emphasized sacred orientation in the Early Intermediate to an emphasized secular orientation in the Late Intermediate:

Thus the audiencia may have evolved as an architectural form in the highly religious-ceremonial context of the huacas. Through time they could have become associated with the administrative activities of the compounds, activities which are represented in their most developed form by the audiencia-storage complexes at Chan Chan. (Keatinge et al. 1975:129)

There is no question that religion and ideology remained important elements in the political organization of the Chimu empire, but they did not appear to have played the transcendent role that they played in the preceding Early Intermediate Period. A number of factors can be seen as influencing the relative decline of the ideological power base. The Chimu polity expanded by conquest, and as a result it is highly probable that many of the subordinate populations did not share the religious ideology of the Chimu kings. Consequently, the use of this ideology for purposes of legitimization would have had limited effectiveness, leading to greater reliance on secular economic and physical means of gaining the compliance of the populations. In terms of the native Chimu population, the strength of the army and the substantial accumulation of economic wealth by the kings provided them with increased potential for applying secular sanctions, thus reducing the need for the legitimizing use of ideology.

The secularized Chimu polity marks the end of the autochthonous development of the state on the coast of Peru. In the middle of the fifteenth century the Chimu were conquered by the highland Inca, and shortly thereafter the coast, along with the rest of Peru, came under the domination of the Spanish. The above brief outline of more than three thousand years of political evolution on the Peruvian coast demonstrates, however sketchily, the applicability of a power framework for understanding the long-term process of state development. Viewed in terms of power relationships between leaders and their populations, the development of the state on the Peruvian coast can be seen to follow predictable patterns, and many of the archaeological manifestations observed in coastal societies can be more readily and fully explained. By looking at communal labor projects, fortifications, warriors, religious art, population size, and subsistence systems as potential expressions of interrelated power variables, a much more comprehensive picture of coastal political evolution can be drawn than if they are looked at as in any way separate or independent of each other.

[Chapter 9]

Conclusions and Prospects

The twin questions of why and how the governmental institutions of state level societies first arose have been extensively debated in the past and will undoubtedly continue to be debated in the future. The attempted test and synthesis of the conflict and integration models offered in chapter 4 will not put an end to the philosophical struggle between the two schools of thought. Nor will the review of specific theories in chapter 5 bring to a sudden halt further theorizing about how specific states arose. The theoretical and empirical study of the evolution of the state is still in a stage of adolescence, and decisive answers to myriad questions cannot be provided at this point. However, both the synthesis and the review do point out that competing theories or models may indeed complement rather than contradict each other and can be brought together into a more coherent whole. Instead of proclaiming victory for any one position, it would seem to be more productive to acknowledge that the emergence of the state involved both conflict and integrative elements, and that trade, warfare, irrigation, and perhaps one or more additional factors may have each served as different routes to statehood.

Bringing these all together is not simply an abdication to eclecticism; rather, the cumulative work of different theorists points out certain overarching patterns that appear to be characteristic of the general process of state formation. Specifically, the initial centralization of a social system involves a process of integration through trade, warfare, irrigation, or some other means. The integrative process itself, in turn, results in stratification of the system, with a leadership group gaining increased access to basic resources by controlling either their production or procurement. This control then provides that leadership group with an economic base for exerting coercive power over the rest of the population.

With an economic power base as a starting point, I have argued in chapters 6 and 7 that the leaders in emergent states can be expected

to initiate and/or exploit additional physical and ideological p
bases in order to supplement and insure the continuity of their exe
of power. Thus, developed state power structures will be built on s
form of economic foundation with an overlay of physical and i
logical elements. These general arguments about the developmer
state power relationships can serve as a broad framework for ir
preting particular patterns that are observed in the archaeological
cord of prehistoric societies. Specific interpretations have been offe
above for a number of such patterns observed in complex societies of
the New World: 1) the efflorescent appearance of monumental architecture and other communal labor projects in Formative Olmec
sites in Mesoamerica and Initial Period/Early Horizon coastal sites in
Peru can be explained as manifestations of the emergence of coercive
state power relationships; 2) major differences in labor expenditure
between Olmec sites and the site of Teotihuacán can be explained as
differences in the nature of the economic base and the potential extension of power of the respective leaders; 3) the strong correlation
between religious iconography and the construction of monumental
architecture on the coast of Peru can be explained as the use of an
ideological power base to legitimize the exercise of power by societal
rulers; 4) the correlation between warfare and religion in Moche art
can be similarly explained; 5) the secularization of the power structure
in the Peruvian Late Intermediate Period can be explained as the
increased effectiveness of secular economic and physical bases of
power.

While not conclusively documented, these examples nevertheless
illustrate how a focus on power can provide significant insight into
similarities and differences between state societies as well as into both
long- and short-term processes of state evolution. Basically, little of
what I have argued is totally new to the literature on early states, but
I have tried to integrate diverse ideas into a single comprehensive
framework that has greater strength than a series of individual parts
considered separately. Furthermore, I believe the framework can be
expanded beyond the basic outline presented in previous chapters,
and that it brings to light and emphasizes critical questions that need
to be addressed through research if we are to arrive at a satisfactory
understanding of the processes of state evolution.

Possible areas for expansion of the framework might include a consideration of urbanization, cultural collapse, revolution, and the re-

lationship between chiefdoms and states. In regard to urbanization, for example, Wheatley (1971, 1972) has pointed out that the world's first urban centers consistently have a strong ceremonial orientation. Looked at in terms of power, this pattern may be seen as a manifestation of states' leaders attempting to exercise both ideological and physical power over their populations. Prior to the modern innovations of radio and television, exploitation of an ideological base in the process of legitimization required face-to-face contact between the power holders and the respondents. The costs of exercising such a base thus are greater when a population is dispersed than when they are clustered together. It is cheaper to support one priest who can preach to a thousand people at a time than to support ten priests who preach to a hundred people at a time. Furthermore, people may be more cheaply and efficiently controlled by a police force when they are aggregated into a city than when they are spread out over the countryside. People may thus be drawn or forced into cities ostensibly for economic, ceremonial, defensive, or any number of other reasons, but once there, they would be significantly more susceptible to the exercise of physical and ideological power by their leaders. Undoubtedly there have been other causal variables influencing the process of early urbanization, but reducing the power costs of state leaders offers some interesting possibilities for investigation.

Similarly, a focus on power may provide an alternative perspective on the collapse of early states and on the potentially related phenomenon of peasant revolutions. As argued earlier, the initial economic power base in early states is specifically to support additional physical and ideological bases, and together the three form a stable governing power structure. If this is indeed the case, then a weakening of the economic base seriously threatens the stability of the entire power structure. While intensified exploitation of the physical and ideological bases might temporarily shore up the attenuated structure, they both have limited potential without continued economic support. A police force is extremely expensive to maintain in the first place, and increasing its size increases its cost without proportionate increases in its effectiveness (see Bierstedt 1950). On the other hand, while intensifying the ideological base may significantly enhance the "legitimacy" of the power structure, at the bottom line the effectiveness of an ideological base is dependent on more substantive economic and physical means of exerting power. (You can get people to believe in paying taxes, but extracting payment without some form of economic or physical sanctions is somewhat more difficult.)

Beyond the basic limitations of the other two power bases, the loss or debilitation of the economic base introduces an additional structural weakness into the power structure. Whereas with the three bases interacting together there is a balanced triadic relationship, elimination of one of the three produces in inherently more unstable dyadic relationship. As Georg Simmel points out (1950:135–36), in a triad there is always a mediator to resolve conflicts between any two components, but in a dyad the mediator is lacking. Consequently, in a state with a weakened economic power base, exercising power over the population is not only more expensive and less effective, but the power structure itself is more open to internal conflict and strife. Such a state is thus more susceptible to collapse either through self-destruction of the power structure, revolution of the population, or a combination thereof.

The Classic Mayan Collapse (Culbert 1973—particularly Willey and Shimkin 1973 and Sanders 1973), for example, would appear to fit this pattern quite nicely. In this case, the initial economic power based on control over subsistence resources and trade goods was weakened by environmental deterioration and external events. Accompanying this weakening, warfare and the military increased in importance, and religious architecture reached a frantic peak. The decline of economics, along with the rise of religion and the role of the military took place over the course of at least two hundred years, before a total collapse put an end to the entire system. Although I have admittedly oversimplified an extremely complex situation, I believe the Mayan case illustrates how a particular historical event can be fit into a wider processual model based on a consideration of power.

Another area of research where the concept of power may be of some use lies in the transition from chiefdoms to states. It is virtually accepted as fact in the anthropological literature that a chiefdom or ranked stage is antecedent to the emergence of the state in the universal scheme of cultural evolution (White 1959; Steward 1955; Fried 1967; Service 1971a, 1975; Adams 1975). However, if we look at the emergence of initial state-level power structures, the necessity of an antecedent chiefdom-type of organization comes into question. In each of the specific theories of state formation reviewed above, societies come under various pressures to centralize and consolidate their organizational structures, and it is the very process of centralization and consolidation that gives certain members of those societies power by controlling the production or procurement of basic resources. It is not a necessary component in the theories that the societies *must* be hierarchically arranged prior to undergoing the transformation. In other words it is equally possible that both ranked and unranked societies, chiefdoms, and tribes may have responded in similar ways to similar pressures and emerged as states. Thus, we may find chiefdoms preceding states in the archaeological record of some areas, as is the case in the Cotton Preceramic on the coast of Peru; and we may also find states that seem to blossom out of almost nowhere, as may be the case at San Lorenzo in the Olmec area (Coe and Diehl 1980). I believe, in fact, that the absence of a preceding chiefdom stage may be one of the major reasons behind resistance to the idea that the Olmec were at a state level.

Consideration of power may also help to explain why some chiefdoms do *not* evolve into states. Whereas all chiefs may exercise ideological power, and some may even exercise limited physical power, environmental conditions may prevent chiefs in some areas from ever gaining the necessary economic power base. Specifically, in areas where all basic resources are naturally available and/or where subsistence production is decentralized, it simply may not be possible for leaders to gain control over the production or procurement of basic resources. Thus, in the northwest coast, the hunting and gathering subsistence mode, coupled with the relative abundance of resources, blocked the path of anyone seeking control over production or procurement activities. In Hawaii, where Earle (1978) has demonstrated decentralized production and distribution of resources, the chiefs would have had no way to establish the coercive economic base necessary to move on to statehood. (Introduction of guns by early Europeans changed the aboriginal system dramatically, however, and did provide a very effective coercive means for exercising power.) I would predict similar inabilities on the part of chiefs in other islands of Polynesia as well, and at least a similar *kind* of pattern in other world areas where chiefdoms flourished and states did not emerge aboriginally (e.g., parts of Africa and the Circum-Caribbean).

Before leaving chiefdoms, I should return to a problem alluded to several times earlier: what are the potentials and limitations in the scope of power exercised in chiefdoms? In preceding chapters I have presented an argument that comes dangerously close to claiming that whenever you have monumental architecture you have state-level society. Phrased somewhat differently, does monumental architecture necessarily represent state-level power being exercised in order to get populations to do things they would not otherwise do? If so, such architecture would serve as another nice, tidy pigeonholing mechanism for archaeologists. In fact, this kind of claim has a long history in the literature, and an equally long history of being assaulted on all sides. On the one hand, archaeologists are constantly looking for markers to tell them what they are working with, and on the other they eschew simplistic attempts to equate single phenomena, such as monumental architecture, writing, or cites, with complex political organization of the state.

However, I do not think I have made this simplistic kind of equation. In Shang China, for example, where except for the wall at Chengchou, truly monumental architecture is lacking, I would still argue that the coercive power structure of a state is present. In this case, as Chang amply demonstrates (1980: 236–38), instead of building monuments to legitimize their position, the Shang leaders used their power to build personal wealth and increase their own well-being.

But what about the other way around? Does the *presence* of monumental architecture signify a state-level power structure? Are the massive mounds of the Mississippian cultures in North America, for example, manifestations of the coercive power relationship expected in state societies? I do not know. I do not believe, however, that a negative answer is necessarily self-evident. I think we need a great deal more information about the compliance costs to the populations involved in building such mounds and about potential bases of power available to the leaders of the societies, before we can provide definitive statements about the nature of their respective forms of political organization. While a great deal of energy has been expended to prove the presence of social ranking in these societies, I think insufficient attention has been paid to the possibility of stratification and accompanying institutions of the state (cf. Sears 1954).

For some reason, most people seem willing to believe that the basically noncoercive power of a chief is sufficient to induce a population to contribute its energy toward the construction of massive mounds and other large-scale communal labor projects. Yet the evidence that has been cited to date is less than convincing.

In one of the very few cases where ethnographic analogs have been used to deal with the question, Renfrew (1973b:138–41) turns to Borneo for cases of cooperative construction of monuments by relatively small prestate communities. In particular, he cites a Borneo man who, in exchange for all his worldly goods, has a monument raised to himself. This "monument" built by the community consists of a mound of rocks "higher than the long-house is off the ground, and twice the width anyone can leap" (Harrisson 1959:12; cited in Renfrew 1973b:139). He cites another case where single large stones were transported from "a distant place" and erected as memorials. He then argues that if such a practice were carried out annually or as part of an annual cycle, very impressive monuments could eventually result. But he goes on to state: "I do not know of an ethnographic instance where the erection of such monuments takes place as part of a regular annual festivity of this kind" (1973b:140). While the details of the Borneo cases are a little sketchy, the "monuments" being constructed do not seem to be remotely analogous to the accomplishments of the Olmec, Mississippian, Initial Period Peruvians, or any number of other possible prehistoric states (nor does Renfrew make such a claim).

The experimental and ethnographic work done by Erasmus (1965) and Kaplan (1963) in Mesoamerica is frequently cited as evidence that considerable large-scale construction is possible without the exertion of coercive power by a state power structure. However, in spite of the high quality of their work, it is not particularly germane to the question at hand. In both cases, they were working with people who ultimately were part of a highly stratified, capitalist economic system. While labor may well be contributed voluntarily under such conditions, it is necessarily within the context of a *state*. It thus tells us absolutely nothing about what may or may not happen in chiefdoms. There are too many external variables that cannot be factored out in order to draw any kind of reasonable analogy. The coercive power of a state, particularly in such modern states as are found in Mesoamerica today, is always a potentially influencing variable, *whether or not it is directly manifested in any specific social situation.*

The problem of whether chiefdoms build monumental architecture is neither minor nor esoteric, and it is not going to be easily resolved. On an empirical level, much more ethnohistorical research needs to be done on the organization and practices of early chiefdoms that existed prior to the influences of invading colonial states. However, while we may find no positive evidence in the ethnohistoric record, it is still a distinct possibility that some *pre-contact* chiefdoms may in fact have constructed giant monuments in the absence of any kind of coercive state power structure. Archaeologists thus cannot depend wholeheartedly on the ethnohistoric record to provide the answers. It is necessary to design and implement research that will reveal the nature of the power structure in prehistoric societies where large and small mounds are found. For example, is there a potential economic power base that might have been exploited by the Mississippian leaders? If so, what would have been the means of exercising this base, and what would have been the refusal costs to the population? If not, what kind of power base was being exploited by the leaders to get their populations to contribute so much labor? These are the kinds of empirical questions that need to be explicitly considered if we are ever going to understand the organization of the Mississippians or any other complex prehistoric polity.

On a theoretical level, the issue of monumental architecture in chiefdoms has broad ramifications beyond debates over whether a particular society is a chiefdom or state. It is tied into larger questions about the basic nature of the relationship that pertains between a population and its governing body. Do people willingly contribute large-scale, nonsubsistence labor in response to the demands of an essentially noncoercive and beneficient leadership? Or, is such labor contributed only when the societal leaders have extensive coercive power at their command?

Both of these, in turn, can be subsumed under larger questions about why populations obey the demands of their leaders and what is the role of government in complex societies. Once again, we come full circle back to the conflict/integration debate, and are faced with fundamental problems that political scientists have been attacking since at least the time of Plato and Aristotle. These problems are not likely to go away of their own accord, and to my mind they constitute the primary research domain that can and should be addressed in the archaeological investigation of state evolution. Archaeology is the only discipline that can tell us how government began, the nature of the world's first governments, and the role those governments played in the organization of their respective political systems.

In arguments outlined above, I have come to the conclusion that while integration played a major role in the original coalescence of governmental institutions, maintenance of a system of stratification and coercion lie at the heart of the first true governments. Empirical support for this position is not great, but new data are required to provide more conclusive answers about the emergence and development of governmental institutions in state-level societies. The data presently at hand have allowed us to make great strides in the study of state evolution, and they provide an excellent background for directing future research. However, it is time to begin asking new questions and establishing new priorities if archaeology is to fulfill its ultimate potential as a political science.

References

Adams, Richard E. W. 1977. "Rio Bec Archaeology and the Rise of the Maya Civilization." In Richard E. W. Adams, ed., *The Origins of Maya Civilization*, pp. 77–100. Albuquerque: University of New Mexico Press.

Adams, Richard N. 1975. *Energy and Structure: A Theory of Social Power*. Austin: University of Texas Press.

Adams, Robert McC. 1966. *The Evolution of Urban Society: Early Mesopotamia and Prehispanic Mexico*. Chicago: Aldine.

Adams, Robert McC. and Hans J. Nissen. 1972. *The Uruk Countryside*. Chicago: University of Chicago Press.

Allchin, Bridget and Raymond Allchin. 1968. *The Birth of Indian Civilization*. Harmondsworth: Penguin Books.

Allen, W. L. and J. B. Richardson, III. 1971. "The Reconstruction of Kinship from Archaeological Data: The Concepts, the Methods and the Feasibility." *American Antiquity*, 36:41–53.

An, Chin-huai. 1957. "The Ancient Remains of Cheng'chou." *Wenwu*, 8:16–20.

Anders, Martha B. n.d. "Formal Storage Facilities in Pampa Grande, Peru. A Preliminary Report of Excavations." Manuscript, Cornell University, Ithaca, N.Y.

Andrews, Anthony P. 1974. "The U-shaped Structures at Chan Chan, Peru." *Journal for Field Archaeology*, 1:241–64.

Apter, David. 1968. "Government." *International Encyclopedia of Social Sciences*, David L. Sills, ed. New York: Macmillan and Free Press.

Asad, Talal. 1973. "The Beduin as a Military Force: Notes on Some Aspects of Power Relations Between Nomads and Sedentaries in Historical Perspective." In C. Nelson, ed., *The Desert and the Sown: Nomads in Wider Society*, pp. 98–115. Berkeley: Institute of International Studies.

Austin, John. 1873. *Lectures on Jurisprudence.* 4th ed. (orig. 1840). Robert Campbell, ed. London: F. D. Linn.

Balandier, Georges. 1970. *Political Anthropology.* New York: Pantheon Books.

Barker, Ernest. 1947. Introduction to *Social Contract: Essays by Locke, Hume, and Rousseau,* Ernest Barker, ed. New York: Oxford University Press.

Barton, Roy F. 1949. *The Kalingas: Their Institutions and Custom Law.* Chicago: University of Chicago Press.

Bawden, Garth. 1977. "Galindo and the Nature of the Middle Horizon in Northern Coastal Peru." Ph.D. dissertation, Harvard University, Cambridge.

Bell, Roderick, David V. Edwards, and R. Harrison Wagner, eds. 1969. *Political Power: A Reader in Theory and Research.* New York: Free Press.

Bennett, Wendel C. 1944. *The North Highlands of Peru: Excavations in the Callejon de Huaylas and at Chavín de Huantar.* Anthropological Papers of the American Museum of Natural History, vol. 39, part 1.

—— 1950. *The Gallinazo Group: Viru Valley, Peru.* Yale University Publications in Anthropology, no. 40.

Benson, Elizabeth P. 1972. *The Mochica, a Culture of Peru.* New York: Praeger.

Benson, Elizabeth P., ed. 1971. *Dumbarton Oaks Conference on Chavín.* Washington, D.C.: Dumbarton Oaks Research Library and Collection, Trustees for Harvard University.

Bernal, Ignacio. 1968. "Views of Olmec Culture." In Elizabeth P. Benson, ed., *Dumbarton Oaks Conference on the Olmec,* pp. 135–42. Washington, D.C.: Dumbarton Oaks Research Library and Collection, Trustees for Harvard University.

—— 1976. *The Olmec World.* Doris Heyden and Fernando Horcasitas, tr. Berkeley: University of California Press. Paperback.

Bierstedt, Robert. 1950. "An Analysis of Social Power." *American Sociological Review,* 15:730–38.

Binford, Lewis R. 1972. *An Archaeological Perspective.* New York: Academic Press.

Bird, Junius. 1948. "Preceramic Cultures in Chicama and Viru." *Society for American Archaeology Memoir,* 4:21–28.

Blanton, Richard E. 1976. "The Origins of Monte Albán." In Charles

E. Cleland, ed., *Culture Change and Continuity: Essays in Honor of James Bennett Griffin*, pp. 223–32. New York: Academic Press.

Bohannon, Paul. 1968. "Law." *International Encyclopedia of Social Sciences*, David L. Sills, ed. New York: Macmillan and Free Press.

—— 1977. "Anthropology and the Law." In Sol Tax and Leslie G. Freeman, eds., *Horizons of Anthropology*, 2d ed., pp. 290–99. Chicago: Aldine.

Borhegyi, Stephan F. 1965. "Archaeological Synthesis of the Guatemalan Highlands." In Gordon R. Willey, ed., *Handbook of Middle American Indians*, vol. 2: *Archaeology of Southern Mesoamerica*, part 1, pp. 3–58. Austin: University of Texas Press.

Boserup, Ester. 1965. *The Conditions of Agricultural Growth*. Chicago: Aldine.

Braun, David P. and Stephen Plog. 1980. "Tribalization in Prehistoric North America." Paper presented at the 79th Annual Meeting of the American Anthropological Association, Washington, D.C.

Brown, James A., ed. 1971. *Approaches to the Social Dimensions of Mortuary Practices*. Society for American Archaeology, Memoir 25.

Buikstra, Jame. 1976. *Hopewell in the Lower Illinois Valley: A Regional Study of Human Biological Variability and Prehistoric Mortuary Behavior*. Northwestern Archaeological Program Scientific Papers, vol. 2, Evanston.

Bullard, William R., Jr. 1960. "Maya Settlement Pattern in Northeastern Peten, Guatemala." *American Antiquity*, 25:355–72.

Carneiro, Robert L. 1970. "A Theory of the Origin of the State." *Science*, 169:733–38.

—— 1978. "Political Expansion as an Expression of the Principle of Competitive Exclusion." In Ronald Cohen and Elman R. Service, eds., *Origins of the State: The Anthropology of Political Evolution*, pp. 205–24. Philadelphia: Institute for the Study of Human Issues.

—— 1979. "Conference Synthesis." Paper presented at the conference "The Transition to Statehood in the New World: Toward a Synthesis," Hamilton College, Clinton, N.Y.

Chagnon, Napoleon. 1968. *Yanomamo: The Fierce People*. New York: Holt, Rinehart & Winston.

Chang, Kwang-chih. 1976. *Early Chinese Civilization: Anthropological Perspectives*. Cambridge: Harvard University Press.

—— 1977. *The Archaeology of Ancient China*. 3d ed. New Haven: Yale University Press.

—— 1980 *Shang Civilization*. New Haven: Yale University Press.

Cheng, Te-k'un. 1960. *Archaeology in China: Shang China*, vol. 2. Cambridge, England: Heffner.

Childe, V. Gordon. 1936. *Man Makes Himself* (paperback ed., 1951). New York: New American Library, Mentor Books.

—— 1942. *What Happened in History* (paperback ed. 1964). Harmondsworth: Penguin Books.

—— 1972. "The Urban Revolution." In Mark P. Leone, ed., *Contemporary Archaeology*, pp. 43–51. Carbondale: Southern Illinois University Press. Reprinted from *Town Planning Review* 21:3–17 (1950).

Ch'u, T'ung-tsu. 1961. *Law and Society in Traditional China*. Paris: Mouton.

Claessen, Henry J. M. and Peter Skalnik. 1978. *The Early State*. The Hague: Mouton.

Cobean, R. H., Michael D. Coe, E. A. Perry, Jr., K. K. Turekian and D. P. Kharkar. 1971. "Obsidian Trade at San Lorenzo Tenochtitlan, Mexico." *Science*, 174:666–71.

Coe, Michael D. 1962. "An Olmec Design on an Early Peruvian Vessel." *American Antiquity*, 27:579–80.

—— 1963. "Cultural Development in Southern Mesoamerica." In B. J. Meggers and C. Evans. eds., *Aboriginal Cultural Development in Latin America: An Interpretive Review*, pp. 27–44. Washington, D.C.: Smithsonian Miscellaneous Collections, vol. 146, no. 1.

—— 1965. *The Jaguar's Children: Pre-Classic Central Mexico*. New York: Museum of Primitive Art.

—— 1968a. "San Lorenzo and the Olmec Civilization." In Elizabeth P. Benson, ed., *Dumbarton Oaks Conference on the Olmec*, pp. 41–78. Washington, D.C.: Dumbarton Oaks Research Library and Collection, Trustees for Harvard University.

—— 1968b. *America's First Civilization*. Eau Claire, Wisc.: Hale.

Coe, Michael D. and Richard Diehl. 1980. *In the Land of the Olmec*, vol. 1:. *The Archaeology of San Lorenzo Tenochtitlan*; vol. 2: *The People of the River*. Austin: University of Texas Press.

Coe, William R. 1965. "Tikal: Ten Years of Study of a Maya Ruin in the Lowlands of Guatemala." *Expedition* 8 (1).

Cohen, Ronald. 1978. "Introduction." In Ronald Cohen and Elman

R. Service, eds., *Origins of the State: The Anthropology of Political Evolution*, pp. 1–20. Philadelphia: Institute for the Study of Human Issues.

Conrad, Geoffrey. 1981. "Cultural Materialism, Split Inheritance, and the Expansion of Ancient Peruvian Empires." *American Antiquity*, 46:3–26.

Covarrubias, Miguel. 1957. *Indian Art of Mexico and Central America*. New York: Knopf.

Culbert, T. Patrick, ed. 1973. *The Classic Maya Collapse*. Albuquerque: University of New Mexico Press.

Dahl, Robert A. 1968. "Power." *International Encyclopedia of Social Sciences*, David L. Sills, ed. New York: Macmillan and Free Press.

—— 1969. "The Concept of Power." In Roderick Bell et al., eds., *Political Power: A Reader in Theory and Research*, pp. 79–93. New York: Free Press. Reprinted from *Behavioral Sciences*, 2:201–15 (1957).

Daniel, Glyn. 1968. *The First Civilizations*. New York: Apollo Editions.

Day, Kent C. 1974. "Monumental Architecture at Chan Chan, Peru." Ph.D. dissertation, Harvard University, Cambridge.

—— 1975. "Midseason Report: ROM Lambayeque Project." Royal Ontario Museum, Toronto. Mimeo.

—— 1976. "Storage and Labor Service; Two Aspects of Ancient Peruvian Socio-Economic Organization." Paper presented at seminar on "Chan Chan: City and Hinterland", School of American Research, Sante Fe.

Dean, Jeffrey, Alexander J. Lindsay, Jr., and William J. Robinson. 1978. "Prehistoric Settlement in Long House Valley, Northeastern Arizona." In Robert C. Euler and George Gumerman, eds., *Investigations of the Southwestern Anthropological Research Group: An Experiment in Archaeological Cooperation*, pp. 25–44. Flagstaff: Museum of Northern Arizona.

DeBary, William T., Wing-Tsit Chan, and Burton Watson, comps. 1960. *Sources of Chinese Tradition*, vol. 1. New York: Columbia University Press.

Deetz, James D. F. 1965. *The Dynamics of Stylistic Change in Arikara Ceramics*. Illinois Studies in Anthropology no. 4. Urbana: University of Illinois Press.

Diamond, Stanley. 1974. *In Search of the Primitive*. New Brunswick, Transaction Books.

Donnan, Christopher B. 1978. *Moche Art of Peru*. Los Angeles: Museum of Cultural History, University of California.

Drucker, Philip. 1952. *La Venta, Tabasco: A Study of Olmec Ceramics and Art*. Bureau of American Ethnology Bulletin 153. Washington, D.C.

—— 1965. *Cultures of the North Pacific Coast*. San Francisco: Chandler.

Drucker, Philip, Robert F. Heizer, and J. J. Squier. 1959. *Excavations at LaVenta, Tabasco, 1955*. Bureau of American Ethnology Bulletin 170. Washington, D.C.

Durkheim, Emile. 1893. *Division of Labor in Society*. George Simpson, tr. New York: Free Press, 1933.

Earle, Timothy K. 1977. "A Reappraisal of Redistribution: Complex Hawaiian Chiefdoms." In Timothy K. Earle and Jonathon E. Ericson, eds., *Exchange Systems in Prehistory*, pp. 213–28. New York: Academic Press.

—— 1978. "Economic and Social Organization of a Complex Chiefdom: The Halelea District, Kaua'i, Hawaii." Museum of Anthropology, Ann Arbor, University of Michigan Anthropological Papers no. 63.

Easton, David. 1957. "An Approach to the Analysis of Political Systems." *World Politics*, 9:383–400.

—— 1965. *A Systems Analysis of Political Life*. New York: Wiley.

Emmett, Dorothy. 1954. "The Concept of Power." *Proceedings of the Aristotelian Society*, 54:1–26.

Engel, Frederic. 1966. "Le Complexe Preceramique d'El Paraiso (Perou)." *Journal de la Societe des Americanistes*, 54:43–96.

Engels, Friedrich, 1891. *The Origin of the Family, Private Property, and the State*. Eleanor Burke Leacock, ed. New York: International Publishers, 1972.

Erasmus, Charles J. 1965. "Monument Building: Some Field Experiments." *Southwestern Journal of Anthropology*, 21:277–301.

Euler, Robert C. and George J. Gumerman. 1978. *Investigations of the Southwestern Anthropological Research Group: An Experiment in Archaeological Cooperation*. Flagstaff: Museum of Northern Arizona.

Fairservis, Walter A., Jr. 1975. *The Roots of Ancient India*. 2d ed. Chicago; University of Chicago Press.

Fanon, Franz. 1966. *The Wretched of the Earth*. New York: Grove Press.

Fei, Hsiao-t'ung. 1953. *China's Gentry*. Chicago: University of Chicago Press.

Feldman, Robert A. 1977. "Life in Ancient Peru." *Field Museum of Natural History Bulletin*, 48:12–17.

Ferguson, Adam. 1819. *An Essay on the History of Civil Society*. 8th ed. Philadelphia: A. Finley.

Flannery, Kent V. 1972. "The Cultural Evolution of Civilizations." *Annual Review of Ecology and Systematics*, 3:399–426.

Flannery, Kent V., ed. 1976. *The Early Mesoamerican Village*. New York: Academic Press.

Flannery, Kent V. and Joyce Marcus. 1976. "Evolution of Public Building in Formative Oacaca." In Charles E. Cleland, ed., *Cultural Change and Continuity: Essays in Honor of James Bennett Griffith*, pp. 205–22. New York: Academic Press.

Fogelson, Raymond D. and Richard N. Adams, eds. 1977. *The Anthropology of Power*. New York: Academic Press.

Frankfort, Henri. 1951. *The Birth of Civilization in the Near East*. Garden City, N.Y.: Doubleday.

Fried, Morton H. 1960. "On the Evolution of Social Stratification and the State." In Stanley Diamond, ed., *Culture in History: Essays in Honor of Paul Radin*, pp. 713–31. New York: Columbia University Press.

—— 1961. "Warfare, Military Organization, and the Evolution of Society." *Anthropologica*, 3:134–47.

—— 1967. *The Evolution of Political Society: An Essay in Political Anthropology*. New York: Random House.

—— 1968. "State: The Institution." *International Encyclopedia of Social Sciences*, David L. Sills, ed. New York: Macmillan and Free Press.

—— 1975. *The Notion of Tribe*. Menlo Park, Calif.: Cummings.

—— 1978. "The State, the Chicken, and the Egg, or What Came First." In Ronald Cohen and Elman R. Service, eds., *Origins of the State: The Anthropology of Political Evolution*, pp. 35–48. Philadelphia: Institute for the Study of Human Issues.

Gay, C. T. E. 1967. "The Oldest Paintings in the New World." *Natural History*, 76(4):28–35.

—— 1972. *Chalcacingo*. Portland, Ore.: International Scholarly Book Service.

Gearing, Frederick. 1962. *Priests and Warriors: Social Structures for*

Cherokee Politics in the 18th Century." American Anthropological Association Memoir 93.

Gluckman, Max. 1940. "The Kingdom of the Zulu of South Africa." In Meyer Fortes and E. E. Evans-Prichard, eds., *African Political Systems*, pp. 25–55. New York: Oxford University Press.

—— 1955. *Custom and Conflict in Africa.* Oxford: Blackwell.

Goldman, Irving. 1970. *Ancient Polynesian Society.* Chicago: University of Chicago Press.

Grebinger, Paul. 1973. "Prehistoric Social Organization in Chaco Canyon, New Mexico: An Alternative Reconstruction." *The Kiva*, 39:3–24.

Grennes-Ravitz, Ronald A. 1974. "The Olmec Presence at Iglesia Vieja, Morelos." In Norman Hammond, ed., *Mesoamerican Archaeology: New Approaches*, pp. 99–108. Austin: University of Texas Press.

Grove, David. 1968. "The Pre-Classic Olmec in Central Mexico: Site Distribution and Inferences." In Elizabeth P. Benson, ed., *Dumbarton Oaks Conference on the Olmec*, pp. 179–85. Washington, D.C.: Dumbarton Oaks Research Library and Collection, Trustees for Harvard University.

—— 1974. "The Highland Olmec Manifestation: A Consideration of What It Is and Isn't." In Norman Hammond, ed., *Mesoamerican Archaeology: New Approaches*, pp. 109–28. Austin: University of Texas Press.

—— 1978. "Olmec Monument Mutilation." Paper presented at the 77th Annual Meeting of the American Anthropological Association, Los Angeles.

Grove, David C., Kenneth G. Hirth, David E. Buge, and Ann Cyphers. 1976. "Settlement and Cultural Development at Chalcatzingo." *Science*, 192:1203–10.

Gumplowicz, Ludwig. 1899. *The Outlines of Sociology.* 2d English language edition. Irving L. Horowitz, ed. New York: Paine-Whitman, 1963.

Haas, Jonathan. 1975. "Huaca Excavations at the Site of Pampa Grande, Peru." Paper presented at the 41st Annual Meeting of the Society for American Archaeology, St. Louis.

—— 1977. "The Nature of Prehistoric Government." Paper presented at the 76th Annual Meeting of the American Anthropological Association, Houston.

—— 1980. "Troubles with Tribes: An Archaeological Approach to an Anthropological Problem." Paper presented at the 79th Annual Meeting of the American Anthropological Association, Washington, D.C.

—— n.d. "Excavations on Huaca Grande: An Initial View of the Elite at Pampa Grande, Peru." Manuscript.

Hammond, Norman. 1977a. "Ex Oriente Lux: A View from Belize." In Richard E. W. Adams, ed., *The Origins of Maya Civilization*, pp. 45–76. Albuquerque: University of New Mexico Press.

—— 1977b. "The Earliest Maya." *Scientific American*, 236:116–33.

Harris, Marvin. 1968. *The Rise of Anthropological Theory*. New York: Crowell.

—— 1974. *Cows, Pigs, Wars, and Witches: The Riddles of Culture*. New York: Vintage Books.

—— 1975. *Culture, People, Nature*. New York: Crowell.

—— 1977. *Cannibals and Kings*. New York: Random House.

—— 1979. *Cultural Materialism: The Struggle for a Science of Culture*. New York: Random House.

Harrisson, Tom. 1959. *World Within*. London: Cresset Press.

Harsanyi, John C. 1969. "Measurement of Social Power, Opportunity Costs, and the Theory of Two-Person Bargaining Games." In Roderick Bell, et al., eds., *Political Power: A Reader in Theory and Research*, pp. 226–38. New York: Free Press. Reprinted from *Behavioral Science* 7:67–80 (1962).

Hastings, C. Mansfield and Michael E. Moseley. 1975. "Adobes of Huaca del Sol and Huaca de la Luna." *American Antiquity*, 40:196–203.

Hatch, James W. 1976. "Status in Death: Principles of Ranking in Dallas Culture Mortuary Remains." Ph.D. dissertation, Pennsylvania State University, University Park.

Haury, Emil. 1976. *The Hohokam*. Tucson: University of Arizona Press.

Haviland, William A. 1967. "Stature at Tikal, Guatemala: Implications for Ancient Maya Demography and Social Organization." *American Antiquity*, 36:316–25.

—— 1970. "Tikal Guatamala and Mesoamerican Urbanism." *World Archaeology*, 2:186–98.

Heizer, Robert F. 1960. "Agriculture and the Theocratic State in Lowland Southeastern Mexico." *American Antiquity*, 26:215–22.

—— 1966. "Ancient Heavy Transport, Methods and Achievements." *Science*, 153:821–30.

—— 1968. "New Observations on La Venta." In Elizabeth P. Benson, ed., *Dumbarton Oaks Conference on the Olmec*, pp. 9–40. Washington, D.C.: Dumbarton Oaks Research Library and Collection, Trustees for Harvard University.

Hill, James N. 1970. *Broken K Pueblo: Prehistoric Social Organization in the American Southwest*. Anthropological Papers of the University of Arizona 18.

Hill, James N., ed., 1977. *Explanation of Prehistoric Change*. Albuquerque: University of New Mexico Press.

Ho, Ping-ti. 1976. *The Cradle of the East*. Chicago: University of Chicago Press.

Hobbes, Thomas 1651a. *Philosophical Rudiments Concerning Government and Society*. New York: Lambrecht, 1949.

—— 1651b. *Leviathan*, C. B. Macpherson, ed. Harmondsworth: Penguin Books, 1968.

Hocart, A. M. 1936. *Kings and Councillors*, reprint ed. (1970). Chicago: University of Chicago Press.

Hoebel, E. Adamson. 1954. *The Law of Primitive Man*. Cambridge: Harvard University Press.

Hofstadter, R. 1944. *Social Darwinism in American Thought, 1860–1915*. Philadelphia: University of Pennsylvania Press.

Horowitz, Irving L. 1963. Introduction to *The Outlines of Sociology* by Ludwig Gumplowicz. 2d English language edition (orig. 1899), Irving Horowitz, ed. New York: Paine-Whitman.

Hume, David. *David Hume's Political Essays*, C. W. Hendel, ed. New York: Liberal Arts Press, 1953.

Hunt, Eva and Robert C. Hunt. 1974. "Irrigation, Conflict and Politics: A Mexican Case." In T. E. Downing and McGuire Gibson, eds., *Irrigation's Impact on Society*, pp. 129–58. Anthropological Papers of the University of Arizona 25.

Isbell, William H. 1981. "Comment on Conrad." *American Antiquity*, 46:27–30.

Isbell, William H. and Katharina J. Schreiber. 1978. "Was Huari a State?" *American Antiquity*, 43:372–89.

Jennings, Jesse, ed. 1979. *The Prehistory of Polynesia*. Cambridge: Harvard University Press.

Johnson, Gregory A. 1973. *Local Exchange and Early State Devel-*

opment in Southwestern Iran. Museum of Anthropology, University of Michigan Anthropological Papers 51.

—— 1977. "Aspects of Regional Analysis in Archaeology." In Bernard J. Siegel, ed., *Annual Review of Anthropology,* vol. 6, pp. 479–508. Palo Alto, Calif.: Annual Reviews, Inc.

Joralemon, Peter D. 1971. *A Study of Olmec Iconography.* Studies in Pre-Columbian Art and Archaeology, vol. 7. Washington, D.C.: Dumbarton Oaks Research Library and Collection, Trustees for Harvard University.

Kan, Michael. 1972. "The Feline Motif in Northern Peru." In Elizabeth P. Benson, ed., *The Cult of the Feline,* pp. 69–90. Washington, D.C.: Dumbarton Oaks Research Library and Collection, Trustees for Harvard University.

Kao, Ch'u-hsun. 1959. "The Royal Cemetery of the Yin Dynasty at An-Yang." *Bulletin of the Department of Archaeology and Anthropology, National Taiwan University,* nos. 13/14:1–9

K'ao-ku. 1974. No. 4, Peking.

K'ao-ku Hsueh Pao. 1957. 1:58–71.

Kaplan, David. 1963. "Man, Monuments, and Political Systems." *Southwestern Journal of Anthropology,* 19:397–410.

Keatinge, Richard W. 1979. "Playing for High Stakes: The Roll of Religion in State Formation, or God's Got the Goods." Paper presented at conference on "The Transition to Statehood in the New World: Toward a Synthesis," Hamilton College, Clinton, N.Y.

Keatinge, Richard W., David Chodoff, Deborah Phillips Chodoff, Murray Marvin, and Helaine I. Silverman. 1975. "From the Sacred to the Secular: First Report on a Prehistoric Architectural Transition on the North Coast of Peru." *Archaeology,* 28:128–29.

Keatinge, Richard W. and Kent C. Day. 1973. "Socioeconomic Organization of the Moche Valley, Peru, During the Chimu Occupation of Chan Chan." *Journal of Anthropological Research,* 29:275–95.

—— 1974. "Chan Chan: A Study of Precolumbian Urbanism and the Management of Land and Water Resources in Peru." *Archaeology,* 27:228–35.

Koch, Klaus-Friedrich. 1977. "The Anthropology of Law and Order." In Sol Tax and Leslie G. Freeman, eds., *Horizons of Anthropology,* pp. 300–18. 2d ed. Chicago: Aldine.

Kosok, Paul. 1965. *Life, Land, and Water in Ancient Peru.* New York: Long Island University Press.

Krader, Lawrence. 1968. *Formation of the State.* Englewood Cliffs, N.J.: Prentice-Hall.

Kuo, Pau-chun. 1951. "Report on the Excavation of Yin-hsu in the Spring of 1950." *K'ao Ku Hsueh Pao,* 5:1–61.

Kutscher, Gerdt. 1950. "Iconographic Studies as an Aid in the Reconstruction of Early Chimu Civilization." *Transactions of the New York Academy of Sciences,* Series II, 12(6):194–203.

Lamberg-Karlovsky, C. C. 1972. "Trade Mechanisms in Indus-Mesopotamian Interrelations." *Journal of the American Oriental Society,* 92(2):222–30.

Lanning, Edward P. 1963. "Olmec and Chavín: A Reply to Michael Coe." *American Antiquity,* 28:99–101.

—— 1967. *Peru Before the Incas.* Englewood Cliffs, N.J. Prentice-Hall.

Larco Hoyle, Rafael. 1938. *Los Mochicas.* Lima, n.p.

—— 1941. *Los Cupisniques.* Lima, n.p.

—— 1945. *Los Mochicas.* Buenos Aires: Sociedad Geografica Americana.

Laslett, Peter. 1960. Introduction to *Two Treatises of Government* by John Locke, Peter Laslett, ed. New York: New American Library, Mentor Books.

Lasswell, Harold and Abraham Kaplan. 1950. *Power and Society.* New Haven: Yale University Press.

Lathrap, Donald W. 1965. "Origins of Central Andean Civilization: New Evidence—Review of *Andes 2: Excavations of Kotosh, Peru, 1960,* by Seiichi Izumi and T. Sono." *Science,* 148:796–98.

Leacock, Eleanor. 1963. Introduction to *Ancient Society* by Lewis Henry Morgan, Eleanor Leacock, ed. Gloucester, Mass.: Peter Smith.

—— 1972. Introduction to *The Origin of the Family, Private Property, and the State* by Frederick Engels, Eleanor Leacock, ed. New York: International Publishers.

Lenin, Vladimir, 1918. *State and Revolution.* New York: International Publishers, 1932.

Lenski, Gerhard E. 1966. *Power and Privilege: A Theory of Social Stratification.* New York: McGraw-Hill.

Levy, Janet. 1979. "Evidence of Social Stratification in Bronze Age Denmark." *Journal of Field Archaeology,* 6:49–56.

Lewis, Herbert S. 1978. "Warfare and the Origin of the State: Another Formulation." Paper presented at the Xth International Congress of Anthropological and Ethnological Sciences, New Delhi.

Locke, John. 1690. *Two Treatises of Government*, Peter Laslett, ed. New York: New American Library, Mentor Books, 1960.

Logan, Michael H. and William T. Sanders. 1976. "The Model." In Eric. R. Wolf, ed., *The Valley of Mexico*, pp. 31–58. Albuquerque: University of New Mexico Press.

Longacre, William A. 1970. *Archaeology as Anthropology: A Case Study.* Anthropological Papers of the University of Arizona 17.

—— 1973. "Comment." In Charles L. Redman, ed., *Research and Theory in Current Archaeology*, pp. 329–36. New York: Wiley.

Lowie, Robert H. 1927. *The Origin of the State.* New York: Harcourt.

Lubbock, John. 1870. *The Origins of Civilization, and the Primitive Condition of Man: Mental and Social Condition of Savages.* London: Longmans, Green.

Lumbreras, Luis G. 1971. "Toward a Re-evaluation of Chavín." In Elizabeth P. Benson, ed., *Dumbarton Oaks Conference on Chavín*, pp. 1–28. Washington, D.C.: Dumbarton Oaks Research Library and Collection, Trustees for Harvard University.

—— 1974. *The Peoples and Cultures of Ancient Peru.* Washington, D.C.: Smithsonian Institution Press.

MacNeish, Richard S., Thomas C. Patterson, and David L. Browman. 1975. *The Central Peruvian Prehistoric Interaction Sphere.* Papers of the R. S. Peabody Foundation for Archaeology, no. 7.

Macpherson, C. B. 1968 Introduction to *Leviathan* by Thomas Hobbes, C. B. Macpherson, ed. Harmondsworth: Penguin Books.

Maine, Henry S. 1861. *Ancient Law.* Reprint ed. Gloucester, Mass.: Peter Smith, 1970.

Mair, Lucy. 1962. *Primitive Government.* Harmondsworth: Penguin Books.

Malo, David. 1951. *Hawaiian Antiquities.* Bernice Pahau Bishop Museum Special Publications, no. 2, 2d ed.

Mao, Hsieh-chuin and Yen Yin. 1959. "Dental Condition of the Shang Dynasty Skulls Excavated from Anyang and Huii-Xian." *Vertebata Palasiatica*, 3(2):79–80.

Marcus, Joyce. 1975. "The Rise of the Classic Maya State." Paper presented at the 74th Annual Meeting of the American Anthropological Association, San Francisco.

Meggers, Betty J. 1975. "The Transpacific Origin of Mesoamerican Civilization: A Preliminary Review of the Evidence and Its Theoretical Implications." *American Anthropologist*, 77:1–27.

Menzel, Dorothy, John H. Rowe, and L. E. Dawson. 1964. *The Paracas Pottery of Ica: A Study in Style and Time*. University of California Publications in American Archaeology and Ethnology, vol. 50.

Millon, Rene. 1973. *Urbanization at Teotihuacán, Mexico, Vol. 1, The Teotihuacan Map, Part One: Text*. Austin: University of Texas Press.

—— 1976. "Social Relations in Ancient Teotihuacán." In Eric R. Wolf, ed., *The Valley of Mexico*, pp. 205–48. Albuquerque: University of New Mexico Press.

Millon, Rene, Bruce Drewitt, and George L. Cowgill. 1973. *Urbanization at Teotihuacán, Mexico*, vol. 1: *The Teotihuacán Map, Part Two: Map*. Austin; University of Texas Press.

Moret, A. and G. Davy. 1926. *From Tribe to Empire*, V. Gordon Childe, tr. New York: Knopf.

Morgan, Lewis Henry. 1877. *Ancient Society*. Reprint ed. Eleanor Leacock, ed. Gloucester, Mass.: Peter Smith, 1963.

Morris, Donald R. 1965. *The Washing of the Spears*. New York: Simon and Schuster.

Moseley, Michael E. 1975a. *The Maritime Foundations of Andean Civilization*. Menlo Park, Calif.: Cummings.

—— 1975b. "Prehistoric Principles of Labor Organization in the Moche Valley, Peru." *American Antiquity*, 40:191–96.

—— 1975c. "Chan Chan: Andean Alternative of the Preindustrial City." *Science*, 187:219–25.

Moseley, Michael E. and Carol J. Mackey. 1973. "Chan Chan, Peru's Ancient City of Kings." *National Geographic*, 143(3):318–45.

—— 1974. *Twenty-Four Architectural Plans of Chan Chan, Peru: Structure and Form at the Capital of Chimor*. Cambridge: Peabody Museum Press.

Moseley, Michael E. and Luis Watanabe. 1974. "The Adobe Sculpture of Huaca de los Reyes: Imposing Artwork from Coastal Peru." *Archaeology*, 27:154–61.

Moseley, Michael E. and Gordon R. Willey. 1973. "Aspero, Peru: A Reexamination of the Site and Its Implications." *American Antiquity*, 38:452–67.

Nadel, S. F. 1940. "The Kede: A Riverain State in Northern Nigeria."

In Meyer Fortes and E. E. Evans-Prichard, eds., *African Political Systems*, pp. 165–96. New York: Oxford University Press.

—— 1942 *Black Byzantium*. London, Oxford University Press.

Oberg, Kalvaro. 1940. "The Kingdom of Ankole in Uganda." In Meyer Fortes and E. E. Evans-Prichard, eds., *African Political Systems*, pp. 121–64. New York: Oxford University Press.

Oppenheimer, Franz. 1914. *The State: Its History and Development Viewed Sociologically*. Reprint ed. New York: Vanguard Press, 1926.

Parsons, Jeffrey R. 1976. "Settlement and Population History of the Basin of Mexico." In Eric R. Wolf, ed., *The Valley of Mexico*, pp. 69–100. Albuquerque: University of New Mexico Press.

Parsons, Talcott. 1960. *Structure and Process in Modern Societies*. Glencoe, Ill., Free Press.

Patterson, Thomas C. 1971. "Chavín: An Interpretation of Its Spread and Influence." In Elizabeth P. Benson, ed., *Dumbarton Oaks Conference on Chavín*, pp. 29–48. Washington, D.C., Dumbarton Oaks Research Library and Collection, Trustees for Harvard University.

Patterson, Thomas C. and Edward P. Lanning. 1964. "Changing Settlement Patterns on the Central Peruvian Coast." *Nawpa Pacha*, 2:113–23.

Paulsen, Alison. 1981. "The Archaeology of the Absurd: Comments on 'Cultural Materialism, Split Inheritance, and the Expansion of Ancient Peruvian Empires.'" *American Antiquity*, 46:31–37.

Peebles, Christopher S. 1974. "Moundville: The Organization of a Prehistoric Community and Culture." Ph.D. dissertation, University of California, Santa Barbara.

Peebles, Christopher S. and Susan M. Kus. 1977. "Some Archaeological Correlates of Ranked Societies," *American Antiquity*, 42:421–48.

Peters, Stuart. 1980. "Comments on the Analogy between Biological and Cultural Evolution." *American Antiquity*, 45:596–601.

Porada, Edith E. 1965. "Relative Chronology of Mesopotamia, Part 1, Seals and Trade (6000–1600 B.C.)." In R. W. Erich, ed., *Chronologies in Old World Archaeology*, pp. 133–200. Chicago: University of Chicago Press.

Porter, Muriel N. 1953. *Tlatilco and the Preclassic Cultures of the New World*. Viking Fund Publications in Anthropology, no. 19.

—— 1956. *Excavations at Chupícuaro, Guanajuato, Mexico*. American Philosophical Society, Transactions no. 46, part 5.

Pospisil, Leopold. 1971. *Anthropology of Law: A Comparative Theory*. New York; Harper and Row.

—— 1972. *The Ethnology of Law*. McCalb Modules in Anthropology Module 12. Reading, Mass.: Addison Wesley.

Pozorski, Thomas. 1980. "The Early Horizon Site of Huaca de los Reyes: Societal Implications." *American Antiquity*, 45:100–9.

Price, Barbara J. 1973. "Prehispanic Irrigation Agriculture in Nuclear America." In Morton H. Fried, ed., *Explorations in Anthropology: Readings in Culture, Man, and Nature*, pp. 211–46. New York: Thomas Y. Crowell.

—— 1976. "A Chronological Framework for Cultural Development in Mesoamerica." In Eric R. Wolf, ed., *The Valley of Mexico*, pp. 13–22. Albuquerque: University of New Mexico Press.

—— 1977. "Shifts of Production and Organization: A Cluster Interaction Model." *Current Anthropology*, 18(2):209–34.

—— 1978. "Secondary State Formation: An Explanatory Model." In Ronald Cohen and Elman R. Service, eds., *Origins of the State: The Anthropology of Political Evolution*, pp. 161–86. Philadelphia: Institute for the Study of Human Issues.

Prichard, James B. 1950. *Ancient Near Eastern Texts*. Princeton: Princeton University Press.

Puleston, Dennis E. 1974. "Intersite Areas in the Vicinity of Tikal and Uaxactun." In Norman Hammond, ed., *Mesoamerican Archaeology: New Approaches*, pp. 303–12. Austin: University of Texas Press.

Puleston, Dennis E. and E. W. Callender, Jr. 1967. "Defensive Earthworks at Tikal." *Expedition*, 9(2):40–8.

Rathje, William L. 1970. "Socio-Political Implications of Lowland Maya Burials: Methodology and Tentative Hypotheses." *World Archaeology*, 1(3):359–74.

—— 1971. "The Origin and Development of Lowland Maya Classic Civilization." *American Antiquity*, 36:275–85.

—— 1972. "Praise the Gods and Pass the Metates: A Hypothesis of the Development of Lowland Rainforest Civilizations in Mesoamerica." In Mark P. Leone, ed., *Contemporary Archaeology*, pp. 365–92. Carbondale: Southern Illinois University Press.

Redman, Charles L. 1978. *The Rise of Civilization: From Early Farmers to Urban Society in the Ancient Near East*. New York: Freeman.

Renfrew, Colin. 1972. *The Emergence of Civilization: The Cyclades and the Aegean in the Third Millennium B.C.* London: Metheun.
—— 1973a. "Monuments, Mobilization and Social Organization in Neolithic Wessex." In Colin Renfrew, ed., *The Explanation of Culture Change: Models in Prehistory*, pp. 539–58. Pittsburgh: University of Pittsburgh Press.
—— 1973b. *Before Civilization: The Radiocarbon Revolution and Prehistoric Europe.* New York: Knopf.
Roe, Peter, 1974. *A Further Exploration of the Rowe Chavín Seriation and Its Implications for North Central Coast Chronology.* Dumbarton Oaks Studies in Pre-Columbian Art and Archaeology, no. 13. Washington, D.C.: Dumbarton Oaks Research Library and Collection, Trustees for Harvard University.
Rothschild, Nan Askin. 1975. "Age and Sex, Status and Role, in Prehistoric Societies of Eastern North America." Ph.D. dissertation, New York University, New York.
Rousseau, Jean-Jacques. 1762 and 1755 respectively. *The Social Contract and Discourse on the Origin and Foundation of Inequality Among Mankind*, Leslie G. Crocker, ed. New York: Washington Square Press, Pocket Books, 1964.
Rowe, John H. 1948. "The Kingdom of Chimor." *Acta Americana*, vol. 6, nos. 1 and 2.
—— 1963. "Urban Settlements in Ancient Peru." *Nawpa Pacha*, 1:1–27.
—— 1967. "Form and Meaning in Chavín Art." In John H. Rowe and Dorothy Menzel, eds., *Peruvian Archaeology: Selected Readings*, pp. 72–103. Palo Alto: Peek Publications.
Rowe, John H. and Dorothy Menzel. 1967. "Introduction." In John H. Rowe and Dorothy Menzel, eds. *Peruvian Archaeology: Selected Readings*, Palo Alto: Peek Publications.
Sahlins, Marshall. 1958. *Social Stratification in Polynesia.* Seattle: University of Washington Press.
—— 1968. *Tribesmen.* Englewood Cliffs, N.J.: Prentice-Hall.
Salzman, Philip Carl. 1978. "The Proto-State in Iranian Baluchistan." In Ronald Cohen and Elman R. Service, eds., *Origins of the State: The Anthropology of Political Evolution*, pp. 125–40. Philadelphia: Institute for the Study of Human Issues.
Sanders, William T. 1972. "Population, Agricultural History and Societal Evolution in Mesoamerica." In Brian Spooner, ed., *Popu-*

lation Growth: Anthropology Implications, pp. 101–53. Cambridge: MIT Press.

—— 1973. "The Cultural Ecology of the Lowland Maya: A Reevaluation." In T. Patrick Culbert, ed., *The Classic Maya Collapse*, pp. 325–65. Albuquerque: University of New Mexico Press.

—— 1974. "Chiefdom to State: Political Evolution at Kaminaljuyú, Guatemala." In Charlotte B. Moore, ed., *Reconstructing Complex Societies*, pp. 97–122. Supplement to the Bulletin of the American School of Oriental Research, no. 20.

—— 1976a. "The Natural Environment of the Basin of Mexico." In Eric R. Wolf, ed., *The Valley of Mexico*, pp. 59–68. Albuquerque: University of New Mexico Press.

—— 1976b. "The Agricultural History of the Basin of Mexico." In Eric R. Wolf, ed., *The Valley of Mexico*, pp. 101–60. Albuquerque: University of New Mexico Press.

Sanders, William T., Jeffrey R. Parsons, and Robert S. Santley. 1979. *The Basin of Mexico: Ecological Processes in the Evolution of a Civilization*. New York: Academic Press.

Sanders, William T. and Barbara J. Price. 1968. *Mesoamerica: The Evolution of a Civilization*. New York, Random House.

Sawyer, A. R. 1961. "Paracas and Nazca Iconography." In S. K. Lothrop et al., eds., *Essays in Pre-Columbian Art and Archaeology*, pp. 269–98. Cambridge: Harvard University Press.

Saxe, Arthur A. 1970. "Social Dimensions of Mortuary Practices." Ph.D. dissertation, University of Michigan, Ann Arbor.

Schoeninger, Margaret J. 1979a. "Diet and Status at Chalcatzingo: Some Empirical and Technical Aspects of Strontium Analysis." *American Journal of Physical Anthropology*, 51:295–310.

—— 1979b. *Dietary Reconstruction at Chalcatzingo, A Formative Period Site in Morelos, Mexico*. Museum of Anthropology, University of Michigan, Technical Reports, no. 9.

Seagle, William. 1946. *The History of Law*. New York: Tudor.

Sears, William. 1954. "The Sociopolitical Organization of Pre-Columbian Cultures on the Gulf Coastal Plain." *American Anthropologist*, 56(3):339–46.

Service, Elman R. 1962. *Primitive Social Organization: An Evolutionary Perspective*. New York: Random House.

—— 1971a. *Primitive Social Organization: An Evolutionary Perspective*. 2d ed. New York: Random House.

—— 1971b. *Cultural Evolutionism: Theory in Practice*. New York: Holt, Rinehart and Winston.

—— 1975. *Origins of the State and Civilization: The Process of Cultural Evolution*. New York: Norton. Selections reprinted by permission.

—— 1978. "Classical and Modern Theories of the Origins of Government." In Ronald Cohen and Elman R. Service, eds., *Origins of the State: The Anthropology of Political Evolution*, pp. 21–34. Philadelphia: Institute for the Study of Human Issues.

Shih, Chang-ju. 1933 "Ti Ch'i Ts'e Yin'hsü fu'chüeh: E ch'u kung-tso pao-kao." *An-yang Fa-chueh Pao-Kao*, 4:7–9, 28.

—— 1950. "Yin Weapons in Sets as Excavated from Hsiao-t'un." *Bulletin of the Institute of History and Philology of Academia Sinica*, 22:18–24.

—— 1954. *Annals of Academia Sinica*, no. 1, p. 276.

—— 1959. *Yin-hsu chien-chu Yi-ts'un*. Institute of History and Philology, Academia Sinica, Taipei.

—— 1970. *Pei tsu Mu-tsang*. Institute of History and Philology, Academia Sinica, Taipei.

Shimada, Izumi. 1976. "Socioeconomic Organization at Moche V Pampa Grande, Peru: Prelude to a Major Transformation to Come." Ph.D. dissertation, University of Arizona, Tucson.

—— 1977. "Functional Analysis of Urban Context at Moche V Pampa Grande: A Field Methodology and a Commodity and Labor Flow Model." Paper presented at the 42d Annual Meeting of the Society for American Archaeology, New Orleans.

—— 1978. "Economy of a Prehistoric Urban Context: Commodity and Labor Flow at Moche V Pampa Grande, Peru." *American Antiquity*, 43:569–92.

Simmel, Georg. 1950. *The Sociology of George Simmel*, Kurt H. Wolff, tr. and ed. New York: Free Press.

Spence, Michael W. 1967. "The Obsidian Industry of Teotihuacán." *American Antiquity*, 34:507–14.

—— 1973. "The Development of the Classic Period Teotihuacan Obsidian Production System." Paper presented at the 38th Annual Meeting of the Society for American Archaeology, San Francisco.

Spencer, Herbert, 1876, 1882, 1896. *The Evolution of Society* (selections from *Principles of Sociology*: vol. 1, 1876; vol. 2, 1882; vol. 3, 1896. Edited with Introduction by Robert Carneiro. Chicago: University of Chicago Press, 1967.

Steward, Julian H. 1938. *Basin-Plateau Aboriginal Sociopolitical Groups. Bureau of American Ethnology Bulletin 120.*

—— 1955. *Theory of Culture Change: The Methodology of Multilinear Evolution.* Urbana: University of Illinois Press.

Stinchcombe, Arthur L. 1968. *Constructing Social Theories.* New York: Harcourt Brace & World.

Stirling, Mathew W. 1943. *Stone Monuments of Southern Mexico.* Bureau of American Ethnology Bulletin 138.

—— 1955. *Stone Monuments of the Rio Chiquito, Veracruz, Mexico.* Bureau of American Ethnology Bulletin 157.

Sumner, William Graham and Albert Keller. 1927. *The Science of Society.* New Haven: Yale University Press.

Tainter, Joseph. 1973. "Social Correlates of Mortuary Patterning at Kaloko, North Kona, Hawaii." *Archaeology and Physical Anthropology in Oceania,* 8:1–11.

—— 1975. "The Archaeological Study of Social Change: Woodland Systems in West-central Illinois." Ph.D dissertation, Northwestern University, Evanston, Ill.

Thomas, David Hurst. 1972. "A Computer Simulation Model of Great Basin Shoshonean Subsistence and Settlement Patterns." In David L. Clarke, ed., *Models in Archaeology,* pp. 671–704. London: Methuen.

—— 1973. "An Empirical Test of Steward's Model for Great Basin Settlement Patterns." *American Antiquity,* 38:155–76.

—— 1974. "An Archaeological Perspective on Shoshonean Bands." *American Anthropologist,* 76:11–23.

Thurnwald, Richard. 1935. *Die Menschliche Gesselschaft,* vol. 4. Berlin and Leipzig.

Tolstoy, Paul. 1974. "Mesoamerica." In Shirley Gorenstein, ed., *Prehispanic America,* pp. 29–64. New York: St. Martin's Press.

Topic, John R. and Theresa Lange Topic. 1978. "Prehistoric Fortification Systems of Northern Peru." *Current Anthropology,* 19:618–9.

Topic, Theresa Lange. 1977. "Excavations at Moche, Peru." Ph.D. dissertation, Harvard University, Cambridge.

Trigger, Bruce G. 1978. *Time and Traditions.* New York: Columbia University Press.

Tuck, James A. 1971. "The Iroquois Confederacy." *Scientific American,* 224(1):35–49.

Vico, Giambattista. 1744. *The New Science.* Revised. Thomas G. Bergin and Max H. Fisch, tr. Ithaca, N.Y.: Cornell University Press, 1968.

Vinogradoff, Paul. 1920. *Outlines of Historical Jurisprudence*, vol. 1. London: Oxford.

Voss, Jerome. 1980. "Tribal Emergence During the Neolithic of Northwestern Europe." Paper presented at the 79th Annual Meeting of the American Anthropological Association, Washington, D.C.

Wagner, R. Harrison. 1969. "The Concept of Power and the Study of Politics." In Roderick Bell et al., eds., *Political Power: A Reader in Theory and Research*. pp. 3–12. New York: Free Press.

Wallerstein, Immanuel. 1976. *The Modern World System: Capitalist Agriculture and the Origins of the European World-Economy in the Sixteenth Century* (text edition). New York: Academic Press.

—— 1979. *The Capitalist World-Economy*. London: Cambridge University Press.

Walter, Eugene V. 1969. *Terror and Resistance: A Study of Political Violence*. London: Oxford University Press.

Weaver, Muriel Porter. 1972. *The Aztecs, Maya, and Their Predecessors*. New York: Seminar Press.

Webb, Malcolm C. 1965. "The Abolition of the Taboo System in Hawaii." *Journal of the Polynesian Society*, 74:21–39.

—— 1968. "Carneiro's Hypothesis of Limited Land Resources and the Origins of the State: A Latin Americanist's Approach to an Old Problem." *South Eastern Latin Americanist*, 12(3):1–8.

—— 1973. "The Peten Maya Decline Viewed in the Perspective of State Formation." In T. Patrick Culbert, ed., *The Classic Maya Collapse*, pp. 367–404. Albuquerque: University of New Mexico Press.

—— 1975. "The Flag Follows Trade: An Essay on the Necessary Interaction of Military and Commercial Factors in State Formation." In C. C. Lamberg-Karlovsky and Jeremy A. Sabloff, eds., *Ancient Civilization and Trade*, pp. 155–210. Albuquerque: University of New Mexico Press.

Weber, Max. 1947. *The Theory of Social and Economic Organization*, Talcott Parsons, ed., Talcott Parsons and A. M. Henderson, tr. New York: Free Press.

Webster, David. 1975. "Warfare and the Evolution of the State: A Reconsideration." *American Antiquity*, 40:464–70.

—— 1976. "On Theocracies." *American Anthropologist*, 78:812–28.

Weissleder, Wolfgang. 1978. "Aristotle's Concept of Political Structure and the State." In Ronald Cohen and Elman R. Service, eds., *Origins of the State: The Anthropology of Political Evolution*, pp. 187–204. Philadelphia: Institute for the Study of Human Issues.

Wen-wu. 1974. No. 9, p. 2.

Wheatley, Paul. 1971. *The Pivot of the Four Quarters*. Chicago: Aldine.

—— 1972. "The Concept of Urbanism." In Peter J. Ucko, Ruth Tringham and G. W. Dimbleby, eds., *Man, Settlement, and Urbanism*, pp. 1–37. Cambridge, Mass.: Duckworth.

White, Leslie. 1949. *The Science of Culture*. New York: Farrar, Straus & Giroux.

—— 1959. *The Evolution of Culture: Civilization to the Fall of Rome*. New York: McGraw-Hill.

Wicke, Charles R. 1971. *Olmec: An Early Art Style of Precolumbian Mexico*. Tucson: University of Arizona Press.

Willey, Gordon R. 1951. "The Chavín Problem: A Review and Critique." *Southwestern Journal of Anthropology*, 7:103–44.

—— 1953. *Prehistoric Settlement Patterns in the Viru Valley*. Bureau of American Ethnology Bulletin 155.

—— 1971. *An Introduction to American Archaeology*, vol. 2: *South America*. Englewood Cliffs, N.J.: Prentice-Hall.

Willey, Gordon R. and Dimitri Shimkin. 1973. "The Maya Collapse: A Summary View." In T. Patrick Culbert, ed., *The Classic Maya Collapse*, pp. 457–501. Albuquerque: University of New Mexico Press.

Williams, Leonard, David Hurst Thomas, and Robert Bettinger, 1973. "Notions to Numbers: Great Basin Settlements as Polythetic Sets." In Charles Redman, ed., *Research and Theory in Current Archeology*, pp. 215–38. New York: Wiley.

Winch, Peter. 1972. "Man and Society in Hobbes and Rousseau." In Maurice Cranston and Richard S. Peters, ed., *Hobbes and Rousseau: A Collection of Critical Essays*, pp. 233–53. Garden City, N.Y.:. Doubleday.

Winter, Marcus. 1974. "Residence Patterns at Monte Albán." *Science*, 186:982–87.

—— 1976. "The Archaeological Household Cluster in the Valley of Oaxaca." In Kent V. Flannery, ed., *The Early Mesoamerican Village*, pp. 25–30. New York: Academic Press.

Winter, Marcus C. and Janes W. Pires-Ferreira. 1976. "Distribution of Obsidian Among Households in Two Oaxacan Villages." In Kent V. Flannery, ed., *The Early Mesoamerican Village*, pp. 306–10. New York: Academic Press.

Wittfogel, Karl A. 1957. *Oriental Despotism*. New Haven: Yale University Press.

Wolf, Eric R. 1969. *Peasant Wars of the Twentieth Century*. New York: Harper & Row.

Wolf, Eric R., ed. 1976. *The Valley of Mexico*. Albuquerque: University of New Mexico Press.

Woodbury, Richard B. 1961. "A Reappraisal of Hohokam Irrigation." *American Anthropologist*, 63:550–60.

Woolley, C. Leonard. 1928. *The Sumerians*. Oxford: Clarendon Press

—— 1934. *Ur Excavations: The Royal Cemetery*, vol. 2. London and Philadelphia: Trustees of the British Museum and the Museum of the University of Pennsylvania.

—— 1956. *Ur Excavations: The Early Periods*, vol. 4. London: Oxford University Press.

Wright, Henry T. 1977a. "Recent Research on the Origin of the State." In Bernard J. Siegel, ed., *Annual Review of Anthropology*, vol. 6, pp. 379–98. Palo Alto, Calif.: Annual Reviews, Inc.

—— 1977b. "Toward an Explanation of the Origin of the State." In James N. Hill, ed. *Explanation of Prehistoric Change*, pp. 215–30. Albuquerque: University of New Mexico Press.

Wright, Henry T. and Gregory A. Johnson. 1975. "Population, Exchange, and Early State Formation in Southwestern Iran." *American Anthropologist*, 77:267–89.

Yoffee, Norman. 1979. "The Decline and Rise of Mesopotamian Civilization: An Ethnoarchaeological Perspective on the Evolution of Social Complexity." *American Antiquity*, 44:5–34.

Index